ethno-techno

Writings on performance, activism, and pedagogy

by Guillermo Gómez-Peña

edited by Elaine Peña

Routledge
Taylor & Francis Group
NEW YORK AND LONDON

ethno-techno

The performance of "extreme identity" is familiar to us all through the medium of television (just switch on *Jerry Springer*). So where does this leave the critical practice of artists who aim to make tactical, performative interventions into our notions of race, culture, and sexuality?

Guillermo Gómez-Peña has spent many years developing his unique style of performance-activism: his theatricalizations of postcolonial theory. In *Ethno-Techno: Writings on performance, activism, and pedagogy*, he pushes the boundaries still further, exploring what's left for artists to do in a post-9/11 repressive culture of what he calls "the mainstream bizarre".

Extensive photos document his artistic experiments. The text not only explores and confronts his political and philosophical parameters, it offers an insight into one of the most daring, innovative, and challenging performance artists of our age.

Guillermo Gómez-Peña is a performance artist and writer, and Artistic Director of San Francisco-based company La Pocha Nostra. His pioneering work in performance, video, radio, installation, poetry, journalism, and cultural theory explores crosscultural issues, immigration, the side effects of globalization, the politics of language, "extreme culture," and the digital divide. His previous books include *Warrior for Gringostroika* (1993), *The New World Border* (1996), and *Dangerous Border Crossers* (2000).

First published 2005
by Routledge
270 Madison Ave, New York, NY 10016

Simultaneously published in the UK
by Routledge
2 Park Square, Milton Park
Abingdon, Oxon OX14 4RN

Routledge is an imprint of the Taylor & Francis Group

Designed and typeset in Bauhaus and Akzidenz Grotesque
by Keystroke, Jacaranda Lodge, Wolverhampton
Printed and bound in Great Britain
by TJ International Ltd, Padstow, Cornwall

Library of Congress Cataloging in Publication Data
Gómez-Peña, Guillermo.
Ethno-techno : writings on performance, activism, and pedagogy/
Guillermo Gómez-Peña ; edited by Elaine Peña.
p. cm.
Includes bibliographical references and index.
1. Performance art–United States–20th century. 2. Gómez-Peña, Guillermo.
3. Mexican American art. 4. Politics in art. 5. Minorities in art. 6. Art and race.
I. Peña, Elaine. II. Title.
NX456.5.P38G67 2005
700–dc22 2004021796

British Library Cataloguing in Publication Data
A catalogue record for this book is available from the British Library

ISBN 0–415–36247–4 (hbk)
ISBN 0–415–36248–2 (pbk)

DEDICATORY

To my adored mother Martha
who has waited so long on this earth
just to make sure I don't fuck up real bad;
to make sure that my son grows up
with a connection to our remote past
Madre mía, every word I've written here
is largely thanks to you
Please stay a little longer
'cause we still need you so badly

Doña Martha Peña de Gómez.
Mexico City, 1942.

CONFESSION

Today, I'm tired of ex/changing identities in the net.
In the past eight hours,
I've been a man, a woman and a s/he.
I've been Black, Asian, Mixteco, German,
and a multi-hybrid replicant.
I've been ten years old, twenty, forty-two, sixty-five.
I've visited twenty-two meaningless chat rooms
I've spoken seven broken languages.
(I speak in tongues)
As you can see, I need a break real bad;
I just want to be myself for a few minutes.

El Webback

contents

illustrations

acknowledgments

Earlier versions of "In Defense of Performance" appeared in *Art Papers*, July/August 2003, pp. 22–7, and in the book *Live Art and Performance* edited by Adrian Heathfield (Tate, 2004), pp. 76–85. The version published here is the complete one.

An early version of "*Culturas-in-extremis*" under the title "The New Global Culture: Somewhere between corporate multiculturalism and the mainstream bizarre" was published in *TDR* T169, 45, 1 (spring 2001), pp. 7–30. The version published here is substantially different.

Different versions of "An Open Letter to the National Arts Community" appeared in dozens of publications and cyber-magazines, in various countries and languages, including *Contemporary Theatre Review*, 12, 2 (May 2004).

"Letter to an Unknown Thief" appeared under the title of "Utterance 8: Letter to an unknown thief" in *Performance Research*, 4, 2 (summer 1999), pp. 96–7.

Excerpts of "Brownout 2" appeared in *Performance Research*, 8, 3 (September 2003), pp. 126–35.

"Theatricalizations of Postcolonial Theory" appeared under the title of "A Latino Philosopher Interviews a Chicano Performance Artist" in *Nepantla*, 2, 3 (2001), pp. 539–54.

"The Minefields of Utopia" appeared under the title of "Navigating the Minefields of Utopia: a conversation" in *TDR* T174, 46, 2 (summer 2002) pp. 66–96. This version was excerpted by the author.

The images from photographer Arturo Vason were part of *The Ex-Centris Project* at the Liverpool Biennial of Contemporary Art International Exhibition 2002, a collaboration between the Liverpool Biennial, Bluecoat Arts Centre and the Live Art Development Agency.

The images from Hugo Glendinning were part of *Ex-Centris* (Live Culture at Tate Modern, 2003), produced by the Live Art Development Agency and Adrian Heathfield in collaboration with Tate Exhibitions and Events departments.

Introduction and thanks

Guillermo Gómez-Peña

I am an interdisciplinary intellectual. To me, every idea demands a different artistic language to express it. Certain ideas, impulses, and metaphors can be better expressed through live performance, installation, or video; others require the written word. Those ideas which depend on the word still need to find their own format. In dialogue with my colleagues, they eventually become essays, chronicles, performance scripts, poems, or hybrids of sorts. And in the spirit of border culture, many of these texts get recycled back into other formats and genres. This collection of recent writings, which starts precisely when my last book in English (*Dangerous Border Crossers*, Routledge, 1998) ends, exemplifies the various intertwined roads, tunnels, and bridges I have utilized lately to migrate, talk back, articulate questions, and reposition myself within my conceptual map.

I truly believe that this, my seventh book and my second one with Routledge, is my most political so far. Why? Because I feel that our dangerous times demand it. The new lords of war and censorship are personally invested in the destruction of critical culture. In fact most of the texts included here were written in direct response to the formidable political, cultural, and philosophical dilemmas we are facing as members of an international community of progressive thinkers and art-makers in a bizarre world controlled by greedy politicians, warmongers, and cynical corporations who feel utter contempt for critical art. It's a personal thing.

This book is also my most "traditional" to date. Unlike my previous publications, whose structure and style were as hybrid and experimental as the very ideas presented, *Ethno-Techno* responds to two extremely pertinent challenges posed by my dear colleague, Routledge editor Talia Rodgers: First, to attempt to explain my position vis-à-vis the contemporary performance field and the challenges my colleagues and I face as politicized artists and public intellectuals in the post-9/11 era. Second, to articulate the working methods, strategies, and pedagogy of my eccentric San Francisco-based performance organization, La Pocha Nostra, in the hope that other practitioners can choose to apply these ideas in their own work. I have accepted both challenges wholeheartedly.

This book may also be my most collaborative written publication to date. Last October (2003), when I began to imagine the book, I asked performance theorist Elaine Peña to help me revise each chosen text and envision a conceptual structure for the complete manuscript. Her job here as "editor" was more complex than usual—I'd say epiphenomenological. She challenged me to rewrite certain pieces, and to edit or extend others. She insisted we not include writings that were not in direct response to Talia's original challenges, and forced me to become (hopefully) a better, more reflective, and more focused writer. I truly loved this rigorous editing process, and treasure my new friendship with her.

In the process, I also asked my British sister Rachel Rogers to help me cowrite and piece together perhaps the most difficult section, the one on pedagogy and La Pocha Nostra's working methods. Having worked on at least six major performance projects with me over the same number of years, she was able to help me put down on paper the infamous "Pocha method" and (hopefully, again) make it readable, understandable, and fun. After all, we have had a huge amount of fun during the workshops and rehearsals.

So, it is thanks to Talia, Elaine, and Rachel that this book was made possible. I thank them immensely for their generosity, rigor, valor, and trust. They were more than willing to jump blindfolded into the border abyss, without a parachute—no pinche questions asked.

I also wish to thank my dear colleagues who cowrote specific texts with me, including Eduardo Mendieta, Lisa Wolford, Elaine Katzenberger, and Silvana Straw; and my assistant, Allison Wyper, who helped correct the awkward Spanish syntax of certain sections. The innumerable members and associates of La Pocha Nostra who have ventured into *Terra ignota performatica* with me in the past few years are also a crucial part of this book. Among others I wish to acknowledge Michelle Ceballos, Juan Ybarra, Kari Hensley, Nola Mariano, Emiko R. Lewis, Guillermo Galindo, Suzanne Stephanac, Violeta Luna, Monica Lleó, Lois Keidan, Orlando Britto, Fiona Winning, Harley Strumm, Ansuman Biswas, Kazuko Hohki, Marlene Cancio, Ulla Berg, Diana Taylor, Richard Schechner, Richard Gough, Marco Barrera, Cristina

King, Cesar Martinez, and many others whose names I simply couldn't fit on this page. Locos and Locas, you know who you are. You are the only people I know who are crazier than me. Thanks for jumping into the flames with me. Thanks for protecting my back.

Most importantly, I wish to thank my beloved lifetime compañera Colombian writer and curator Carolina Ponce de Leon. Amidst her epic projects, she has had to endure "el monstruo" Gómez-Peña sitting in front of his computer—a stationary intellectual—for over four months, and that's not an easy task. She fed me, caressed me, and helped me domesticate my bloodthirsty border demons and vampires throughout the whole pinche process of putting together this manuscript. Ay, Leona, what would I do without you? What would the entire universe be without you?

This said, let us begin to venture into the rocky and unpredictable cartography of my mind, a planet where theory becomes practice overnight, where identities are constantly morphing into other identities and personae, and where "I" and "we" are constantly shifting faultlines. Dear reader, in my performance country, you don't need your ID and no passport is necessary. Welcome to the Mex-files . . .

Pedagogic interventions in the mainstream bizarre

Elaine Peña

"Have the courage to be happy."

Augusto Boal, *Legislative Theatre: Using performance to make politics* (1998)

La frontera es lo único que compartimos/The border is all we share.[1] This claim made by Gómez-Peña over ten years ago in an open letter to the national arts community needs to be reconsidered. Initially written in the context of theorizing a paradigm shift—one that rotated the axis of East Coast/West Coast to a North/South position—this idea of shared borders is presently being appropriated and swallowed by the mainstream bizarre. In what follows, Gómez-Peña reevaluates "border-sharing" by examining contemporary political and cultural challenges in the United States. More importantly, he responds to these challenges. Gómez-Peña and his La Pocha

1 See Gómez-Peña, "The Multicultural Paradigm: An open letter to the national arts community," *Negotiating Performance: Gender, sexuality, and theatricality in Latin/o America*. Edited by Diana Taylor and Juan Villegas. Durham, NC: Duke University Press, 1994, p. 20.

Nostra colleagues generously offer us their critical performance pedagogy—the micrologistics of their rehearsal, performance, and production methodologies. They reveal their process. Their modes of communication continually traverse local, national, and global borders. We hope they cross disciplinary and professional boundaries as well.

Gómez-Peña's initial "border-sharing" claim is still pertinent, but its efficacy has been packaged and shipped by corporate America and her global cronies. We all saw this coming. The inauguration of the North American Free Trade Agreement (NAFTA) in 1985 signaled the accelerated transformation from "shared borders" to profit and commodities. The Zapatista uprising alerted us to the injustices accompanied by free market negotiations: The gross violations of human rights (particularly in Juarez, Chihuahua), the pervasive racism and classism that plagues millions of illegals in the United States, and suburbia sex-trade networks. Meanwhile, the Clinton administration veiled the realities of its neo-liberal agenda by strategically extending a hand (from the White House down) to "American" concerns—feminist, race, and multicultural issues—while simultaneously eliding the economics of their struggles.

To be fair, Gómez-Peña anticipated the worst. In 1994 he wrote, "the permanent condition of political emergency and cultural vulnerability we live in leaves no other choice. If our actions are not daring, inventive, and unexpected, they won't make a difference, *and border reality, with its overwhelming dynamics, will supersede us in an instant*" (emphasis mine).[2] It has. Hyperpatriotism from Gulf Wars (Parts I and II) twists our dreams of border-sharing. Accelerated trade liberalization (NAFTA, CAFTA, FTAA) threatens to culturally, politically, and economically recolonize the Americas. Equally disturbing, "daring, inventive, and unexpected" extreme identity performances are now seen everywhere, everyday, on reality television, and talk and news shows. These are foundational layers of the mainstream bizarre, what Gómez-Peña calls, "a superficial fascination the global media has with 'extreme behavior,' with high-definition images of hardcore violence and explicit sexuality, this fascination with revolution-as-style, with stylized hybridity and superficial transculture."[3]

2 ibid., p. 22.

3 Guillermo Gómez-Peña and Eduardo Mendieta, "A Latino Philosopher Interviews a Chicano Performance Artist," *Nepantla* 2.3 (2001), see this volume, pp. 245–57.

"The serpent has finally bit its own tail"[4]

In 2003, Gómez-Peña addressed this conundrum in another letter to the national arts community. Unlike his 1994 letter, this message does not exude hope of border-sharing. Gómez-Peña is fearful. His fear is instantiated by post-9/11 paranoid patriotism, extreme depletion of arts funding, and witnessing bodies and psyches "internalizing the pain of the larger sociopolitical body and the confusion of the collective psyche."[5] He suggests this mainstream bizarre consumes previous discussions of what it means to be "radical," "revolutionary," or "progressive." Under the radar it is eating away at distinctions between multiculturalism, transculturalism, and interculturalism as well as semantic arguments differentiating performance from theater. Gómez-Peña asks us to "remember." How could we forget?

Questions arise: What does an artist do when the society they are critically mirroring is already mirroring itself? How do we negotiate this moment of philosophical vertigo, of refractory realities? What are our methodologies? Where are our lines of communication? What tactics and strategies may we deploy, and when? These predicaments are at the heart of the following exploration of performance, pedagogy, and activism.

Gómez-Peña's 2003 letter to the national arts community also raises challenging questions. He and his La Pocha Nostra colleagues ask:

1. What are our new roles as artists and intellectuals in this cartography of terror?
2. What concrete actions can we realistically undertake as a sector (and not as disenfranchised individuals), to reclaim our stolen civil self and our legitimate right to create and to articulate our artistic visions?
3. How to keep these questions alive, discuss survival strategies with our local and national communities and present our case empathetically to the press and to sympathetic members of the political class?[6]

Working through these questions requires complete inclusivity. This is not to suggest that inclusivity has never been a goal; rather, the madness of our present circumstances necessitates articulating the obvious. One starting point may be to look toward our recent past for clues, paradigms, and methods. In conversation with many, Gómez-Peña's 1994 letter advocated radical performance that produces

4 See Gómez-Peña, "*Culturas-in-Extremis*," in this volume, pp. 45–64.
5 ibid.
6 See Gómez-Peña, "Open Letter to the National Arts Community," (2003), in this volume, pp. 65–71.

dialogue between artist and spectator, spectator and community, and community and imagined community. He suggests,

> All we can aspire to is beginning a dialogue. This document is a humble contribution. I ask you to join in. A whole generation of artists and intellectuals has begun the dialogue. It is mostly artists, writers, and arts administrators (not politicians, scientists, or religious leaders) who are leading the effort. And from these people, the most vocal and enlightened are women.[7]

Again, stating the obvious—"the most vocal and enlightened are women"—is necessary, but it is important to ask: What are the possibilities and repercussions of dialogue shared dominantly among artists, writers, and arts administrators in the mainstream bizarre? Questioning our lines of communication and our positionalities shifts our focus to process—what methods do we use to communicate our ideas?

Pedagogy and performance in the mainstream bizarre

Working through these questions requires that we state what may be another obvious point: Dialogue among "artists, writers, and arts administrators" is productive but no longer sufficient. We must share ideas across disciplines, across professions, in different spaces. Concomitantly, Jill Dolan argues for dialogue that is situated in vernacular language, not jargon.[8] Further, we must move with circuits of power, with capital, with labor, with commodities to create think tanks and networks of communication capable of permeating the cavernous space of the mainstream bizarre. Creating dialogue across disciplinary and professional boundaries as well as local and national contexts is an extremely ambitious proposition. However challenging, this project is valiantly undertaken by innumerable scholars/activists/artists.[9] It is

7 See Gómez-Peña, "The Multicultural Paradigm: An open letter to the national arts community," p. 26.

8 Jill Dolan, *Geographies of Learning: Theory and practice, activism and performance*. Middletown, Conn.: Wesleyan University Press, 2001.

9 The project has been taken up by many most recently by: Augusto Boal, *Legislative Theatre: Using performance to make politics* (Trans. Adrian Jackson, London: Routledge, 1998) and *Theatre of the Oppressed* (Trans. Charles A. and Maria-Odila Leal McBride, New York: Theatre Communications Group, 1985); Paulo Freire, *Pedagogy of the Oppressed* (Trans. Myra Bergman Ramos, New York: Continuum, 1970); Baz Kershaw, *The Politics of Performance: Radical Theatre as Cultural Intervention* (London: Routledge, 1992); David Róman, *Acts of Intervention: Performance, Gay Culture, and AIDS* (Bloomington, Ind.: Indiana University Press, 1998); Chela Sandoval, *Methodology of the Oppressed* (Minneapolis, Minn.: University of Minnesota Press, 2000).

continued here by Gómez-Peña and his La Pocha Nostra colleagues with a focus on process and with a new understanding of art as a "total crossover culture jam" event.

Gómez-Peña and his La Pocha Nostra colleagues put forth performance strategies and radical pedagogy that privileges the transformative possibilities of performance in rehearsal *and* the staged product. These performance strategies speak to a wide range of students and experienced practitioners. Pocha workshops and rehearsals create bridges between different spheres of production, particularly if one presupposes that not all students will become performance artists. They will be city clerks, service-industry workers, beauticians, lawyers, scientists, social workers, librarians, rock stars, teachers, and philanthropists. The knowledge and critical thinking they develop, no matter how ephemeral, will be carried in their bodies and distributed across disciplinary and professional boundaries. This is hope. Gómez-Peña suggests performance pedagogy, "challenges authoritarian hierarchies and specialized knowledge by attempting to create temporary utopian spaces where interdisciplinary dialogue and imagination can flourish. These utopian spaces are framed by, but not contained within a pentagon-shape of radical ideas whose vertices are community, education, activist politics, new technologies, and experimental aesthetics."[10] Maintaining an analysis situated in historical political economy and exploring connections between the local and the global also grounds the relationship among performance, pedagogy, and activism.

Examining the local and the global is of particular importance in the mainstream bizarre. The Lysistrata Project (2003) and worldwide antiwar protests are representative examples of how utopian projects are made reality when the desire to create embodied dialogue across locales is matched with intermedia collaboration (radio and Internet) and interdisciplinary/interprofessional discussion. Harry J. Elam wrote of the production: "Performers knew that they were linked at once to a cause larger than themselves and to greater numbers around the world. The readings constituted not simply localized events but a global spectacle, [. . .] operating at once in ways that are both local and global."[11] Analogously, Dwight Conquergood expands conceptions of "local" space as an active component of "global" space:

> A boundary is more like a membrane than a wall. In current cultural theory, "location" is imagined as an itinerary instead of a fixed point. Our understanding of a "local context" expands to encompass the historical, dynamic, often traumatic, movements of people, ideas, images, commodities and capital. [. . .]

10 See "La Pocha Nostra's Basic Methodology", in this volume, pp. 95–135.
11 Harry J. Elam, "Theater and Activism." Editorial. *Theatre Journal* 55.4 (2003).

> We are now keenly aware that the "local" is a leaky, contingent construction, and that global forces are taken up, struggled over, and refracted for site-specific purposes.[12]

Attending to the relationship between local and global contexts offers us another way to analyze politics vis-à-vis performance. Gómez-Peña and his La Pocha Nostra colleagues practice this theoretical connection by producing regenerative sources of labor. Working within a structural system comprised of concentric and overlapping circles, their performance praxis has far-reaching and regenerative effects across local and international borders. Compiling their performance models, methods, and documents, gathering what Diana Taylor suggests are "repertoires and archives,"[13] increases the possibility of sustaining dialogue and social change.

The following collection of essays, chronicles, performance scripts, and strategies contributes to this proposal. The utility of these texts and methods is that they may be applied in multiple contexts: The classroom, performance laboratories, museums, theaters, the streets, radio, and cyberspace. They themselves are having an identity crisis (which somehow mirrors the logic of the mainstream bizarre). This malleability is both productive and necessary.

Chicago, Illinois
April 2004

12 Dwight Conquergood, "Performance Studies Interventions and Radical Research," *The Drama Review* 46.2 (2002): 145.
13 Diana Taylor, *The Archive and the Repertoire: Performing cultural memory in the Americas*, Durham, Ind.: Duke University Press, 2003.

track ONE

INTRODUCTORY ESSAYS AND CHRONICLES

This first section offers critical essays and chronicles written between 1999 and 2004. Appearing here for the first time in English, "On the Other Side of the Mexican Mirror" (2002) autoethnographically draws the political and economic inconsistencies of US–Mexico relations into sharp focus. Gómez-Peña situates himself as a border artist reflecting on "postnational Mexicans" and their bittersweet relationship with "homeland." He also examines their role in the construction of a virtual nation inside the USA called "Latinoamerica del Norte."

"In Defense of Performance" is a hybrid chronicle and dream diary in which the artist draws "a poetical portrait of the performance artist standing on a map of *his* performance art field." Gómez-Peña attempts to make the field accessible and "hip" to young artists and students by framing performance processes and products as intensely collaborative and interactive–spaces to think, create, and change.

The artist confronts his philosophical parameters and political certainties in "*Culturas-in-Extremis*: Performing against the cultural backdrop of the mainstream bizarre." He connects the mainstream bizarre's fraught political undercurrents with performance art and the body. He focuses on the mainstream's infatuation with extreme behavior and with the display of extreme bodies. Further, Gómez-Peña reflects on the role of performance artists in the new century. He calls attention to spaces of possibility but concentrates on areas of tension–how and where may we tactically intervene in the mainstream bizarre?

In "An Open Letter to the National Arts Community," Gómez-Peña critically examines waning arts-funding in the United States and our current culture of fear in relation to the Bush administration.

Elaine Peña

Natural-born matones.
Guillermo Gómez-Peña and Carmel Kooros. *El Mexterminator Project*, 1998. Photo: Eugenio Castro.

1

On the other side of the Mexican mirror

(Essay/Chronicle, 2003. Revised 2004)

I wish to acknowledge El Andar *magazine editor Julie Reynolds who helped me revise the very first version of this text.*

I

I left Mexico City in 1978 to study art in California, "the land of the future" as my lost generation saw it. Too young to be a *hipiteca* and too old to be a *punketo*, I was a twenty-two-year old interstitial rebel, a writer and artist who couldn't find space to breathe in the suffocating official culture of Mexico. There, the art and literary cartels were structured in an ecclesiastical fashion, accountable to one untouchable *capo*. He was the archbishop and final arbiter of what was acceptable as "high culture" and "Mexican-ness," *Don* Octavio Paz.

In those days, identity in Mexico was a static construct, yet intricately connected to national territory and language. A Mexican was someone who lived in Mexico and who spoke Spanish like a Mexican. *Punto.* There weren't many alternative ways of being Mexican. Despite the fact that we came in all shapes, colors, and even races, *mestizaje* (the mixed race) was the official *dictum* and master narrative. Whether we liked it or not, we were the bastard children of Hernán Cortez and La Malinche—product of a colonial rape and a cultural cesarean—eternally condemned to come to terms with this historical trauma. The millions of *indios*, the original proto-Mexicans, were portrayed as living in a parallel (and mythical) time and space outside *our* history and society. The paternalistic *indigenista* jargon of the government and the intelligentsia reduced indigenous people to infantilized, colorful ethnographic specimens that seemed to be cosponsored by the Department of Tourism and *National Geographic*. Their photographic image, folklore, and traditions were "nuestros"—ours—but not their misery, joblessness, and despair.

Not surprisingly, many chose to leave.

Those who dared to migrate *al otro lado*—to the other side—became instant traitors, inauthentic and bastardized Mexicans destined to join the ranks of the infamous *Pochos* who were the other forgotten orphans of the Mexican nation-state. And so, when I crossed the border, I unwittingly started my irreversible process of *Pocho*-ization or de-Mexicanization.

When I arrived in the USA, I innocently engaged in what turned out to be taboo behavior: I began to hang out with Chicanos (politicized Mexican-Americans) and to write in Spanglish (the tongue of the *Pochos*) about our hybrid identity that was demonized by both countries. I found that once you cross the border you could never really go back. Whenever I tried, I always ended up "on the other side," as if walking on a Moebius strip. My ex-*paisanos* on the Mexican side of the line made a point of reminding me that I was no longer "a true Mexican," that something, a tiny and mysterious crystal, had broken inside of me forever. After five years of "returning," in their minds I had forgotten the script of my identity. Even worse, I had "shipwrecked" on the other side (Octavio Paz used this loaded metaphor in a controversial essay that once angered the Chicano intelligentsia).

Six months after my arrival in Los Angeles, I decided to spend twenty-four hours in a public elevator wrapped in an Indian fabric bound with rope. I can only speculate in retrospect, but perhaps I did this as a way of expressing my profound feelings of cultural loneliness. I was unable to move or communicate verbally. My total anonymity and vulnerability seemed to grant my involuntary audience the freedom to confess to me intimate things about their lives—things I didn't want to hear—but also to abuse me verbally, and even to kick me. I overheard two adolescents discussing the possibility of setting me on fire. A dog peed on me, and at night, the security guards decided to pull a prank "on the weird artist." They threw me into an industrial trashcan, where I spent the last two hours of my first performance piece in the USA.

The strong emotional responses from my involuntary audiences made me realize what an ideal medium performance was to insert my existential and political dilemmas into the social sphere. Today, as I look back, I see this performance as a metaphor of my painful birth in a new country, of my new identity, "the Chicano," and of my new language, performance art.

II

For decades, both the US government and Mexico's Partido Revolucionario Institucional (PRI) had been immersed in a stubborn chess game of defensive nationalisms. Both sides saw the border between them as a straight line, not our Moebius strip; a dead-end, not an intersection. For the USA, the border was the scary beginning of the Dantean Third World, and therefore "the most sensitive zone of national security." For Mexico, *la frontera* was a conceptual wall that marked the outer limits of Mexican-ness against the mighty *gringo* Otherness.

Neither country understood (or they pretended not to understand) the political and cultural significance of the great Mexican migration that was taking place. In its more generous moments, Mexico saw us migrants as helpless *mojados* at the mercy of the Immigration Naturalization Service (INS), and with a few exceptions didn't do much to defend us. Despite the nationalistic jargon of its *politicos*, Mexico's hands were permanently tied by loans from the Washington bosses and secret commitments to business partners in the North. The *gringos* conveniently saw us as a primary source of America's social ills and financial tribulations, especially during tough economic times. To put it bluntly, we were perceived as a bunch of transnational criminals, gang members, drug lords, Hollywood-style greaser bandits, and job thieves—and we were treated accordingly. One country was relieved we were gone; the other was afraid to have us. Luckily, since we were Catholic, we accepted our postnational limbo stoically. After all, our goal was not to attain happiness on earth, but simply to make a decent living and send money back to our families in Mexico.

We simply couldn't escape our marked bodies. Being a Mexican "alien" in southern California meant to wake up every day and choose to remain so by consciously performing our Mexicanness. Whether we liked it or not, consciously or not, we became part of a culture of resistance. Just to look "Mexican" or speak Spanish in public was in itself an act of political defiance. Walking the lonely streets of southern California often entailed the possibility of being harassed or even busted by the police.

Our position vis-à-vis mainstream Californian culture was paradoxical to say the least. We were everywhere and nowhere. We were both the largest "minority" in the state and the least represented in the hierarchies of power. We were the undisputed backbone of the economy and the omnipresent bogeyman in the Anglo imagination. We were California's romantic backdrop and favorite food, and at the same time we were its epic fear: A gallant mariachi morphing back and forth into Godzilla.

If it hadn't been for Chicanos and other US Latinos, I probably would have died of loneliness, nostalgia, and invisibility. Chicanos taught me a different way of thinking about myself as an artist and as a citizen. Through them, I discovered that my art could be developed as a means to explore and reinvent my multiple and ever-shifting identities (something that had been unthinkable in Mexico). Thanks to this epiphany, I began to see myself as part of a larger US Chicano/Latino culture in a permanent process of reinvention. I was no longer a nostalgic immigrant yearning to return to a mythical homeland. I learned the basic lesson of *el movimiento*: I began to live "here" and "now," to fully embrace my brand-new contradictions and my incipient process of politicization as a much-touted "minority,"—to "reterritorialize" myself, as theorists would say.

And so my painful process of Chicanoization began.[1]

III

For an entire decade I was asked by Chicano nationalists and hardliners to pay expensive dues, and submit myself to thorough identity searches and blood tests. My desire to "belong" far outweighed my impatience and I waited stoically for my "conversion." During this time I was struck by an existential predicament which caused me to shed many tears, create performances ridden with pathos, and engage in obsessive inner questioning: How to ground my multiple repertoires of identity in a country which does not even regard me as a citizen? What are the crucial factors that determine degree of Chicanoization? Time spent as a politicized Mexican in the US, or a long-term commitment to *our* grassroots institutions and *causa*? Did I ever become a full Chicano? If so, when exactly did this happen? The day I was busted for talking back to a cop, or the day my father died and my umbilical cord with Mexico broke for good? Perhaps it happened when my ex-Mexican *paisanos* began to see me as Other?

Today, after twenty-four years of crossing that bloody border back and forth by foot, by car, and by airplane, as I write this text I wonder, does it even matter anymore when it happened? I realize that the space between my remote Mexican past and my Chicano future is immense and my identity can zigzag across it freely.

Eventually, it was my art and my literature that granted me the full citizenship denied to me by both countries. I invented my own conceptual country. In the "inverted cartography" of my performances and writings, Chicanos and US Latinos became the mainstream culture, with Spanglish as the *lingua franca*, and

1 A detailed description of the art projects reflecting my process of "Chicanoization" can be found in my first two books, *Warrior for Gringostroika*, Greywolf Press, 1993; and *New World Border*, City Lights, 1996.

Mexican artists in search of aggressive US curator to domesticate them.
Guillermo Gómez-Peña, Juan Ybarra and Violeta Luna at Gómez-Peña's home, Mexico City, 2003. Photo: Miguel Velasco.

monocultural Anglos became an ever-shrinking minority (*Waspbacks* or *Waspanos*) unable to participate in the public life of "my" country because of their unwillingness to learn Spanish and embrace our culture. My performance colleagues and I would often invite "all immigrants and people of color" to enter the theater or the museum first, then "all bilingual people and interracial couples," and finally "all monolingual Anglos." We began to treat our audiences as "exotic minorities" and temporary foreigners in "our" America. In a nutshell, we assumed a fictitious center and pushed the dominant culture to the margins. Art critics described this radical epistemology as "reverse anthropology" and "Chicano cyber-punk art." To me it was just a humorously heightened form of social realism.

IV

On January 1, 1994, the Zapatistas staged their legendary insurrection in Chiapas as NAFTA came into effect with its promise of "unifying" Mexico, the USA and Canada in a free-trade zone. Bringing the needs of indigenous Mexicans into the national political discussion for the first time, the Zapatistas effectively used poetic allegories, cyber-communiqués, and wild performance strategies to broadcast their worldview and effect change. Mexico has never been the same. Nor have US–Mexico relations. *Zapatismo* forced Mexico to reflect on its unrecognized plural identities and multiple crises. The country's endemic economic distress and racial divides were framed in the context of a call for democratic process: For "a place at the table for all Mexicans," not just those affiliated with the oligarchic structure that had ruled the country for so long. The Zapatista lesson was crystal clear: Democracy in Mexico could only exist if we acknowledged and incorporated its forbidden diversity. In the words of Subcomandante Marcos, this diversity included not just indigenous peoples, but also women, gays, youth, and even those on the other side of the national mirror: The Chicanos and "undocumented" Mexicans. With the rise of the Zapatistas, many forgotten and forbidden Mexicos, including those beyond the border, were resurrected. These Other Mexicos included the indigenous populations excluded from *National Geographic* spreads and tourist maps and the *Pochos* living beyond the border.

Zapatismo played an enormous role in the awakening of the *sociedad civil* (civil society) on both sides of the border. From the grass roots up, this movement challenged the PRI's stranglehold on state power and, paradoxically, helped the conservative Vicente Fox get elected as president some years later. It also reenergized the Chicano movement on this side of the border, which was under attack by virulent anti-immigration politicians and cultural backlashers. By 1996, Marcos was practically an honorary Chicano rocker, the avatar of Rage Against the

Machine. Many Chicano and border activists, artists, and intellectuals, including myself, made the obligatory pilgrimage to the *Chiapaneca* jungle. We were in search of a utopian political site in which to locate our voices and aspirations, but couldn't find it. Instead, we found yet another Mexico, *el profundo*. This Mexico was very different from those in the photo albums and distorted memories of our immigrant families, or those in the TV shows of Televisa. In this other Mexico, indigenous men and women were risking their lives on behalf of all the orphans of the two nation-states.

Eight years later, my heart continues to be with them.

V

NAFTA sponsored several mirages. Among others, it created the illusion that the US–Mexico border was fading away to allow the exchange of products, capital, "global media," and corporate dreams. Unfortunately, the free transit of people and ideas, especially from South to North, and respect for labor, human rights, and environmental standards weren't part of the original deal. It was clear that both governments favored open borders going from North to South and carefully supervised borders from South to North. It's not a coincidence that along with the implementation of NAFTA we witnessed the construction of a sinister metallic border wall that eerily resembles the old Berlin Wall. This gesture of despotic arrogance coincided with the implementation of Operation Gatekeeper and the radicalization of the "English-Only" movement.

The new wall contradicted the borderless rhetoric of the free-traders, revealing their true intentions. For the Northern countries, the wealthy ones who invented "the Global Project," the evil other was no longer the Eastern bloc; it was now the southern hemisphere, especially Latin America and Africa. The unfortunate Immigration Act of 1996 and California's Proposition 187 clearly targeted brown and black immigrants, formalizing this new paradigm shift. Other "Western" nations followed suit, criminalizing their own immigrant populations. Eventually, the coordination of anti-immigrant efforts became the only fiber sustaining the phony structure of globalization.

Given this backdrop, it became clear to many artists and intellectuals on both sides of the border that what we really needed was a "Free Art Agreement." From 1995 to 1998, many binational cultural initiatives that bypassed government agencies were created on both sides. Our main objective was to create an ongoing exchange of thorny ideas, noncommercial artwork, and literature across the border. Visionary artists and cultural impresarios from both countries took advantage of the rhetorical freeways created by NAFTA and used the expansive freedom of digital technologies to network and collaborate. For a while it felt as if we were getting somewhere. Experimental Mexican art, Spanglish poetry, *rock en español*, border and Chicano culture were considered "hip" and taken seriously in the US cultural milieu. Simultaneously, Mexico became aware of the importance of Chicano art and culture.

But it soon became clear that the cultural power-brokers on both sides were more interested in the financial benefits and the hype of the "international" art market than in visionary ideas. The border region became an Art Expo, grant-writing replaced critical art and thought, and "the border paradigm" replaced multiculturalism as the chic discourse and subject matter for biennials and international festivals. A burgeoning Mexican "Naftart" market offering a *maquiladora* (assembly plant) type of art was created strictly for foreign consumption. It caught the attention of collectors, impresarios, and cultural ventriloquists in the US commercial art circuits, ever hungry for new flavors and exotic cultures. Of course, the more acid, critical, and outrageous voices were left out of the binational fiesta.

VI

In the year 2000, the PRI's opposing candidate, Vicente Fox, made an appeal to Mexicans living in the USA. These voters were traditionally anti-PRI, favoring the PRD, a more progressive party. Fox asked us to return and vote in border towns. Many of us went, although there were not enough ballots for us when we got there. Still, we trusted Fox and celebrated his victory. Why? First and foremost, because he had democratically defeated the seventy-one-year-old PRI—a monumental achievement, bigger, perhaps, than winning the soccer World Cup. Fox was charismatic, frank, and photogenic—he even looked a bit like super-ranchero singer Vicente Fernández.

A few months after his victory, born-again-Christian cowboy George W. Bush defeated Al Gore in a voting process filled with irregularities and *corruptelas* that paradoxically resembled the old PRI practices so criticized by Washington in the past. The Mexican independent press jokingly called for a delegation of unemployed PRI politicians to travel to Washington and train the clumsy Republican Party in more sophisticated and discrete corruption methods.

Though Fox came from the corporate right, he began to behave more like a European social democrat. In his first official trip to *El Norte*, he told US President Clinton, Canadian Prime Minister Jacques Chretien, and then-candidates "Gush and Bore" of his utopian vision of US–Mexico relations. He wanted to: (1) Create "a trinational fund" that would eventually equalize the Mexican economy with its northern partners and slowly erase the border; (2) reform NAFTA on behalf of

Mexican workers; and (3) guarantee respect for the human rights of migrants. US and Canadian politicians flipped out. Chicanos and US Latinos, even I, flipped out. Why? Fox's "border project" sounded like a progressive Chicano activist proposal. The mirror of ideology was suddenly hanging upside down.

Fox's emotional inaugural speech was even more perplexing than his "border project." Alone, with little support behind him, and before an audience of adversaries—Mexico's calcified politicians and an international TV audience of skeptics—he promised indigenous peoples that he would implement the sensitive San Andrés Accords. These peace proposals had been negotiated but never introduced to Congress by the PRI after their uneasy "ceasefire" with the Zapatistas. If this weren't enough, he boldly told the political dinosaurs sitting before him that "no corruption would be tolerated," and that "the *peces gordos* will end up in jail." Later on, he even welcomed the *Marcha Zapatista* into Mexico City, and allowed masked Comandante Esther to address the country at the Palace of San Lazaro.

Fox's multi-ideological stances seemed to announce the beginning of a new, more enlightened era, surgically marked by the beginning of the new century. He formed an eclectic working team composed of business impresarios and politicians from all parties. He even appointed prominent leftist intellectuals to key cabinet positions, and invited several artists to join the foreign service as cultural attachés. (Let's pause here for a moment and imagine Jorge Bush appointing Native American poet and activist Susan Shown Harjo as Secretary of Foreign Affairs, Chicana writer Ana Castillo as the head of the INS, and performance artist Karen Finley as cultural attaché in the UK—long dramatic pause—unthinkable, *¿qué no*?)

VII

In 2001, US–Mexico relations became a priority for both presidents. Or so they said over and over. From a distance, Fox and Bush seemed to be infatuated with one another. Whenever they got together, they behaved like nineteenth-century hacienda-owners who loved to chat in each other's language about boots, cattle, quaint border culture, and, of course, *negocios*. Both Mexicans and Chicanos were carefully waiting and watching with binoculars as the new *rancheros* in power introduced a series of unprecedented proposals to improve border relations. Perhaps the most outrageous was the "regularization" of three million undocumented Mexicans in the US, an unquestionable step in the right direction, but a hard one to believe.

One couldn't help but ask out loud: Were these *cheros* for real? Did Jorge Bush really mean it, or was he trying to appeal to us as part of his greater plan to seduce Latino votes to assure the survival of his party? After all, up to that point the nativist Republicans had been extremely aggressive toward immigrants. What then, was

Bush's secret Mexican agenda? Water, electricity, petroleum, the need to find a powerful ally to implement his "Free Trade Area of the Americas"?[2]

The abrupt transformation of political structures in Mexico proved to be much more complicated than Fox's good intentions, Messianic personality, and media-savvy combined. Dissent erupted from all directions. The President was soon besieged by the passive-aggressive PRI who constantly stonewalled his new legislation, by the far right in his own party, and the drug lords and corrupt *judiciales* on whom he had declared war.

Fox was suddenly more lonely and sober than ever. Graffiti in downtown Mexico City read: "Fox . . . Fox You." His short-lived affair with the citizenry was over, and so were his outrageous promises of instant economic prosperity "for all Mexicans." To complicate things even more, the tragedy of 9/11 prompted the Bush administration to shift its foreign policy 180 degrees toward Afghanistan and "the War on Terror." As the Jetsons carpetbombed the Flintstones, Bush's Mexican *amigo* faded into the dusty background of a bad spaghetti western, and the many border projects concocted by Bush, Fox and Associates were indefinitely postponed.

VIII

Under the pretense of "national unity," and "national security," a frightening culture of intolerance, patriotism, paranoia, and isolationism has permeated our private and public lives. These cautionary measures further poisoned our already precarious relationship with Mexico and Canada. With the country in a state of "maximum alert," its two borders have been tightened considerably since 9/11; "suspicious [brown] immigrants" are rounded up and kept indefinitely in detention centers, and the *migra*—the border patrol—has doubled in numbers and ferocity. The border, once hailed by free-traders as the porous gateway for goods and services, is now "the entryway for potential terrorists." The "information superhighway" of the past administration, which promised to shorten the gap between cultures and communities, is now the largest surveillance system on earth.

These kamikaze measures have practically destroyed the US–Mexico border economy which is so crucial for both countries. They have forced 25 percent of the undocumented Mexican labor force to return home, crestfallen, and have frightened off potential tourists and binational entrepreneurs. As James Clifford told me

2 In Quebec City, Canada, on April 20, 2001, the heads of thirty governments of North, South, Central America, and the Caribbean met in secret with hundreds of corporations to negotiate the terms for the creation of a "Free Trade Agreement of the Americas." The proposal was designed by Bush and his cadre. The project was soon derailed by 9/11.

recently, "the question is how long can the US government afford this tightening of the border? [*Dramatic pause.*] Not long. Let's not forget that in contemporary politics, business weighs much more than fear." I hope with all my heart that James is right.

IX

In addition to the myriad challenges that President Fox faces in Mexico, he's got a formidable one on this side of the border: The fulfillment of his promise to develop a respectful, ongoing relationship with Mexicans and post-Mexicans living in the USA. These laborers literally sustain the economy of both countries. Like Bush, Fox knows we can no longer be ignored. Despite their self-serving hope that we might be induced to keep their respective parties in power, I truly hope that both presidents and the strange men behind them will soon realize that postnational Mexicans perform extremely beneficial roles for both nations as binational brokers and entrepreneurs, informal ombudsmen and diplomats, chroniclers and intercultural interpreters.

But reconciliation won't be easy. Understandably, we are wary. We've been profoundly hurt by the Mexican government's legacy of abandonment and by a history of institutionalized racism in the USA, which since 9/11 has become officialized through the Homeland Security Office. Besides, it is clear to most Mexican-Americans, even apolitical ones, that the dubious historical relationship between *Los Pinos* (the Mexican presidential house) and the White House is in some way responsible for us being here.

And so we came, like so many orphans from other countries seeking the gold at the end of the rainbow, only to find hardships, citizen vigilantes, and punitive immigration laws. In this painful process of becoming Chicanos, or *Americanos* in the widest sense of the Spanish term, we built invisible bridges between past and future, South and North, memory and identity, indigenous America and high-technology, art and politics. These handmade bridges may be more useful to contemporary US–Mexico relations than the rhetorical ones supposedly built by NAFTA and the global media.

Our numbers have only continued to grow. We now constitute an archipelago that spreads from North County, San Diego to Homestead, Florida, from East Los Angeles to East Harlem, and from San Antonio to Kodiak Island. We are thirty-five million postnational Mexicans, acculturated (or Chicanoized) to varying degrees, and involved, often silently, in every aspect of American culture, economy, and public life. In chorus with at least ten million other US Latinos, our mere existence demands the creation of a new cartography—a virtual nation in which Latinos, documented or not, can enjoy the same rights and privileges as other "Americans." I am not merely suggesting liberal tolerance or empty acknowledgments. I am talking about an imaginary place where difference is actually encouraged. This place would house theories and methods that could become the source of future political projects.

This "other Latin America," part of the larger Third World within the First, with a population larger than that of Canada and Australia put together, is currently being coimagined and drafted by Spanglish poets, hip-hop artists, fusion musicians, radical scholars, performance artists, and independent filmmakers.

In the year 2003, both the US and Mexico's monolithic visions of nationhood are being confronted by multiplicity, hybridity, tolerance, and *autogestion ciudadana* (citizen negotiation)—direct products of the border wound. It is the new South reminding *El Norte*, and the new North warning *El Sur*, in Spanglish and from the grass roots up, that no democratic vision of the future can be fully realized without including the Other—which, it turns out, is no longer so "other." As ghost citizens of a borderless nation, we may soon have to redefine the meanings of a long list of dated twentieth-century terminology. Words such as "alien," "foreigner," "immigrant," "minority," "diaspora," even "border," and "American" may no longer be useful to explain our new condition, identity, and dilemmas.

X

Two years ago, when Mexico and the USA finally allowed "dual citizenship" for the first time ever, many colleagues and I decided to apply. We hit the jackpot. We exchanged our green card for a gold one, and went from being partial, incomplete citizens to becoming full citizens in both countries (see "On Dual Citizenship", pp. 159–60). Our rationale for applying was: If our two countries were engaged in a seductive rhetoric of "free exchange," it was only logical that all Mexican-Americans should become dual citizens, and vote in both countries (what a scary thought, *¿qué no*?). It was only logical that we should demand to be treated as true partners in the project of imagining a more enlightened future for both countries . . . even if this logic only applies in the realms of the symbolic and the emotional.

For the moment, the image in the border mirror is frozen. I am extremely worried about Bush's and Ashchoft's notions of "America" and "homeland." "Their" cartography seems to have very little room for "us."

XI

When Arnold Schwarzenegger announced his controversial campaign to run for Governor of California, I began to have this recurring nightmare. I quote from my dream diary:

> **The stage is a mythical Chicano urbanscape, a composite city made out of generic Los Angeles skyscrapers, a pseudocolonial church, the Golden Gate Bridge, and the Alamo. In the background, the Hollywood hills (with the word "Haliwud") are framed by two techno-Aztec pyramids. In the apocalyptic skies lingering over my bed, I can see several taco-shaped UFOs squirting *salsa picante* all over, which creates an amazing aurora-borealis effect.**
>
> **I clearly see a central image: This muscular and mustachioed Vato Loco covered with "pinto" tattoos and bearing huge female breasts under his latex mariachi vest. It's *El Mexterminator* himself, defender of the rights of undocumented migrants and border-crossers, and archenemy of the *migra* (border patrol). He's got a robotic bleeding heart, and a techno-jalapeño phallus that squirts guacamole into the eyes of hysterical border-patrolmen running amok in the lower part of the stage, the dream stage, I mean. His "homeboys" are backing him up. They are tiny green aliens, slowly morphing into chihuahua guerrillas, who in turn morph into robo-lowriders.**
>
> **The *tableaux* get even more complex: A gorgeous blonde woman in a mariachi hat and a tight, bright-gold superhero jumpsuit stamped with the words "la mera chingona" patiently awaits her lover on the Mexican side of the border wall.**
>
> **Suddenly, out of the blue, "America's favorite killing machine," Terminator 4 himself steps into the middle of the screen and screams in his computerized macho voice: "Enough fun, you 'meskins'! You've run out of time! Let's shoot the real film!" Then he begins to shoot indiscriminately at everything and everyone while screaming: "Hasta la vista, cabrones!" until I wake up, all agitated.**

Why am I so anxious about a cheesy action-movie actor? Let's recapitulate a bit. Schwarzenegger started campaigning on the very same week his movie *Terminator 3* came out. His political mentor was Mr. Pete Wilson, the American version of France's Jean-Marie Le Pen. Despite his well-known anti-immigration stances and a dozen accusations of sexual groping, Schwarzenegger was actually elected with the help of the votes of women and Latinos. Why? Has the border between pop culture and social reality been thoroughly erased? To the astonishment of the international community, yet another unapologetic neomacho rose to power in the Bush era. Clearly, his mandate was to protect his version of the American dream in a world of undetermined turmoil and out-of-control borders, to make California an all-too-real movie in which his brutish alter ego defends the state against migrants, terrorists, gang members, feminists, poor people, and all evil-doers and "predators" who stand in his way.

Mexico's reaction was immediately felt. From the streets to the senate, the whole country protested a known racist with no political experience whatsoever becoming "governator" of the state with the most complex cultural and business relationship with Mexico. But, as Mexicans expected, the US press did not report Mexico's outrage. Why? Americans have never really cared about what Mexico thinks, especially in the Bush era, where isolationism and unilateralism are perceived as mere byproducts of patriotism.

Perhaps this feeling of despair and abandonment is what fuels my recurring dream. I mean, to realize that our immediate future as postnational Mexicans in the USA is a movie in which the main roles are those of a fundamentalist cowboy and a cyborg-killer. Will El Mexterminator be able to defend himself from the Terminator? I wonder what will be the terms and context of this inevitable fight? Culture? Politics? Demography? A cyber-punk flick directed by a Chicano?

2

In defense of performance

(Essay/Chronicle, 2003)

Question
"Excuse me, can you define performance art?"

Answers
"A bunch of weirdos who love to get naked and scream about leftist politics." (Yuppie in a bar)

"Performance artists are . . . bad actors." (A "good" actor)

"You mean, those decadent and elitist liberals who hide behind the art thing to beg for government money?" (Politician)

"It's . . . just . . . very, very cool stuff. Makes you . . . think, and shit." (My nephew)

"Performance is both the antithesis of and the antidote to high culture." (Performance artist)

"I'll answer you with a joke: What do you get when you mix a comedian with a performance artist? . . . A joke that no one understands." (A friend)

INTRO

For twenty years, journalists, audience members, and relatives have asked me the same two questions in different ways: What "exactly" is performance art? And what

El Techno-Shaman and his possessed performance assistant.
Guillermo Gómez-Peña and Agatha Gothe-Snape. Performance Space, Sydney, 2000.
Photo: Heidrun Lohr.

makes a performance artist be, think, and act like one? In this text, I will attempt to elliptically answer these questions by drawing a poetical portrait of the performance artist standing on a map of the performance-art field. I will try to write with as much passion, valor, and clarity as I can, but take heed: The slippery and ever-changing nature of the field makes it extremely hard to define in simplistic terms. As my conceptual *padrino* Richard Schechner told me after he read an early version of this text,

> the "*problem*," if there is a problem, is that the field "in general" is too big and encompassing. It can be, and is, whatever those who are doing it say it is. At the same time, and for the same reason, the field "in specific" is too small, too quirky, too much the thing of this or that individual (artist, scholar) who is doing the doing.

With this in mind, I will, in this text, attempt to articulate "my thing"—to map my own performance field, so to speak. In doing so, I will try to join my many colleagues, the rest of the citizens of *my* performance map, in the common goal of critiquing "high art," consumer culture, and global politics, as well as narrowminded notions of identity, community, and art-making.

To be congruent with my performance praxis, I will constantly cross the borders between theory and chronicle, between personal and social realms, in hopes of coming across some interesting cross sections and bridges.

I am fully aware that my voice within this text is but one in a crowd of subjectivities. By no means am I attempting to speak for others, to establish boundaries and checkpoints in the performance field, or to outlaw any art practice that is not captured by my camera. If the reader detects some conceptual contradictions in my writing—especially in my strategic use of the dangerous pronoun "we" or in my capricious placement of a border—I beg you to cut me some extra slack: I am a contradictory *vato*, and so are most performance artists I know.

THE CARTOGRAPHY OF PERFORMANCE

I The map

First, let's draw the map.

I see myself as an experimental cartographer. In this sense I can approach a definition of performance art by mapping out the "negative" space (as in photography, not ethics) of its conceptual territory. Though our work sometimes overlaps with experimental theater, and many of us utilize spoken word, *stricto sensu*, we are neither actors nor spoken-word poets. (We may be temporary actors and poets but we abide by other rules, and stand on a different history.)[1] Most performance artists are also writers, but only a handful of us write for publication. We theorize about art, politics, and culture, but our interdisciplinary methodologies are different from those of academic theorists. *They* have binoculars; *we* have radars. Performance artists spend the bulk of our time "scanning" rather than "focusing," as theorists do, settling on one spot and then pulling out the binoculars. When performance-studies scholars refer to "the performance field," they often mean something different than

1 The history of performance art has been largely written from the ethnocentric perspective of the European and "American" (as in US) avant-garde and does not acknowledge other histories of indigenous and ritual performance. In the Americas, pre-Columbian performance practices may have more to do with the history of performance art than with theater, but this is a territory I am not trained to defend.

what performance artists mean: A much broader field that encompasses all things performative, including anthropology, religious practice, pop culture, and sports and civic events. While *we* chronicle our times, unlike journalists or social commentators, our chronicles tend to be non-narrative, symbolic, and polyvocal. It's a different way of chronicling. If we utilize humor, we are not seeking laughter like our comedian cousins. We are more interested in provoking the ambivalence of melancholic giggling or painful smiles, though an occasional outburst of laughter is always welcome.

Many of us are exiles from the visual arts, but we rarely make objects for display in museums and galleries. In fact, our main artwork is our own body, ridden with semiotic, political, ethnographic, cartographic, and mythical implications. Unlike visual artists and sculptors, when we create objects, they are meant to be handled and utilized without remorse during the performance. We actually don't mind if these objects get worn out or destroyed. In fact, the more we use our performance "artifacts," the more "charged" and powerful they become. Recycling is our main modus operandi. This dramatically separates us from most costume-, prop-, and set-designers, who rarely recycle their creations.

At times we operate in the civic realm, and test our new personae and actions in the streets, but we are not "public artists" per se. The streets are mere extensions of our performance laboratory—galleries without walls. Many of us think of ourselves as activists, but our communication strategies and experimental languages are considerably different from those utilized by political radicals and antiglobalization activists.

We are what others aren't, we say what others don't, and we occupy cultural spaces that are often overlooked or dismissed. Because of this, our multiple communities are composed of esthetic, political, ethnic, and gender rejects.

II The sanctuary

For me, performance art is a conceptual "territory" with fluctuating weather and borders, a place where contradiction, ambiguity, and paradox are not only tolerated, but encouraged. Every territory a performance artist stakes (including this text) is slightly different from that of their neighbor. We converge in this overlapping terrain precisely because it grants us special freedoms often denied to us in other monocultural/unidisciplinary realms. In a sense, we are hardcore dropouts from our original *métiers* and communities, embarking on a permanent quest to develop a more inclusive system of political thought and esthetic praxis. It's a lonely and largely misunderstood journey, but most performance artists I know, including myself, love it.

"Here" tradition weighs less, rules can be bent, laws and structures are constantly changing, and no one pays much attention to hierarchies and institutional power. "Here," there is no government or visible authority. "Here," the only existing social contract is our willingness to defy authoritarian models and dogmas, and to keep pushing the outer limits of culture and identity. It is precisely in the sharpened borders of cultures, genders, *métiers*, languages, and art forms that we feel more comfortable, and where we recognize and befriend our colleagues. We are interstitial creatures and border citizens by nature—insiders/outsiders at the same time—and we rejoice in this paradoxical condition. In fact, in the act of crossing a border, we find temporary emancipation.

Our performance country is a temporary sanctuary for other rebel artists and theorists expelled from monodisciplinary fields and separatist communities. It's also an internal place, invented by each of us according to our own political aspirations and deepest spiritual needs; our darkest sexual desires and obsessions; our troubling memories and relentless quest for freedom. As I finish this paragraph I bite my romantic tongue. It bleeds. It's real blood. My audience gets really excited because the blood is real.

III The human body

Traditionally, the human body, our body, not the stage, is our true site for creation and *materia prima*.[2] It's our empty canvas, musical instrument, and open book; our navigation chart and biographical map; the vessel for our ever-changing identities; the centerpiece of the altar, so to speak. Even when we depend too much on objects, locations, and situations, our body remains the matrix of the piece.

Our body is also the very center of our symbolic universe—a tiny model for humankind (humankind and humanity are the same word in Spanish: *Humanidad*)—and

2 Richard Schechner problematizes my body argument: If the human body is the ultimate site of performance, "where do you put 'virtual' artists who operate only on the web using Avatars or wholly digitized beings?" Richard raises a hairy predicament: Should we consider the "virtual bodies" real? One of my "readers" who chose to remain anonymous also problematizes my body argument: "As Gómez-Peña says, the question of whether a web action can be considered a performance is critical and too important to leave unanswered. If, as many have suggested, online events are in some sense performative–take Electronic Disturbance Theater (EDT) for example–then the definition of performance offered here comes under pressure. I realize that performance artists feel, rightly, that digital work has been unduly lauded in the past, but that moment is probably past. The question for now is how to redraw the boundaries so that EDT and its like are part of performance but MTV online isn't."

at the same time, a metaphor for the larger sociopolitical body. If we are capable of establishing all these connections in front of an audience, hopefully others will recognize them in their own bodies.

Our scars are involuntary words in the open book of our body, whereas our tattoos, piercings, body paint, adornments, performance prosthetics, and/or robotic accessories, are deliberate phrases.

Our body/corpo/arte-facto/identity must be marked, decorated, intervened culturally, mapped out, chronicled, repoliticized, and recaptured by the camera. When our body is ill or wounded, our work inevitably changes. Bob Flanagan, Ron Athey, Franco B., and others have made us beautifully aware of this.

Our bodies are also occupied territories. Perhaps the ultimate goal of performance, especially if you are a woman, gay, or a person "of color," is to decolonize our bodies and make these decolonizing mechanisms apparent to our audience in the hope that they will get inspired to do the same with their own.

Though we treasure our bodies, we don't mind constantly putting them at risk. It is precisely in the tensions of risk that we find our corporeal possibilities and *raison d'être*. Though our bodies are imperfect, awkward-looking, and frail, we don't mind sharing them, bare naked, with the audience, or offering them in sacrifice to the video camera. But I must clarify here: It's not that we are exhibitionists (at least not all of us). In fact, it's always painful to exhibit and document our imperfect bodies, riddled with racial, cultural, and political implications. We just have no other option. It's like a "mandate," for lack of a better word.

IV My "job"

Do I have a job? [*Dramatic pause.*]

My job may be to open up a temporary utopian/dystopian space, a "de-militarized zone" in which meaningful "radical" behavior and progressive thought are allowed to take place, even if only for the duration of the performance. In this imaginary zone, both artist and audience members are given permission to assume multiple and ever-changing positionalities and identities. In this border zone, the distance between "us" and "them," self and other, art and life, becomes blurry and unspecific.

My job may also be to raise questions. I do not look for answers; I merely raise irritating questions. In this sense, to use an old metaphor, my job may be to open the Pandora's box of our times—smack in the middle of the gallery, the theater, the street, or in front of the video camera—and let the demons loose. Others that are better trained—the activists and academics—will have to deal with them, fight them, domesticate them, or attempt to explain them.

Once the performance is over and people walk away, my hope is that a process of reflection gets triggered in their perplexed psyches. If the performance is effective (I didn't say good, but effective), this process can last for several weeks, even months. The questions and dilemmas embodied in the images and rituals I present can continue to haunt the spectator's dreams, memories, and conversations. The objective is not to "like" or to "understand" performance art, but to create a sediment in the audience's psyche.

V Identity survival kit

Performance has taught me an extremely important lesson that defies all essentialisms: I am not straitjacketed by identity. I have a repertoire of multiple identities and I constantly sample from them. My collaborators and I know very well that with the strategic use of props, make-up, accessories, and costumes, we can actually reinvent our identity in the eyes of others, and we love to experiment with this unique kind of knowledge. In fact, social-, ethnic-, and gender-bending are an intrinsic part of our daily praxis, and so is cultural transvestism. In performance, impersonating other cultures and problematizing the very process of impersonation can be an effective strategy of what I term "reverse anthropology."[3] In everyday life, however, as potential victims of ethnic-profiling and racism, impersonating other cultures can literally save our lives.

To give the reader an example: When my Chicano colleagues and I cross international borders, we know that to avoid being sent to secondary inspection, we can wear mariachi hats and jackets and instantly reinvent ourselves as "amigo entertainers" in the eyes of racist law enforcement. It works. "Welcome back amigos," they tell us. But even then, if we are not careful, our fiery gaze and lack of coolness might denounce us.

VI The irreplaceable body

Our audiences may vicariously experience other possibilities of esthetic, political, and sexual freedom they lack in their own lives. This may be one of the reasons why, despite innumerable predictions over the past thirty years, performance art hasn't died, nor has it been replaced by video or made outdated by new technologies and

3 By "reverse anthopology" I mean pushing the dominant culture to the margins and treating it as exotic and unfamiliar. Whether conscious or not, performance challenges and critiques the ideological products of anthropology and its fraudulent history and yet still utilizes parts of the discipline's methodologies.

robotics. Stelarc's early 1990s warning that "the body [was] becoming obsolete" turned out to be untrue. It is simply impossible to replace the ineffable magic of a pulsating, sweaty body immersed in a live ritual in front of our eyes. It's both shamanic and communal.

In my opinion, no actor, robot, or virtual avatar can replace the singular spectacle of the body-in-action of the performance artist. I simply cannot imagine a hired actor operating Chico McMurtrie's primitive robots, or reenacting Orlan's operations. When we witness Stelarc demonstrating a brand-new robotic bodysuit or high-tech toy, after fifteen minutes, once the novelty wears out, we tend to pay more attention to his sweating flesh than to his prosthetic armor and perceptual extensions. The paraphernalia is great, but the human body attached to the mythical identity of the performance artist in front of us remains at the center of the event.

Recently, Cuban performance artist Tania Bruguera has embarked on an extremely daring project: Abolishing her physical presence during the actual performance. She asks curators in advance to find a "normal person," not necessarily connected to the arts, to replace her. When Tania arrives at the site she exchanges

The Samoan cyborg at *The Museum of Fetishized Identities.*
Brian Fuatta. Performance Space, Sydney, 2000. Photo: Heidrun Lohr.

identities with the chosen person, becoming a mere assistant to their wishes. Curators are flipping out.

TURNING THE GAZE INWARD

VII At odds with authority

Yes. I am at odds with authority, whether it is political, religious, sexual, or esthetic, and I am constantly questioning imposed structures and dogmatic behavior wherever I find them. As soon as I am told what to do and how to do it, my hair goes up, my blood begins to boil, and I begin to figure out ways to dismantle that particular form of authority. I share this personality trait with most of my colleagues. In fact, we crave the challenge of dismantling abusive authority.

We never think twice about putting ourselves on the line and denouncing social injustice wherever we detect it. Without a second thought, we are always ready to throw a pie in the face of a corrupt politician, to give the finger to an arrogant museum director, or to tell off an impertinent journalist, regardless of the consequences. This personality trait often makes us appear a bit antisocial, immature, or overly dramatic in the eyes of others, but we just can't help it. It's a visceral thing, and at times a real drag. I secretly envy my "cool" friends.

VIII Siding with the underdog

We tend to see our probable future reflected in the eyes of the homeless, the poor, the unemployed, the diseased, and newly arrived immigrants. We perceive our "underworld" as overlapping with theirs.

Because of this bohemian mythology, we are often attracted to those who barely survive the dangerous corners of society: Hookers, winos, lunatics, and prisoners whom we perceive as our spiritual brothers and sisters. Although we feel a strong spiritual kinship with them, our material realities are different. Unfortunately, they often drown in the same waters in which we swim—the same waters, just different levels of submersion.

Our politics are not necessarily ideologically motivated. Our humanism resides in the throat, the skin, the muscles, the heart, the solar plexus, and the genitalia. Our empathy for social orphanhood expresses itself as a visceral form of solidarity with those peoples, communities, or countries facing oppression and human-rights violations, with those victimized by imposed wars and unjust economic policies. Unfortunately, as Ellen Zacco recently pointed out to me, "[we] tend to speak for them, which is quite presumptuous." I cannot help but agree with her. Those of us who enjoy certain privileges in the field must be extremely watchful regarding our Messianic tendencies.

IX Clumsy activists

With a few venerable exceptions (Ricardo Dominguez, Felipe Ehrenberg, Suzanne Lacey, Tim Miller, Keith Hennessy, and a few others), performance artists make clumsy political negotiators and terrible community-organizers. Our great dilemma here is that we often see ourselves as activists and, as such, we attempt to organize our ethnic, gender-based, or professional communities. But the results, bless our hearts, are often poor. Why? Our passion and rage are simply too combative for regulated protest, and we get easily lost in logistics and pragmatic discussions. Besides, our iconoclastic personalities, antinationalistic stances and experimental proposals often put us at odds with conservative sectors within these communities. However, we never learn the basic lesson: Performance artists function at a level that is not exactly in tune with the needs and necessities of everyday life and everyday resistance. Organizing and negotiating are definitely not our strengths. Others, better skilled, must help us organize the basic structure for our shared madness—never the other way around.

We are much better at performing other important community roles such as *animateurs*, reformers, alternative semioticians, inventors of brand-new metafictions, choreographers of surprising collective actions, media pirates, and/or "cultural DJs."[4] In fact, our esthetic strategies (not our coordinating skills) can be extremely useful to activists, and they often understand that it is in their best interest to have us around. I secretly advise several activists. Others, like Marcos and Superbarrio who are consummate performance activists, continue to inspire me.

X A matter of life or death

The cloud of nihilism is constantly chasing me around, but I somehow manage to escape it. It's a daily macabre dance right on the border between hope and despair. Whether conscious or not, deep inside I truly believe that what I do actually changes people's lives, and I have a real hard time being cool about it. Performance is a matter of life or death to me. My sense of humor often pales next to my sobriety when it

4 A term coined by my compañera Carolina Ponce de León.

comes to committing to a life/art project. If I suddenly decide to stop talking for a month (to, say, investigate "silence"), walk nonstop for three days (to reconnect with the social world or research the site-specificity of a project), or cross the US–Mexico border without documents to make a political point, I won't rest until I complete my task, regardless of the consequences. This can be maddening to my loved ones, who must exercise an epic patience with me. They must live with the impending uncertainty and the profound fear of my next commitment to yet another transformative existential project. Bless the hearts and hands of our lifetime *compañeros/compañeras*—always waiting for us and worrying about us; bless their tears and their laughter which often remind us that what we do, after all, may not always be a matter of life or death.

XI Dreaming in Spanish

I dreamt in Spanish that one day I decided to never perform in English again. A partir de ese momento, me dediqué a presentar mis ideas y mi arte estrictamente en español y solo para públicos estadounidenses atónitos que no entendían nada. Mi español se hizo cada vez mas retórico y complicado hasta el punto en que perdí todo contacto con mi público. A pesar de los ataques de los críticos racistas, me empeciné en hablar español. Entonces, mis colaboradores se molestaron y empezaron a abandonarme. Eventualmente me quede completamente solo, hablando en español, entre fantasmas conceptuales angloparlantes. Afortunadamente I woke up one day and I was able to perform in English again. I wrote in my diary: "Dreams tend to be much more radical than 'reality.' That's why they are much closer to art than to life."

XII An urban legend

At times, our performance universe can be threatening to our loved ones. Our perceived "extreme behavior" on stage, paired with our frequent association with sexual radicals, social misfits, and eccentrics, can make our loved ones feel a bit "inadequate" or "lightweight" next to our bizarre performance universe.

To complicate things even more, the highly sexualized energies and naked bodies roaming around the space before a performance can easily become a source of jealousy for our partners who often have a hard time differentiating between the real and the symbolic. The great paradox here is, despite our (largely symbolic) sexual onstage eccentricities and our willingness to perform nude, we tend to be quite loyal and committed to our partners and family. Our kinkiness is an urban legend and pales in comparison to that of US talk-show guests and Catholic priests.

XIII Necessary and unnecessary risks

Though performance artists are always risking our lives and physical integrity in the name of art, we rarely kill ourselves and absolutely never kill others. In twenty years of hanging out and working with performance artists, I have never met a murderer, have only lost three colleagues to the demons of suicide, and two to miscalculation during an actual performance.[5]

In the process of finding the true dimensions and possibilities of a new piece, I must confess that a few times I have idiotically put myself, and my audience, at risk, but somehow nothing extremely grave has ever happened . . . yet.

I quote from a script:

> **Dear audience, I've got forty-five scars accounted for, half of them produced by art, and this is not a metaphor. My artistic obsession has led me to carry out some flagrantly stupid acts of transgression, including: Living inside a cage as a Mexican Frankenstein; crucifying myself as a mariachi to protest immigration policy; crashing the Met as El Mad Mex led on a leash by a Spanish dominatrix . . . I mean [*to an audience member*], you want me to be more specific than say, drinking a bottle of Mr. Clean to exorcize my colonial demons? or handing a dagger to an audience member and offering her my plexus? [*Pause*] "Here . . . my colonized body"–I said, and she went for it, inflicting my forty-fifth scar. She was only twenty, *boricua*, and did not know the difference between performance, rock and roll, and street life. Bad phrase, delete . . .**

XIV Embodied theory

I quote from my performance diaries:

> **My intelligence, like that of shamans and poets, is largely symbolic and associative. My system of thought tends to be both**

5 As I was revising this text, I received a phone call from a friend in New York. The body of Spalding Gray was found in the East River. He had been missing for over two months.

> **emotionally and corporeally based. In fact, the performance always begins in my skin and muscles, projects itself onto the social sphere, and returns via my psyche, back to my body and into my bloodstream, only to be refracted back into the social world via documentation. Whatever thoughts I can't embody, I tend to distrust. Whatever ideas I can't feel way deep inside, I tend to disregard. In this sense I can say that for me performance is a form of embodied theory . . . Because of this, in the eyes of my relatives and nonartist friends, I appear to be a bit self-involved, as if the entire universe revolved around my psyche and body. My main struggle is precisely to escape my subjectivity–the imprisonment of my personal obsessions and solipsistic despair–and performance becomes the only way out; or rather, the way for the personal paradigm to intersect with the social . . .**

XV Dysfunctional archives

Performance artists have huge archives at home, but they are not exactly functional. In other words, "the other histories of art" are literally buried in damp, moldy boxes stored in the closets of performance artists worldwide. And—let's face it—most likely no one will ever have access to them. Much worse, some of these boxes, containing one-of-a-kind photos, performance documents, rare magazines, and master audios and videos, get lost in the process of moving to another home, city, project, or lover—or, to a new identity.

If every art and performance-studies department from every university made the effort to rescue these endangered archives from our clumsy hands, an important history would be saved, one that rarely gets written about precisely because it constitutes the "negative" space of culture (as in esthetics not ethics).

XVI Everyday life

If I were to *anthropologize* my everyday life, what would I find? (I quote from a series of personal emails with a Peruvian friend who struggles to understand "what is my everyday life like in San Francisco when I'm not on the road.")

Dear X,

The nuts and bolts of everyday life are a true inferno. To put it bluntly, I simply don't know how to manage myself. Typically, I am terrible with money, administrative matters, grant-writing, and self-promotion—and often rely on the goodwill of whoever wishes to help. I have no medical or car insurance. I don't own my home. I travel a lot, but always in connection to my work, and rarely have vacations, long vacations, like normal people do. I am permanently in debt, but I don't mind it. I guess it's part of the price I have to pay not to be permanently bothered by financial considerations. If I could live without a bank account, a driver's license, a passport, and a cell phone, I would be quite happy, though I am fully aware of the naïveté of my anarchist aspirations. Many of my colleagues here are in a similar situation. What about performance artists in your country?

. . . No, my most formidable enemy is not always the right-wing forces of society but my own inability to domesticate quotidian chaos and discipline myself. In the absence of a nine-to-five job, traditional social structures, and the basic requirements of other disciplines (i.e., rehearsals, curtain calls, and production meetings in theater, or the tightly scheduled lives of dancers or musicians), I tend to feel oppressed by the tyranny of domesticity and get easily lost in the horror vacui of an empty studio or the liquid screen of my laptop. Sometimes, the screen of my laptop becomes a mirror, and I don't like what I see. Melancholy rules my creative process . . . No, I don't think melancholy is a personality trait of all Mexican artists.

. . . Performance is a need. If I don't perform for a long period of time, say two or three months, I become unbearable and drive my loved ones crazy. Once I am onstage again, I instantly overcome my metaphysical orphanhood and psychological fragility and become larger than life. Later on at the bar, I will recapture my true size and endemic mediocrities. The irreverent humor of my collaborators and friends contributes to this "downsizing process."

. . . My salvation? My salvation lies in my ability to create an alternative system of thought and action capable of providing some sort of ritualized structure to my daily life . . . No, I take it back. My true salvation lies in collaboration. I collaborate with others in hopes of developing bridges between my personal obsessions and our social universe. . . . True. I'm kind of . . . "weird" in the eyes of my neighbors and relatives. I talk to animals, to plants, and to my many inner selves. I like to piss outdoors and get lost in the streets of cities I don't know. I love make-up, body decoration, and flamboyant female clothing. I particularly love to cyborgize ethnic clothing. You've seen my robo-mariachi suits. Paradoxically I don't like to be stared at. I am a living, walking contradiction. Aren't you? Aren't we all?

. . . I collect unusual figurines, talismans, souvenirs, tchotchkes, and costumes connected to my "cosmology," in the hope that one day they might be useful in a piece. It's my "personal archeology," and it dates back to the day I was born. With it, wherever I go, I build altars to ground myself. And these altars are as eclectic and complex as my personal esthetics and my many composite identities.

. . . Why? I am extremely superstitious, but I don't talk much about it. I see ghosts and read symbolic messages everywhere. Deep inside I believe there are unspoken metaphysical laws ruling my encounters with others, the major changes in my life, and my creative process (everything is a process to me, even sleeping and walking). My shaman friends say that I am "a shaman who lost his way." I like that definition of performance art.

XVII Celebrity culture

(Censored by the Editor)

[redacted]

XVIII I dreamt I was a pop celebrity

I dreamt I was a performance artist who was "discovered" by an LA entertainment producer. In order to "refine" my act, he forced me to rehearse twelve hours a day. Eventually I became a sort of hybrid between Lenny Bruce and Antonio Banderas. One night, I was performing my over-rehearsed material for a huge audience at a sports arena when suddenly I . . . forgot my lines. I stood still, trembling under a follow spot. After an eternal pause (in dreamtime), the audience began to applaud. They probably thought my hesitation was a conceptual decision, and loved it.

I flipped out and began to free-fall inside my psyche as if spiraling into another dream. While falling, I recapitulated my life as a performance artist. At the end of a fast-paced succession of images, I realized that *that* life had been much more interesting than my new life as a Latino pop celebrity. I opened my eyes and found myself once again at the sports arena. I got depressed. I opened a bottle of gasoline (which just happened to be there), poured it over my head, and lit myself on fire. The audience went wild again and applauded my pitiful "bozo" act. At that point, I awoke with tears of perspiration, sat on the edge of my bed, and thought to myself: "*Qué* weird—only in a dream can one reconcile an extreme performance esthetic with the basic requirements of a pop-cultural spectacle. *Qué* pinche weird."

PERFORMANCE VIS-À-VIS THEATER AND THE ART WORLD

XIX Performance and theater

Before I cross the next dangerous border, I must acknowledge the important contributions of experimental theater (the Living Theater, the Performance Group, Jodorowsky, etc.) to the development of performance, as well as the most recent influence that performance art has had over theater, every time theater is in crisis. Having said this, I will now attempt to venture into the extremely dangerous border-zone between theater and performance with the clear understanding that my project is not to put performance on a binary with theater. Despite the fact that they often occupy the same stage, there are some methodological differences: (As I begin to list these differences, Schechner warns me in an email: "I would say that some distance needs to be made theoretically separating theater that presents dramas (plays) from theater that is 'direct' or presents the performer without plays.")

Although most experimental and antinarrative forms of theater are often in dialogue with performance art, their texts tend to have a beginning, a dramatic crisis (or a series of dramatic crises), and an end. Whereas a performance "event" or "action" is just a segment of a much larger "process" not made available to the audience, and not necessarily made explicit in the event. In this sense, *stricto sensu*, it has no beginning or end. We simply choose a portion of our process and open the doors to expose the audience to it.

Most Western theater structures (even those of ensemble theaters and rebel theater collectives) tend to be somewhat hierarchical with a specialized division of labor (the leader or visionary, the best actors, the supporting actors, and the technical team each taking care of their specific task); whereas the structure of performance tends to be more horizontal, decentered, and constantly in flux. In performance, every project demands a different division of labor. And when we do solo work, we become the producer, writer, director, and performer of our own material. We even design the lights, the sound, and the costumes. There's nothing heroic about this. In fact, sometimes it gets to be a real drag, and we long for the support system of theater.

In drama theater, the actors are not usually the authors. On the other hand, in performance art the performers are almost always the authors. In most theater practice based on text, once the script is finished, it gets memorized and obsessively rehearsed by the actors, and it will be performed almost identically every night. Even the most audacious experimental theater offers highly staged chaos and premeditated hypertextuality. In performance, whether text-based or not, the script is just a blueprint for action, a hypertext contemplating multiple contingencies and options, and it is never "finished." Every time I publish a script, I must warn the reader: "This is just one version of the text. Next week it will be different."

Rehearsals in the traditional sense are not that important to us. In fact, performance artists spend more time researching the site and subject matter of the project, gathering props and objects, studying our audiences, brainstorming with collaborators, writing obscure notes that no one will ever read, and preparing ourselves psychologically, than "rehearsing" behind closed doors. It's just a different process.

Concurrently, a powerful mythology of antihero and countercultural avatar surrounds the performance artist. Audiences don't really mind that Annie Sprinkle is not a trained actress or that Ema Villanueva is not a skilled dancer. Audiences attend the performance precisely to be witnesses to our unique existence (a convergence of legend and flesh), not to applaud our virtuosity.

Onstage, performance artists rarely "represent" others. Rather, we allow our multiplicity of selves and voices to unfold and enact their frictions and contradictions in front of an audience. "To 're-present' would mean to be 'different' from what we are doing," says Brazilian performance artist Nara Heeman. "Our embodied knowledge and images are only possible because they are truly *ours*." Whether we are trained or not (most of the time we aren't), this separates performance artists from theater monologists performing multiple characters: When Anna

Deveare-Smith, Elia Arce, or Eric Bogosian "perform" multiple personae, they don't exactly "represent" them or "act" like them. Rather, they morph in and out of them without ever disappearing entirely as "themselves." Perhaps they occupy a space between acting and being themselves. At one point in their lives, certain theater monologists like Spalding Grey (RIP) and Jesusa Rodriguez decided to cross the thin line into performance in search of extra freedom and danger. We welcome them.

Clearly, there are many exceptions to the rule on both sides of the mirror, and there are many mirrors around.

XX Art criminals

Performance artists get easily criminalized. The highly charged images we produce, and the mythologies that embellish our public personae, make us recognizable targets for the rage of opportunistic politicians and conservative journalists looking for blood. They love to portray us as either promiscuous social misfits, gratuitous provocateurs, or "elitist" good-for-nothing bohemians sponsored by the "liberal establishment." Unlike most of my colleagues, I don't entirely mind this mischaracterization, for I believe it grants us an undeserved respectability and power as cultural antiheroes.

Conservative politicians are fully aware of the unique power of performance art. And when funding-cut time arrives, performance is the first one to go. Why? They claim it is because we are "decadent," "elitist," or (in the USA) "un-American." In fact US Republicans love to portray our work as some kind of bizarre communist pornography, but—let's face it—the fact is that these ideologues know it is extremely hard to domesticate us. When a politician attacks performance art, it is because they get irritated when they see their own parochial and intolerant image reflected upside-down in the mirror of art. The horrible faces of Helms, Buchanan, and Giuliani immediately come to mind.

XXI A performance artist dreams of being an actor

I dreamed I was a good actor, not a performance artist, but an actor, a good one. I could realistically represent someone else in a movie or a theater play, and I was so convincing as an actor that I would become that other person, forgetting completely who I was. The "character" I represented in my dream was that of an essentialist performance artist, someone who hated naturalistic acting, social and psychological realism, someone who despised artifice, make-up, costumes, memorizing lines, being directed.

Brownsheep.
Gigi Oltavaro. Galeria de la Raza, San Francisco, 2000. Photo: Eugenio Castro.

In my dream, the performance artist began to rebel against the actor, myself. He did shit like not talking for a week, or only moving in slow motion for a whole day, or putting on tribal make-up and hitting the streets just to challenge people's sense of the familiar. He was clearly fucking with my mind, and I, the "good actor," got so confused that I ended up having an identity breakdown and didn't know how to act anymore. I adopted a stereotypical fetal position and froze inside a large display case for an entire week. Luckily it was just a dream. When I finally woke up, I was the same old confused performance artist, and I was extremely thankful for not knowing how to act.

XXII Time and space

Notions of time and space are complicated in performance. We deal with a heightened "now," and "here," with the ambiguous space between "real time" and "ritual time," as opposed to theatrical or fictional time. (Ritual time is not to be confused with slow motion.) We deal with "presence" and "attitude" as opposed to "representation" or psychological depth, with "being here" in the space as opposed to "acting." Schechner elaborates in another email: "In performance art the 'distance' between the really real (socially, personally, with the audience, with the performers) is much less than in drama theater where just about everything is pretend—where even the real (a coffee cup, a chair) becomes pretend."

Like time, space to us is also "real," phenomenologically speaking. The building where the performance takes place is precisely that very building. The performance occurs precisely in the day and time it takes place, and at the very place it takes place. There is no theatrical magic, no "suspense of disbelief." Again, the thorny question of whether performance art exists in virtual space or not remains for me unanswered.

Performance is a way of being in the space, in front of or around an audience; a heightened gaze, a unique sense of purpose in the handling of objects, commitments, and words and, at the same time, it is an ontological "attitude" toward the whole universe. Shamans, fakirs, coyotes, dervishes, and Mexican *merolicos* understand this quite well. Many drama actors and dancers unfortunately don't.

XXIII "Art with a capital A" and art institutions

Our relationship with the art world is bittersweet, to say the least. We have traditionally operated in the cultural borders and social margins where we feel the most comfortable. Whenever we venture into the stark postmodern luxury of the mainstream chic—for example, to present our work in a major museum—we tend to feel a bit out of place. During our stay, we befriend the security guards, the cleaning personnel, and the staff in the educational department. The chief curators watch us attentively from a distance. Only the night before our departure will we be invited for drinks.

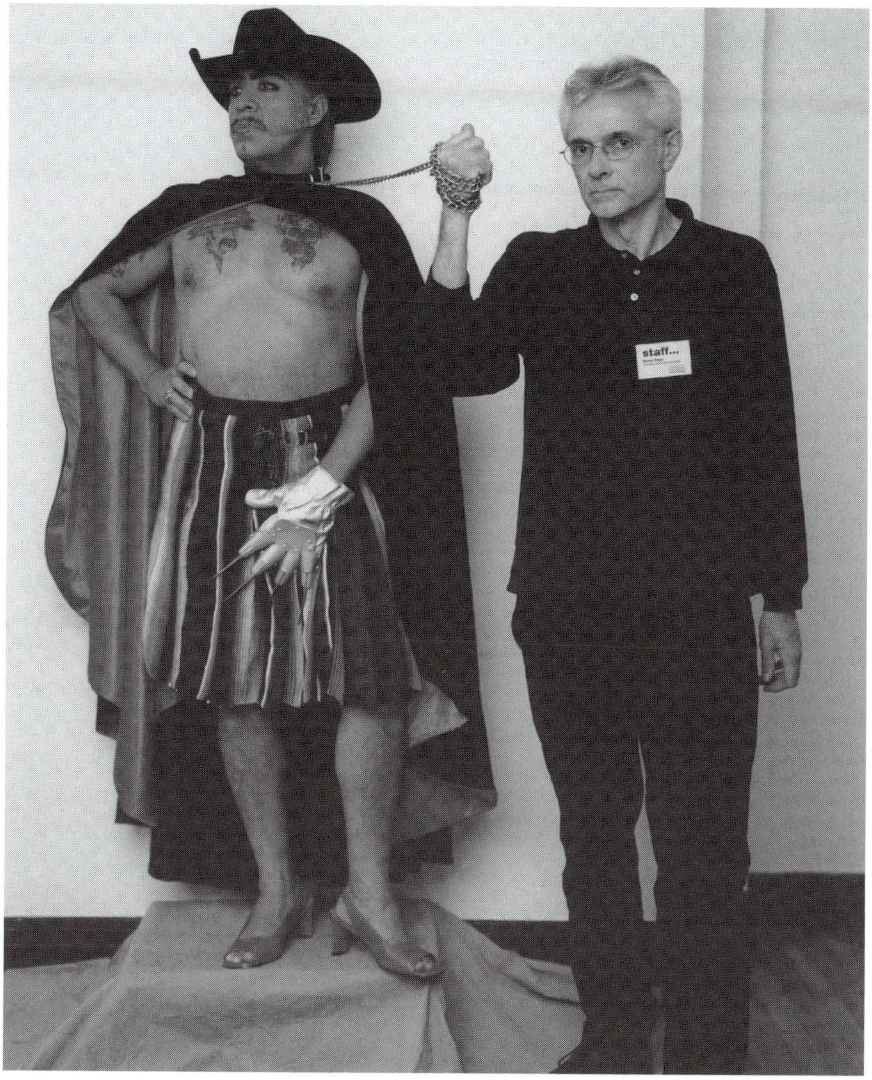

British curator presents his newly discovered specimen to his colleagues back home.
Bryan Biggs and Guillermo Gómez-Peña. Liverpool Biennial, 2002. Photo: Manual Vason.

Mainstream art institutions have a love/hate relationship with us (or rather with what they perceive we represent). Whenever they invite us in, they tremble nervously as if secretly expecting us to destroy the walls of the gallery, scratch a painting with a prop, or pee in the lobby. It's hard to get rid of this stigma, which comes from the days of "the NEA 4" (1989–91), when performance artists were characterized by politicians and mainstream media as irresponsible provocateurs and cultural terrorists. Every time I complete a project in a big institution, the director pulls me aside the day before my departure and tells me: "Guermo, thanks for having been so . . . nice." Deep inside, he may be a bit disappointed that I didn't misbehave more like one of my performance personae.

XXIV Marginalizing lingo

Nomenclature and labeling have contributed to the permanent marginalization of performance art. Since the 1930s, the many self-proclaimed "mainstream art worlds" in every country have conveniently referred to performance artists as "alternative" (alternative to what? The "real" or "serious" stuff?), "peripheral" (to their own self-imposed "center"), "experimental" (meaning "permanently in the testing phase"), or "heterodox" (at mortal odds with tradition). If we are "of color" (who isn't?), we are always labeled as "emerging" (the condescending human version of the "developing countries"), or as "recently discovered," as if we were specimens of an exotic esthetic tribe. Even the word "radical," which we often use ourselves, gets utilized by the "mainstream" as a red light, with the perilous subtext: "Unpredictable behavior. Handle at your own risk."[6]

These terms keep pushing the performance-art field toward the margins of the "legitimate" one—the market-based art world—the big city from which we constitute the dangerous barrios, ghettos, reservations, and banana republics. Curators, journalists, and cultural impresarios obsessed with "the margins" visit our forbidden cities with a combination of eroticized fear and adventuresome machismo.

Caught between the old marginalizing lingo and the new "everything shocking goes" type of ethos of the mainstream bizarre, the field is badly in need of restaking its territory—redefining the now-dated binary notions of center/periphery and mainstream/subculture. Perhaps one useful strategy might be for us, *locos* and

6 Since 9/11, the connotations and implications of this marginalizing terminology have shifted dramatically. Words such as "radical," "transgressive," "revolutionary," and "rebellious" have been tainted overnight with the blood of generic "terrorism," and with the connotations of "evil" in the Bush doctrine.

locas, to occupy a fictional center and push the new dominant culture to its own truly undesirable margins.

XXV The cult of innovation

The performance-art field is obsessed with innovation. This is especially so in the "West" where innovation is often perceived as synonymous with transgression, and as the antithesis of history. Performance defines itself against the immediate past and always in dialogue with the immediate future—a speculative future, that is.

The dominant positive mythology says that we are a unique tribe of pioneers, innovators, and visionaries. This poses a tremendous challenge to us performance *locos* and *locas*. If we lose touch with the rapidly changing issues and trends in "the field," we can easily become "dated" overnight. If we don't produce fresh and innovative proposals and constantly reframe our imagery and theories, we will be deported into oblivion, while thirty others, much younger and wilder, will be waiting in line to replace us.

The pressure to engage in this ongoing process of reinvention (and, in the USA, of "repackaging") forces some exhausted performance artists out of the rat race and others into a rock-and-roll-type lifestyle (without the goodies and exaggerated fame). The performance-art world is not that different in this respect to the merciless world of pop. Only a handful will be granted the privilege, like Bowie or Madonna, of having several reincarnations. There's absolutely nothing romantic about it. Perhaps the only way out of this conundrum may be to work toward the creation of an interactive performance bank, an ongoing dialogue in which all generations contribute and coexist.

XXVI Deported/discovered

The self-proclaimed "international art world" is constantly shifting its attitude toward performance artists. One year we are "in" (if our esthetics, ethnicity, or gender politics coincide with their trends); the next one we are "out." (If we produce video, performance photography, or installation art as an extension of our performances, then we have a slightly better chance to get invited more frequently.) We get welcomed and deported back and forth so constantly that we have grown used to it. And it is only when the art world is in a crisis of ideas that we get asked to participate, and only for a short period of time.

But we don't mind being temporary insiders. Our partial invisibility is actually a privilege. It grants us special freedoms that full-time insiders and "art darlings" don't have. We get to disappear for a while and reinvent ourselves once again, in the shadows and ruins of Western civilization. In twenty-two years of making performance art, I have been deported at least seven times from the art world, only to be (re-)"discovered" the next year under a new light: Mexican, Latino, multi-culti, or Hybrid art? "Ethno-Techno" or "Outsider art"? "Chicano cyber-punk" or "extreme art"? What next? "Neo-Aztec hi-tech post-retro-pop-colonial art"? I patiently await the next label.

XXVII The ethnographic dream

I dreamed my colleague Juan Ybarra and I were on permanent exhibit at a natural history museum. We were human specimens of a rare "post-Mexican urban tribe" living inside Plexiglass boxes, next to other specimens and taxidermied animals. We were hand-fed by museum docents and taken to the bathroom on leashes. Occasionally we would be cleaned with a duster by a gorgeous proprietor who secretly lusted for us.

Our job was not that exciting, but unfortunately, since it was a dream, we couldn't change the script. It went more or less like this: From 10 A.M. to 5 P.M., we would alternate slow-motion ritualized actions and didactic "demonstrations" of our customs and art practices with the modeling of "authentic" tribal wear designed by one of the curators. On Sundays they would open the front of the Plexiglass boxes so the audience could have "a more direct experience of us." We were told by a staff member of the educational department to allow the audience to touch us, smell us, and even change our clothes and alter our body positions. Some people, donors and special guests, were allowed to actually sit on our laps and make out with us if they so wished. It was a drag, an ethnographic shame, but since we were mere "specimens" and not artists, we couldn't do anything about it.

One day, there was a fire, and everyone left the building but us. Suddenly everything outside the Plexiglass boxes was on fire. It was beautiful. I never had that dream again. I guess we died during the fire.

XXVIII Thorny questions

What follows are some of the typical questions asked to me by mainstream journalists . . . followed by some of my typical answers:

Journalist: Is performance art something relatively new?
Gómez-Peña: No. Every culture has had a space allocated to the renewal of

tradition and a space for contestation and deviant behavior. Those who occupy the latter are granted special freedoms.

Journalist: Can you elaborate?

Gómez-Peña: In indigenous American cultures, it was the shaman, the coyote, the Nanabush who had permission from the community to cross the dangerous borders of dreams, gender, madness, and witchcraft. In Western culture this liminal space is occupied by the performance artist: the contemporary antihero and accepted provocateur. We know this place exists and we simply occupy it.

Journalist: I see. The performance artist is the modern bohemian, right?

Gómez-Peña: Yes and no. We are bohemians in a world in which there's no longer a place for bohemians. There's nothing romantic about it.

Journalist: But aren't you interested in crossing over into pop culture?

Gómez-Peña: Not really. A Guatemalan independentist during the secession of his country from Mexico said: "I rather be the head of the mouse than the tail of the lion."

Journalist: I don't get it. What is the function of performance art? Does it have any?

Gómez-Peña: [*Long pause.*] Performance artists are a constant reminder to society of the possibilities of other artistic, political, sexual, or spiritual behaviors, and this, I must say, is an extremely important function.

Journalist: Why?

Gómez-Peña: It helps others to reconnect with the forbidden zones of their psyches and bodies, and to acknowledge the possibilities of their own freedoms. In this sense, performance art may be as useful as medicine, engineering, or law, and performance artists as necessary as nurses, teachers, priests, or taxi-drivers. Most of the time we ourselves are not even aware of these functions.

Journalist: What I want to know is what does performance art do for you?

Gómez-Peña: For me? [*Long pause.*] It is my way to fight or talk back, to recapture my stolen civic self, and piece together my fragmented identity. I'm doing it right now!

Journalist: Mr. Comes Piña [*misspelled, mispronounced*], do you think about these big ideas everyday, all day long?

Gómez-Peña: Certainly not. I'd go mad. Most of the time I'm just going about my everyday life: you know, writing, researching, getting excited by a new project or prop, paying bills, recuperating from the 'flu, waiting anxiously for a phone call to get invited to perform in a city where I have never been.

Journalist: I guess I'm not being clear: What I really want to know is what has performance art taught you?

Gómez-Peña: Ah, you want a soundbite, right?

Journalist: Well . . .

Gómez-Peña: OK, let me think for a moment . . . When I was younger, performance taught me how to talk back. Lately, it is teaching me to listen carefully to others . . . even to stupid people.

XXIX The empty stage

I dreamed of an empty performance stage. Although beautifully lit, it remained empty for a long time and the audience became restless waiting for something original or "extreme" to happen.

There were a few exceptions: Two Goth art students were yawning theatrically in the first row, a very distinguished man with gray hair who looked like a museum director or an Italian businessman was caressing the legs of a young Latina in a red miniskirt, and Vito Acconci (or a Vito-Acconci-looking dude) wearing a silver lounge jacket was nodding to himself as if saying: "Gosh, what has art turned into?"

Suddenly, a nun with a Mexican wrestler mask stood on her seat and began to applaud. At first, it was a lonesome applause. But then, one by one, everyone began to applaud, including the aloof or distracted audience members I mentioned earlier. Their applause become increasingly more desperate. Apparently the performance artists were taking a long break, a pee, or smoking a cigarette in the dressing room. Upon overhearing the boisterous crowd, they returned to the empty stage and did something unscripted and very ordinary that I can't remember. I had an aerial view of the whole thing, but I was also a part of the performance troupe taking a break.

Like performance, this text is incomplete, and will continue to change in the coming months and years. A warrior without glory, I turn off my computer . . .

TO BE CONTINUED . . .

3

Culturas-in-extremis

Performing against the cultural backdrop of the mainstream bizarre

(Essay, 1999–2002)

"Gómez-Peña, you are trapped in between the currents of the global and the concrete. Make up your mind or sink!"

Drunk Mexican art critic at a party

"History begins when I wake up, and it ends when I go to sleep."

Colombian journalist

After I published the first version of this text in TDR, *9/11 changed the whole world overnight. As a "radical" performance artist, and as a writer trying to articulate the vertigo of the new millennium, I was forced to revise every text and performance I was working on. This new version is the product of such obsessive revisions.*

Track #1 Confessions

In the last three years of the twentieth century I stopped writing essays altogether. I concentrated mainly on performance and film scripts, spoken-word poetry, and chronicles of my performance adventures (*Dangerous Border Crossers*, Routledge,

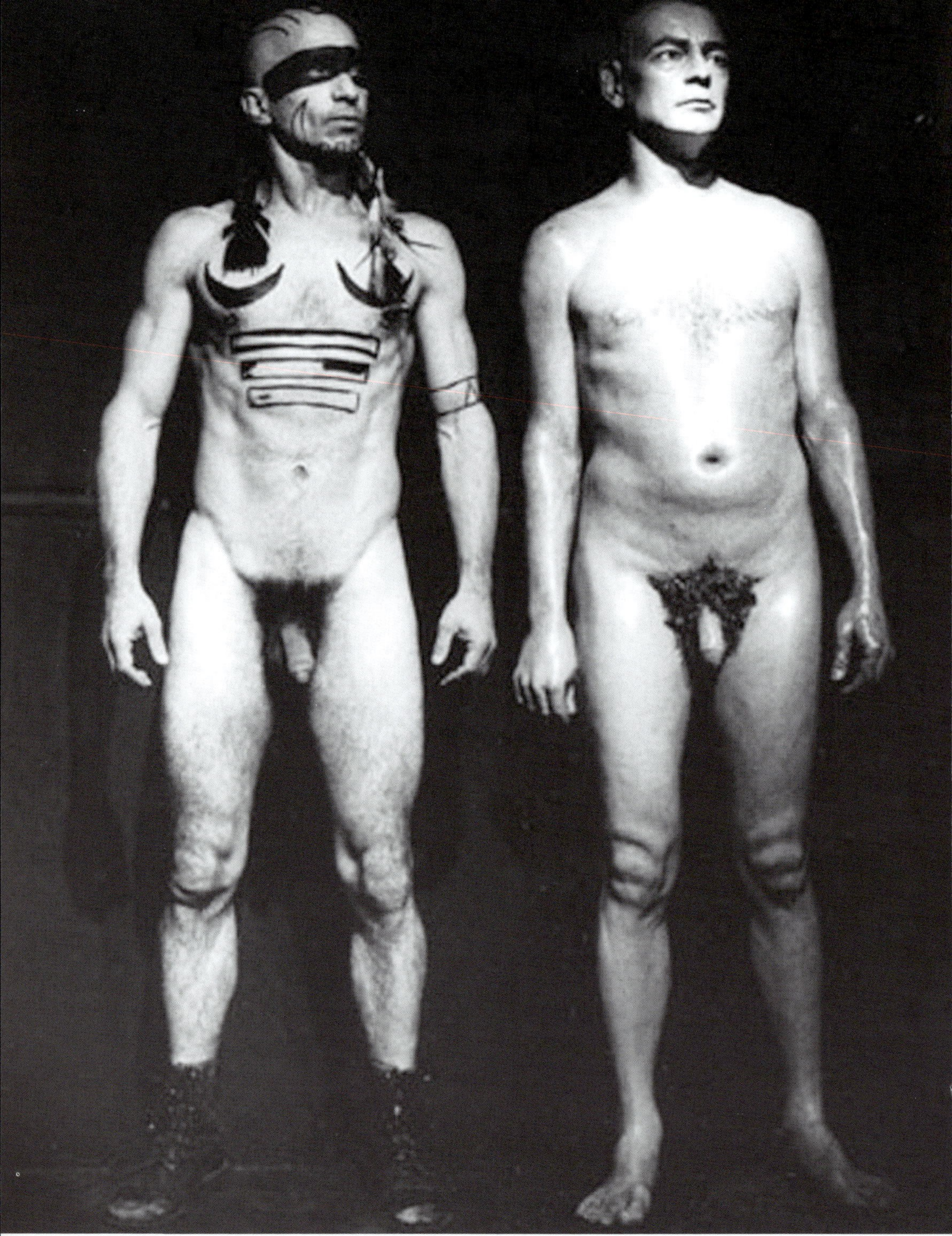

2000). Why? The formidable changes generated by the cult of globalization and virtual capitalism created an unprecedented philosophical vertigo in my consciousness. The larger picture was blurry, so to speak. My confusion worsened due to the rapid socialization of digital technologies and the virulent backlash against humanistic concerns and so-called "identity politics." I was entering a new, terrifying era. All my ideological parameters and political certainties were crisscrossing under my feet. Suddenly, binary models of understanding the world were no longer functional: Us/them, progressive/reactionary, local/global, Third World/First World, alternative/ mainstream, center/periphery, right/wrong, etc., were constantly shifting faultlines in an ever-fluctuating landscape. It truly felt as if I was drunk in the middle of an 8.5 earthquake.

All I could do was mumble in my existential drunken stupor, and clumsily express my inability to assume simplistic positionalities or to unconditionally embrace a cause. All I could do was raise questions, myriad impertinent questions. I must concede that at least my skepticism was proactive, almost militant. As a Chicano, I had no delusions about one day becoming part of the new virtual capitalist project. I was definitely not willing to accept the omnipresent lethargy, much less acritically sing along with the hip dot.com mantra. As a politicized artist, neither suicide nor taking up arms were viable options for me. What I did instead was immerse myself in the epicenter of the finisecular earthquake, in the hope of understanding its causes and nature through direct artistic praxis.

This bipolar condition of ranchero nihilism and proactive humanism became the very substance of my performance work. I performed constantly and everywhere I could: From the streets to chic museums and from community centers to international festivals. The stage became both the ultimate battlefield and the "ground zero" of the search for clarity and valor. The stage became the world and vice versa. I wanted to force myself to be "present" in the crosshairs of change (what corny term, *¿qué no*?) as both cultural witness and social actor. Luckily, this "presence" kept me both politicized and outraged, so my artistic glands continued to produce venom and imagery. Examples of the way I negotiated and articulated this turmoil can be found in some of my performance texts, like *Brownout 2*. These texts function as both blueprints for action and X-rays of my process of reflexivity.

As the new century begins to unfold, I have decided to write this hybrid text (part essay, part chronicle) on global-culture-gone-wrong, and what I perceive to be its main risks and contradictions, artistic and pop-cultural products, major philosophical trends and political dilemmas. Hopefully, my bifocal perspective as a border artist

Living diorama in *The Museum of Fetishized Identities*.
Juan Ybarra with wax figure of Caucasian male. Performance Space, Sydney, 2000. Photo: Heidrun Lohr.

(with one foot on the benign side of globalization and another on the dark side) will provide a unique perspective to my colleagues in the US and the UK.

Inevitably, I am prone to miss the target here and there. As a performance exercise, I am attempting to observe a new world with new eyes, as if my motorboat were reaching the shore of the mainland for the first time—not because I feel like a macho explorer on assignment for the Discovery Channel, but instead because I feel like the survivor of a shipwreck.

As I embark on this conceptual journey, I haven't the least idea where it will take me or when exactly it will end. All I know is that I am willing to walk alone across the spooky bridge of millennial nihilism in the hope of finding some clarity at the end, even if this clarity ends up blinding me. I am sure that in this journey I will come across many distorted images of myself, projections of what I wish I could understand. And that's also fine, for I am unapologetically assuming the contradictory voice of an artist/theoretician, and while writing this text I will exercise the same intellectual and artistic freedoms that my performance work has granted me.

Track #2 Corporate multiculturalism

> **"You may now experience anything you want, become whomever you wish, or purchase whichever cultural, sexual, spiritual, artistic or political experience you desire. You can impersonate other genders or ethnic identities without having to suffer any physical, social, or political repercussions, or be subjected to the rage of the excluded. You don't even need to belong to any 'real' community. And you can do all this from the solitude of your home or by visiting this gallery."**
>
> *(From the program of the performance* Mexotica*)*

"Americans" (or rather USians) arrived in the twenty-first century with acute vertigo, our sense of worth and prosperity as a nation blown out of proportion by the "success" of the new virtual economy, paired with the absence of formidable enemies abroad. The old Soviet menace had been replaced first by mythical enemies, including immigrants and drug lords from south of the border, and later on (after 9/11) by real enemies such as the "terrorists" from the Middle East.

In the international arena, the US's lack of accountability to any legal, moral, or diplomatic institution (other than the World Trade Organization) became apparent. On the domestic front, the backlash against "political correctness" (a euphemism for all humanitarian and humanistic concerns) had thoroughly completed its mission. Sensitive questions of race, gender, and matters of cultural diversity were finally perceived as issues of the past, trembling shadows of the old twentieth century. Given this backdrop, important legacies of the civil rights movement—social programs, cultural projects, and grassroots agencies attending the needs of the disenfranchised—were dismantled. The Darwinian subtext read: "We are (allegedly) installed in a fully globalized, postracist, postsexist, postideological, post-civil rights era, and anyone who thinks otherwise is clearly out of touch with the times. It is finally up to an individual's will and intelligence to overcome the (inconsequential) restrictions imposed by race, gender, and class in order to make a difference (meaning 'in order to become rich')." The *Homo digitalis* was a living proof.

In this unprecedented postdemocratic era, civil, human, and labor rights, education, and art were suddenly perceived as expendable budget items, minor privileges, and nostalgic concerns of "angry minorities" and special-interest groups. Humanism became a mere corporate goal and a trendy marketing strategy for computer firms. According to Apple, "Cesar Chavez . . . Martin Luther King . . . (and) Rigoberta Menchu (thought) different." If this weren't enough, "content" became a hot topic discussed obsessively in seminars by the sponsors of the "new revolution" of cyberspace, and "counterculture" a weekly show on the Bravo channel. The list of buzz words in the new corporate humanism was immense.

To complement this ideology, a "benevolent" and apolitical form of multiculturalism was adopted by corporations and media conglomerates across borders, continents, and virtual space. This global transculture artificially softened the otherwise sharp edges of cultural difference, fetishizing them in such a way as to render them desirable. Under the new corporate logic, it was fine for Blacks to advertise Nikes, and Latinos were definitely OK when we were shaking our butts to "La Vida Loca." Whether the Other was a "gang member" targeted by the LAPD, or an Amazonian Indian fighting ecological devastation, Benetton or the Gap could make them look really cool and sexy. It was no coincidence that the last Latino "boom"—1998/2001—was a dim parade of forgettable pop singers, low-calorie entertainers who could barely speak at all (much less speak Spanish), and one annoying tiny chihuahua whose Mexican accent was actually articulated by an Argentinian actor from LA. The most obvious feature of that finisecular Latinocracy was that, unlike prior booms, it did not include one intellectual—not one social critic, articulate spokesperson, or civil-rights activist.

Corporate multiculturalism proved to be both sexy and profitable—for its sponsors, that is. The sponsors of the Internet, in indirect collaboration with the entertainment industry (Hollywood, "total TV," eco-tourism, the World Music industry, etc.) and the high-art world, created a "global mall" which "we" (as in humankind) could access any time we wished.

They clearly outsmarted us. This unique version of multiculturalism was actually devoid of "real" people of color, true artists, romantic outcasts and "revolutionaries."

The very diversity it claimed to celebrate and sponsor merely performed the passive roles of glossy images and exotic backgrounds, played out by nameless minor actors and sexualized mestizo/mulatto dancers. In this context, so-called "artists of color" didn't seem to perform any meaningful role other than decorators of the omnipresent *horror vacui* and entertainers of a new—more open to "radical behaviors" and much more cynical—consumer class.

Curiously, the social contradictions and hidden violence of this new transculture of denial and rabid consumerism were embodied in the very artifacts it produced. All we needed to do was browse the web or surf the hundreds of channels available on Direct-TV. Suddenly, at the snap of a finger, the multi-spectacle of *amigo* racism, stylish sexism, and eroticized oppression was made available to us. Everything became flat and equalized by high production values and vertiginous editing.

Through the global media networks and the invisible fluids of the Internet, these decontextualized images and colonizing viruses were immediately broadcast to the southern hemisphere, where people had much weaker cultural antibodies to resist them, and certainly lacked the software to talk back. Often, the media emporiums of the "Third World" ended up further exaggerating the imported images, and refracting them back to their own immigrant communities living in the First World, which in turn added yet another layer of distortion to this imagery. Our flaccid identities ended up getting lost somewhere inside this virtual hall of mirrors and multiple video monitors.

My artistic response to corporate multiculturalism came in the form of epic performance extravaganzas mimicking its very practices of representation. My colleagues and I staged "extreme fashion shows" and high-tech expos-gone-wrong, creating total environments where hyperexoticized "artists of color" were on display dutifully performing the stylized desires and intercultural fetishes of the mainstream. We also created stations in which audience members could alter their ethnic identity and "impersonate their favorite cultural Other" through special-effect make-up and costumes we provided, or even "rent an exotic performance artist" for a while. It looked and felt like fun, but it was a painful time and a painful series of performances attempting to articulate it.

(Note: From this point on, all words that appear in quotations are temporarily "meaningless.")

Track #3 Uroboros: The spectacle of the mainstream bizarre

The serpent finally bit its own tail. What ten years ago was considered fringe "subculture" is now mere pop. The insatiable mass of the so-called "mainstream" (remember the film, *The Blob*?) has finally devoured all "margins," and the more dangerous, thorny, and exotic these "margins," the better. In fact, *stricto sensu*, we can say that there are no "margins" left, at least no recognizable ones. "Alternative" thought, "fringe" subcultures, and "radical" behavior, as we knew them, have actually become the mainstream. Nowadays, spectacle replaces content; form gets heightened; "meaning" (remember meaning?) evaporates, or rather, fades out; boredom sinks in and everybody searches for the next "extreme" image or experience. Ethical and political implications are fading memories of the past century.

We are now fully installed in what I term the culture of the mainstream bizarre, a perplexing oxymoron, which reminds me of Mexico's ex-ruling party: El Partido Revolucionario Institucional. Nowhere else is this phenomenon more apparent than in mass media and the Internet, where "radical" behavior, revolution-as-style, and "extreme" images of racialized violence and sexual hybridity have become daily entertainment, mere marketing strategies of a new corporate chic. From the humiliating spectacle of antisocial behavior performed in US network talk shows to TV specials on mass murderers, Aryan supremacists, child killers, religious cults, "extreme" sex, art and sports, predatory animals and natural disasters, and the obsessive repetition of "real crimes" shot by private citizens or by surveillance cameras, we've all become daily voyeurs and participants of a new *cultura in extremis*. Its goal is clear: To entice consumers while providing us with the illusion of vicariously experiencing all the sharp edges and strong emotions that our superficial lives lack. After all, as Elaine Peña says, "we are all made complicit by our economic practices," which reminds me of a graffitos I saw in a Mexico City mall: *Compro luego existo* (I buy therefore I exist). And if I buy Otherness, I conclude, I am supposed to become it.

The mainstream bizarre has effectively blurred the borders between pop culture, performance, and "reality." The new placement of other borders, between audience and performer, between the surface and the underground, between marginal identities and fashionable trends is still unclear.

One thing is clear to me: Artists exploring the tensions between these borders must now be watchful. We can easily get lost in this fun house of virtual mirrors, epistemological inversions, and distorted perceptions—a zone where all desires and fears are imaginary and "content" is just a fading memory. If this happens, performance artists might end up becoming just another "extreme" variety act in the extensive and ever-changing menu of global culture.

What perplexing times for those thinking critically. Traditionally known for our "transgressive" behavior and our willingness to defy dogmas, cultural borders, and moral conventions, performance artists must now compete in outrageousness with sleazebags Howard Stern, Jerry Springer, and MTV's *Jack Ass*. Change channel. Independent filmmakers and video artists now must contend with TV ads and rock videos whose esthetic strategies are directly appropriated from independent film and experimental video, but with a few small differences: They are twice as technically complex and their budgets are logarithmically bigger. Change channel. Public intellectuals (what does "public" mean in this context?) must now attempt to speak to students or write for readers who regard the performative polemicists of MSNBC or Fox News as actual public intellectuals. I know. You know. The difference is obvious: "Content," but since content, *stricto sensu*, no longer matters, difference makes no difference. (The same is true for "depth.")

In this new convoluted logic, Arafat and "the Serial Sniper" will be granted equal status and media coverage as will Mother Teresa and Lady Diana. If Noam Chomsky or Edward Said (RIP) get invited to present an opposing view of Israel to that of MSNBC, the real objective of the host will be to disarm them or make them sound like zealots. After all, dissent can also be spectacle. Latino media may be even worse. Submerged in an ocean of celebrity gossip and chic mindlessness, it invests the banal opinions of J-Lo, Salma Hayek, or Antonio Banderas about "whatever" (sensitive political issues included) with greater weight than the opinions of writers Carlos Fuentes, Richard Rodriguez, or Ana Castillo.

For the moment, I am obsessed with the following questions: If performance artists choose to mimic or parody the strategies of the mainstream bizarre in order to develop new audiences and explore the Zeitgeist of our times, what prevents us from becoming the very stylized freaks we are attempting to deconstruct or parody? And if we are interested in performing for nonspecialized audiences, how can we ensure that our audiences won't misinterpret our "radical" actions and our complex performative identities as mere spectacles of radicalism or stylized hybridity? If our new audiences are more interested in direct stimulation than in content, can we effectively camouflage content as experience?

I have no answers. I only have clues. My dressing room is filled with suspicious mirrors. My computer desktop contains dozens of solipsistic performance scripts.

Track #4 The illusion of talking back

Since the new global culture is supposed to be "interactive," we are granted the illusion of talking back. We can call the TV or radio station, or email them our opinions. We can post our views on any website we like, we can join a chat room or place a classified ad in search of a quorum or accomplices. And someone will respond right away. If we are lucky, we may be invited to a talk show to exhibit (or more accurately, "perform") our miseries. Students, intellectuals, and civic leaders, along with children and housewives randomly chosen by the producer's assistant, may get invited to an electronic town meeting organized by CNN or by the President himself. Our new

Censored.
Juan Ybarra. Mexico City, 2003. Photo: Miguel Velasco.

culture encourages everyone to have an opinion, and to express it (not necessarily an informed opinion, just an opinion). Expression is a kind of placebo or substitute for action. What matters here is the spectacle of participation. No matter how bombastic or "transgressive" our views may be—hey, if they make for good spectacle they will always be welcome (and forgotten immediately).

Citizen participation is encouraged, but not in any significant decision-making process that may effect social change, just in the construction and the staging of spectacle: The great illusory spectacle of citizen participation. The cameras are now pointing in all directions. "Normal people" with "normal" lives can suddenly become reporters, actors, singers, performance artists, filmmakers, and even porn stars. We don't need to have brains, special talents, or a perfect body. In fact, the more "normal" we look and sound, the better. If we are lucky, we might be cast in a "reality TV" show, where "everyone is a celebrity" until they get ousted. If our camcorders are fortunate enough to catch an act of police brutality or a theft, our tapes might become news.

The illusion of interactivity and citizen participation has definitely changed the relationship between live art and its audience. Audiences are increasingly having a harder time just sitting and passively watching a performance, especially younger audiences. They've been trained by TV, SuperNintendo, video games, and the Internet to "interact" and be part of it all. They see themselves as "insiders" and part-time artists. They've got the most recent software to make digital movies and compose electronic music. They burn their own CDs and design their own websites. To them there is nothing esoteric about art. Therefore, when attending a live art event, they wish to be included in the process, talk back to the artist, and if possible, become part of the actual performance. These new audience members are always ready to walk on stage at any invitation from the artist and do something, particularly if participation involves impersonating other cultures or taking off their clothes. It's karaoke time. It's like a live computer game with the added excitement that people, "real people," are watching.

Given this dramatic epistemological shift, artists and art institutions are pressured to redefine our own relationship with our public. The educational departments of museums are trying to figure out how to design more technologically interactive, performative, and "audience-friendly" exhibits. Experimental artists are racking their brains developing new ways to further catch people's attention and implicate new and larger audiences in our performance games. The challenge for performance artists is obvious: If our live "show" is not "exciting," "extreme," or "interactive" enough, our impatient US and European audiences have myriad other options for spending their evening. It's a tight spot in which to be.

Track #5 The finisecular freak crosses the southern border

For years Latin Americans witnessed from the South what we perceived to be a First World culture of unacknowledged excesses and gratuitous extremes. But thanks to global media, satellite TV, the Internet, and the black market, today we, ourselves, play an integral part of this culture, as daily voyeurs and willing participants. Some examples come to mind: The popular Mexican comic books known as *mini-novellas* feature the weekly adventures of characters such as a *lucha libre* wrestler with *priapismo* (a permanent erection) who gets kidnapped and sexually attacked by "extraterrestrial nymphos," and "*Pocachondas*" ("horny Indian maidens who love to torture muscular cowboys"). *Cambio de canal.* Spanish-language tabloid-TV programs such as the recently cancelled *Fuera de la ley* and *Primer impacto* present a disparate repertoire of extreme body images, framed by "bizarre facts and people." Close-ups of corpses at the scene of the crime or the accident, or people with "rare genetic disorders" share the screen with, say, a mob of angry *campesinos* setting a rapist on fire and captured by the camcorder of a bewildered tourist, a recent apparition of the Virgin of Guadalupe, or interviews with witchdoctors and "outrageous artists" such as myself.[1] The old freak show is back in a new high-definition format, and you simply can't take your eyes off the screen. Our lives may suck but the world out there, according to Televisa or Telemundo, is much more bizarre than performance art.

Cambio de canal. The Mexican talk show with the highest ratings right now, *Hasta en las mejores familias* features, among other topics, guests with "peculiar forms of transsexuality," "families engaged in bizarre forms of incest," and "men who love to watch their wives 'do it' with their bosses." Needless to say, most of the guests are working class *mestizos*, which makes the spectacle even more troubling. With an invited audience that includes people with physical deformities and a "jury" formed by a midget, a deaf-mute, and a drag queen, the guests are encouraged to bite each other's heads off—as in the early *Jerry Springer* shows. If they get too violent, a team of flamboyant wrestlers and "gay bodybuilders" (or rather, hetero bodybuilders performing stereotypical "gay behavior") will bring them back to their senses. It's "radical," according to my own family.

1 The Latino tabloid-TV *Primer impacto* covered my Spanglish performance opera *Califas, 2000*. The cameras concentrated mainly on our nude bodies, "antireligious message," and "weird esthetics," which "clearly offended the Latino community." Next day, I became, ipso facto, a one-week outlaw celebrity amongst *taqueros*, homeboys, and bus chauffeurs in the San Francisco Mission District. I also got dozens of emails from old friends I hadn't seen in years. It definitely had much more impact than my participation in the Whitney Biennial.

Cambio de canal. But, it is definitely Peruvian broadcasting that wins first prize in terms of political incorrectness and humiliation. The country's most popular comedy program, *Los cómicos ambulantes*, features an indigenous troupe of fake transsexuals, overweight women in tangas and hypersexualized midgets, all wearing "Indian" wigs. Their comedic specialty is to make fun of the slang and idiosyncratic behavior of campesinos and "dumb *tetonas*" (busty women). During one show, the comedians invited audience members to guess the "weight" of the breasts of a dyed-blonde model, whose "enhanced" body had undergone at least five plastic surgeries. Wearing a microscopic bikini, she looked like a Latina character from a Japanese animé cartoon. For twenty minutes, male audience members stepped in front of the camera to grab her breasts and guess their combined weight. At the end of the program the model sent a kiss to her "eight-year-old son who is watching the show at home. Jorgito, my love, I see you in an hour. Ciao."

There are simply no limits to these shows. Since the genre is so new in Latin America, no legal restrictions have been placed on content, and when intellectuals or citizen groups complain, the ratings simply go up.

Track #6 "Extreme sexuality" and other hollow concepts

Remember the NEA 4? Twelve years ago, performance artists managed to shock the American political class and the mainstream media with their "explicit" sexual images and rituals, and sparked a national conversation about censorship and the role of art.[2] Today, "extreme sexuality" is a hollow concept and a pop cultural genre in Cable TV and the Internet. Baroque forms of racialized transsexuality, teen prostitution, incest, and family love triangles performed by "normal" working-class Americans are displayed daily on talk shows, and sexual fetishes, hardcore S&M, and theatrical sex are regular topics on HBO and Bravo. It's no big deal and we don't hear the ranting of Jesse Helms or the American Family Association anymore.

Howard Stern invites "midget porn stars" and physically challenged women to his TV show and asks them to show their breasts on national TV. Then (if he finds them "sexy"), he offers them a breast enlargement and brings them back to the program after the operation. In another Stern show, titled *I Want to be a Vagina Millionaire*, a midget and a guy with a speech impediment have sex with a prostitute as the cameras follow them into the bedroom.

2 In the early 1990s, Jesse Helms and the American Family Association blacklisted Tim Miller, Holly Hughes, John Fleck, and Karen Finley.

The new "margins" continue to welcome more immigration from the old centers as Anglo males in their thirties, suffused in their neverending crises of masculinity, attend "circle jerk" seminars sponsored and filmed by HBO. Yuppies in search of intense experiences to shatter their lethargy attend vampire clubs in San Francisco and New York, while financiers and politicians explore the wonders of fetishized S&M. In the porn industry, the kinkiest videos, hotlines, and websites are being marketed to average, middle-class people with boring lives and anesthetized bodies. The great paradox here is that behind the spectacle of "extreme sexuality" lies a profound puritanism. For the willing consumer of this new sex industry, the unspoken text seems to be: "I am completely disconnected from my body. I badly need an extreme experience to shake my dormant body up and awaken my senses. Whatever it takes, whatever! . . ."

The sponsors of the mainstream bizarre don't discriminate on the basis of age. Netscape or Yahoo can help lonely suburban teens and kids "navigate" through the user-friendly halls of the great virtual funhouse where online strippers and escorts are already passé. There they can find unimaginable photos to download and video clips to watch: Sex with animals, child porn, "juicy cunts under 17," "the dead babies" website, and the popular "Couple TV" sites which feature amateur couples revealing (or rather "performing") "everything" they do at home from making love to taking a shower to defecating. The menu of eccentricities is unlimited. If the young voyeurs get bored with "extreme sexuality," within seconds they can access other daring sites where they can find neo-Nazi and KKK paraphernalia, militia manifestos, and right-wing terrorist manuals detailing the formula for constructing bombs in the garage. In our new global "democracy," everything, absolutely "everything," is instantly available to us. All we need is a computer, a modem . . . and of course, lots of spare time to exercise our unlimited "freedoms."

I remember with nostalgia the days when for my Chicano colleagues and I to get naked during a performance piece at a Chicano cultural center would trigger a month-long community controversy. I also remember with a melancholic smile when the Walker Art Center outraged the political establishment by presenting Ron Athey, or when Karen Finley was banned in England. Today, things are quite different: Ron gets occasionally invited to direct MTV videos; Karen appears frequently in the TV show *Politically Incorrect*; and an HBO film crew follows my *The Mexterminator Project* on tour. The image of my collaborator, dancer Sara Shelton Mann, crucified nude as a transgender mariachi with a strap-on dildo, which would have sparked riots in Mexico just a few years ago, ends up in the final cut. One of the producers tells me, "Gómez-Peña, I wish you guys had more images like this one." My jaw drops down to my stomach, and I cannot help but think out loud: Is this phenomenon a breakthrough in terms of tolerance for true radical behavior or yet another confirmation that content and difference, in the age of infinite options and multidirectional promises, no longer matter?

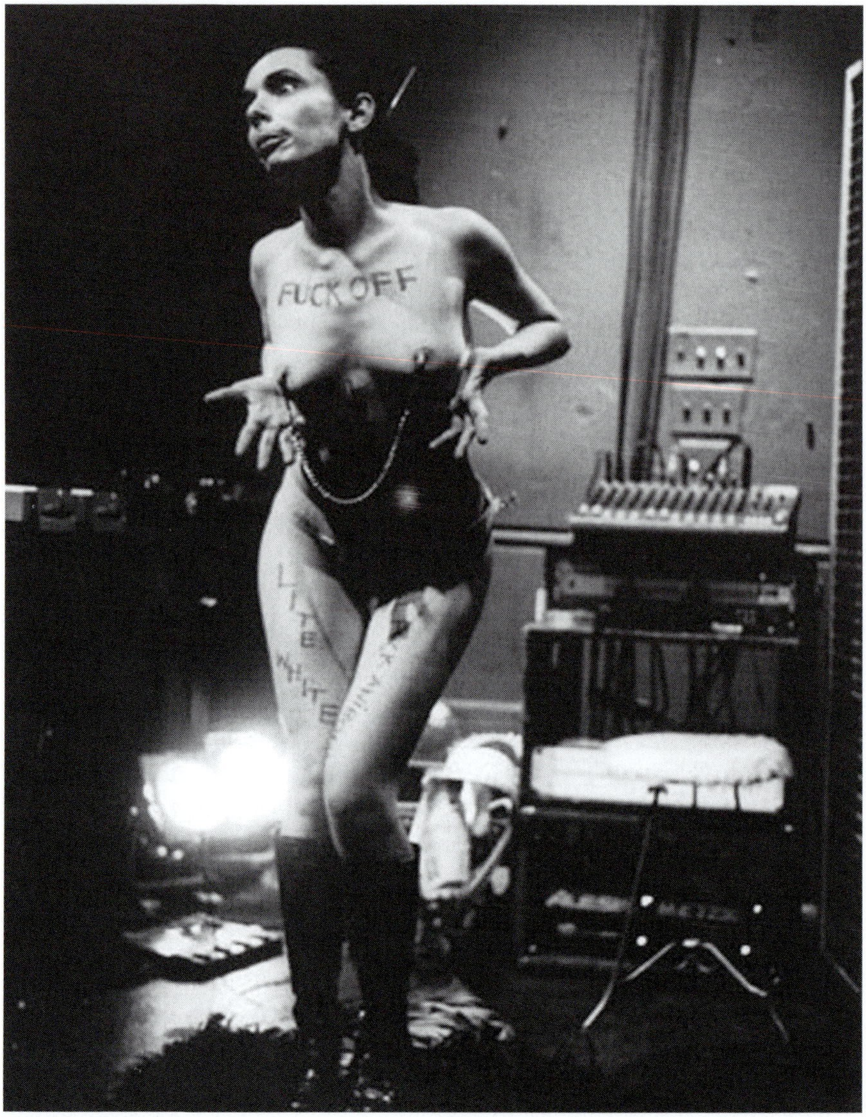

The sexist and racist desires of men performed by Barbara Cole at *The Museum of Fetishized Identities.*

Barbara Cole. Performance Space, Sydney, 2000. Photo: Heidrun Lohr.

Track #7 Altered bodies and wounded bodies

In a culture that acritically glorifies the stylized bizarre, the human body is understandably at the center of it all, for all the wrong reasons. The body is "hot" again, but the spectacle of the altered or wounded body is much hotter. Wherever we turn, we see bodies and body parts reshaped, refurbished, or "enhanced" by implants and prosthetics, steroids and laser surgery, tattoos and piercings; artificial bodies to wear or to watch or both, proudly showing off their liposuctioned asses and "stapled" stomachs, their volcanic breasts and enlarged penises, their reconstructed chins and borrowed noses. These cyborgized bodies reconstructed by high technology, in all states of artificial alteration, appear daily in movies, prime-time TV, fashion and art shows, ads, and websites. They aren't shocking. They are merely "hip."

At the same time, the spectacle of bodies wounded or mutilated by social or political drama went from being a "fringe subculture" to becoming a cliché. Covered with blood, open sores, or prosthetics, mutilated bodies without identity populate both the corporate mediascape and cyberspace. A vertiginous succession of open bodies, bleeding wounds, dissected abdomens, and missing limbs, whether real or staged, may only cause us to blink our eyes once or twice. Why? I can only speculate: These bodies have been silenced, decontextualized, emptied of drama and emotion, stripped of their humanity and identity. And, as inattentive spectators, we have clearly lost our capability to empathize with them and feel outrage over the violent causes of their mutilation.

The combined spectacle of the altered and the wounded body has generated an interest in the strange intersection of performance (and performative photography), (para-)ethnography, a fringe of cybertheory, estheticized porn, forensic medicine, and "role-playing." But the new areas of interest are quite different from last century's fascination with the body extreme. It is clearly no longer the "beautiful" or (fictionalized) "natural" body (with its cultural specificities and ideological implications) or theatricalized nudity as in the films of Fellini, Jodorowsky, or Pasolini. It is definitely not *el cuerpo político*, or *el cuerpo cartográfico*, as in performance art, either. It's the "bizarre" combination of pathology and Eros, of implied violence and high style, of the medical and the criminal realms. It is the morgue, the surgical table, the biogenetic lab, the forensic dossier, as well as the "extreme" sex club, tabloid TV, and the porn websites with their myriad subcategories.

The new objects of fascination are a depoliticized "extreme" body, stripped of all implications, and the suffering, eroticized body of a (willing or accidental) victim. Whether we like it or not, when performance artists "perform," as far as the audience is concerned, our bodies fall in the very same category. Our formidable challenge in this respect is how to rehumanize, repoliticize, and decolonize our own bodies wounded by the media and intervened upon by the invisible surgery of pop culture; and to do it in such a way that our audiences are not even aware of it.

Track #8 Collectable primitives of ("in" or "at") the Great International Expo

The modus operandi of the self-proclaimed "international" art world is not any different from that of corporate multiculturalism or the culture of the mainstream bizarre. In the great art mall of "internationalism," artists, a small number of lucky ones, become commodities and trendy neoprimitives. And all we have to contribute to the great multi-culti delicatessen is our ability to generate desire (and a bit of fear) for the global consumer, to perform our stylized (but tamed) "difference" with an obvious understanding of Western "sophistication," and current art trends.

According to the glossy art journals, "internationalism" (*en abstracto*) is the new -ism. It portrays the world as a borderless *mapa mundi digital* where the cultural energy and the art market are constantly shifting from continent to continent, just like the stock market or the programming of the Discovery channel. In this new ball game, more than ever, artists are at the mercy of the international superstar curator, critic, and producer. Unlike their postmodern, multicultural, or postcolonial predecessors, the new global impresarios needn't be concerned with ethical or political boundaries. Ethics, ideology, border issues and postcolonial dilemmas—they all belong to the immediate past.

The new praxis is to engage in a stylistically "radical" but thoroughly apolitical type of transnational multiculturalism that acritically indulges in mild difference. The new praxis flattens and consumes all thorny edges, "alternative" expressions, anti-social behavior, stylized kink, and revolutionary kitsch. One trend or style will follow or overlap with the other as perplexed artists patiently wait to be discovered or rather rediscovered for the hundredth time, this time under a new light—one without implications, continuity, or context. The definition of the photo is much sharper; the text and the context much vaguer.

A combination of rare political phenomena and the caprices of the impresarios themselves often determine the choice of Otherness. One year it's Cuba, then Mexico, then China, and then South Africa. It's the Buena Vista Social Club syndrome. "Third World" art products are seasonally fashionable so long as they pass the quality-control tests imposed by the fashionable centers. The new Third World or "minority" artist is expected to perform trans- and inter-cultural sophistication, unpredictable eclecticism, and cool hybridity.

The debate is simply nonexistent. In fact, debate is considered passé. Those artists, writers, and curators who decide to problematize this neo-retro-colonial praxis are usually deported back to oblivion or pushed aside to the many other parallel (and semi-invisible) art worlds. After all, no one is truly indispensable in the free market of twenty-first-century art.

As artists exhaust our proposals of difference, "rebel" curators venture into the titillating *terra ignota* of "outsider art," the euphemistic term used by the art world to describe the art of prisoners, sex workers, terminally ill patients, "gang members," serial killers, or the mentally impaired, who suddenly become desirable commodities and instant celebrities. Unlike in the early 1990s, the goal is no longer to "help the outsider." Since compassion is passé and the missionary-community arts movement is just a bad memory, the new goal is to voyeuristically observe *their* crisis and borrow *their* image and artifacts (sometimes permanently) to exhibit them in a museum. The framing, of course, will be done by someone who will never understand the drama of the "outsider." For the global impresario, embarked on an eternal art safari, there are still fortunately lots of extreme emotions and dangerous experiences to explore beyond art, ineffable fringes and sordid realities to discover, document, retitle, and bring back to the gallery, the biennial, or the film festival.

Track #9 "Alternative" spirituality and "world" tribalism

In the past years, eclectic forms of spirituality-by-the-numbers and composite animistic beliefs have influenced our daily lives—our relationships to our bodies, the pop-cultural products we consume, and the art produced by young artists. The menu includes Eastern and Western "alternative" beliefs and practices (no need to be more specific), alleged "Native American" rituals and a sampling of "World" tribalism (as in "World" music).

These practices are not exactly "countercultural" (in the ancient sense of the term that is). To say "alternative spirituality" is corporate culture is neither an oxymoron nor a hyperbole. Conservative yuppies with corporate jobs and middle-class housewives seek shamans, acupuncturists, aromatherapists, and healers-by-phone. They shop on the net for ecofriendly products, herbal secrets, and wisdom. During vacation, they embark on long "spiritual quests" somewhere in "Indian country" (a subsidiary of virtual Nirvana), or south of the (old) border. Their "alternative" spirituality is sometimes complemented by a Spartan health program that requires strict diets, gym routines, mineral baths, and "zero tolerance" for drugs, fat, tobacco, and alcohol. For them, as for many people we know, it is hard to distinguish between "enlightenment" and "lifestyle," between desire and depth, between puritanism and transcendence. The word "spirituality" gets lost in the vast in-between space.

Contemporary spirituality has other cultural manifestations. Freed from the unpleasant moral constraints of critical multiculturalism and "political correctness," many young hipsters have selectively borrowed elements from numerous Third World (pet) cultures, to create their own designer tribalism. From San Diego to Manhattan, and from West Berlin to Formentera, the (mostly) white apocalypse youth gathers for postindustrial powwows in an attempt to recapture a lost sense of belonging to a larger "spiritual community." It warms my heart. Their neotribalism is loosely based (allegedly) on crosscultural performance rituals inspired by "ancient rites," and spiced with collective drumming, aficionado performance art, and pop "anarchist" politics. The goal is collective "ecstasy." The neotribal self-made person, a (self-perceived) dropout of Western civilization, meets *tête-à-tête* with the universe to unleash their creative demons and fairies at huge outdoor ritual raves such as the legendary Burning Man Festival in Nevada or the mega-techno festivals in Europe. There, everyone gets to be a performance artist, anarchist, and shaman for a weekend. They build teepees and kivas out of industrial trash. They proudly wear their Rasta dreadlocks, Indian braids, or shaved heads. They showcase their pale, ex-Protestant bodies covered with Celtic, pre-Columbian, Native American, and Maori tattoos. The great project of recapturing pagan ritualism is an expression of the Western need to connect the dots between body, mind, soul, memory, and heart. As a performance artist, I truly understand their dilemma.

In Mexico and other Latin American countries, since the dramatic collapse of *neoliberalismo* (when we finally realized that we were not exactly VIP guests in "the global project") and the emergence of a generalized culture of violence and despair, the practice of *brujeria* (witchcraft) has extended across class, profession, and age. Everyone consults a witch doctor, even the middle class. In Galerias, a popular Mexico City mall, an entire wing called El Pabellon Esotérico is devoted to the occult. There, after shopping or before the movies, you can get a *limpia* (exorcism), purchase talismans to protect your business or your aching heart, or have someone read your cards, pulse, or aura. The amazing performance personae of the mall witches fall into various categories: *Mexica*/Goth, ultra-*indigenista*, gypsy/*hipiteca*, or Californian new age. They draw their moral strength from the following realization: Our unprecedented emptiness and acute social crises cannot be "healed" by institutionalized religion. Catholicism has failed us (as have other formalized religions) and the witch doctors know it. They know that our selves are fractured and incomplete, that our lives are frail, boring, and predictable, and they are ready to provide us with the instant cure: A participatory ritual performance through which we get to experience (or rather to believe we are experiencing) an intensified sense of ourselves and of the many worlds we have lost for good.

Track #10 Performing the Other-as-freak

Performing against the backdrop of the mainstream bizarre has been quite a formidable challenge. My colleagues in La Pocha Nostra and I have explored the spectacle of the Other-as-freak by decorating and "enhancing" our bodies with special-effects make-up, hyperethnic motifs, handmade "lowrider" prosthetics and braces, and what we term "useless" or "imaginary" technology. The idea is to heighten features of fear and desire in the dominant imagination and "spectacularize" our "extreme identities," with the clear understanding that these identities have already been distorted by the invisible surgery of global media. We then pose on dioramas as "artificial savages" making ourselves completely available for the audience to "explore" us, change our costumes and props, and even replace us for a short period of time. In the second part of the "show," people get to choose from a "menu of possible interactions," which changes from site to site. Among other options, they can whip us, handle us roughly with S&M leashes, "tag" (spray paint) our bodies, and point replicas of handguns and Uzis at us.

Ceding our will to the audience and inviting them to participate in what appear to be "extreme performance games" are integral aspects of the new phase of our work. Some vivid examples come to mind: Once, during a La Pocha Nostra performance at the Caradigian Museum in Wales, a Victorian chanteuse (Katherine Adamenko) handcuffed to a period dresser played strip poker with male audience members for three hours. She had no problem getting people to participate and she was so good that never did she have to strip all the way down. On another occasion, during the San Francisco premiere of our Spanglish lowrider opera, *Califas, 2000*, a nude *ranchera* singer with a strap-on dildo (Michelle Ceballos) would be "activated" by audience members strictly through fellatio. Again, people went for it without hesitation. During the international tour of *The Museum of Fetishized Identities*, Mexican performance artist Juan Ybarra politely asked audience members to flagellate him with a flag of the country in which we were performing. Willing audience members immediately formed a line to carry out his instructions, while others screamed "harder, *harder*!" At the opening performance of the 2002 Liverpool Biennial, a British artist named Gaynor Sweeny who joined our troupe at the last moment, with her face made up to look like a traditional geisha, stood on a platform with a museum sign that read "Authentic Asian bride looking for tender British husband," and asked male audience members to write their phone numbers on her nude body. By the end of the night, her body was completely covered by a phone agenda of excited sexual tourists. More recently, while performing in Zurich, we invited an African actress to pose on a diorama in stereotypical "African Queen" regalia. She sat on a throne framed by two taxidermied lions. A museum sign invited men to wash her feet. The otherwise extremely shy Swiss men succumbed to their interracial fetishes.

Regardless of the country or the city where we perform, the results of these border performance experiments reveal a new relationship between performance artist and audience, between the exoticized "foreign" body and the white voyeur. Most interactions are characterized by the lack of political or ethical implications. Unlike, say, ten years ago, when audiences were overly sensitive regarding gender and racial politics, our new audiences are more than willing to manipulate our identity, overtly sexualize us, and engage in (symbolic or real) acts of crosscultural/cross-gender seduction, transgression, even violence.

Unless we detect the potential for real physical harm, we let all this happen. Why? Our objective (at least the conscious one) is to unleash the millennial demons. As performance artists, we wish to understand our new role and place in this culture of extreme spectacle that has been forced upon us in the past five years. In the process of detecting the exact placement of the new borders of tolerance (especially since 9/11), it becomes necessary to open up a *sui generis* ceremonial space—a space where the audience may engage in anthropoetical inquiry and reflect on their new relationship with cultural, racial, and political Otherness.

4

An open letter to the national arts community

(Letter, 2003)

This letter carries the outrage of my saliva and the fears and aspirations of my many artistic communities. Written originally in November 2003, it is one of my humble attempts to contribute to our clarity and valor, in the era of the Blue Dragon. I truly hope that soon it will be dated.

I

Dear colleagues,

Since the mid-1990s, as part of the much-touted "backlash," the US political right managed to successfully demonize and de-fund contemporary art, labeling critical artists as "decadent," "elitist," and "un-American." As a result, the budgets of federal and state arts agencies were progressively sliced down, and soon the efforts of private foundations to pick up the slack became insufficient.

Then came 9/11 . . .

The dramatic attacks on the US provided the Bush administration with the much-needed moral authority to implement a regime of intolerance, censorship, and paranoid nationalism. Their particular brand of religious machismo was not that different from the extremist beliefs of those they allegedly opposed. Their master discourse stated: You are either with "us" (the "good guys") or with "them" (the "evil ones"); "God Bless America!" a hundred times, a thousand times (and no one else).

And artists and intellectuals suddenly found ourselves caught between two forms of fundamentalisms—not really knowing if we were perceived as part of the "us" or the "them."

In this cartography of fear, new and resurrected borders dividing families, communities and nations were drawn overnight; brand-new enemies and abysmal ethical contradictions were imposed upon us all, and the arts communities were no exception.

First came state-sponsored censorship: Movies and art shows containing references to political violence were indefinitely postponed and a long list of innocuous songs alluding to violence and airplanes were banned from the radio. Remember our complete disbelief? Then, a high-tech form of McCarthyism came into effect with Carnivore and other digital surveillance systems, and thousands of "suspicious" websites and virtual networks were dismantled. Finally came the public burnings of books and audio CDs sanctioned by the theological rhetoric of our Holy Attorney General. He was embarked on a personal crusade against Satan himself, speaking in tongues and covering with fabric the breasts of the nude statues of Washington. Even the Teletubbies became an object of his rage. And so, the Talibanization of the USA began. **CARNIVORE XP–386759–493879–988321**

Under this corrupt climate, the corporate-owned electronic and printed media engaged in a "no questions asked" policy. Wrapped in the American flag (made in China), most US journalists began to willingly perform the role of stenographers for the Pentagon. Soon, the USA became the only Western "democracy" in which generals and intelligence agents performed the role of news commentators. And those "liberal" anchormen, correspondents, and commentators like Phil Donahue and Peter Arnet who deviated from the script were instantly fired.

In academia, conservative students began to report on their outspoken professors and their "anti-American" or "antipatriotic" behavior. In some universities like Duke, conservative alumni threatened to withdraw their financial support if those outspoken professors weren't silenced. Those students and teachers who dared to organize against the SuperNintendo policies of the Bush administration were inundated with hate mail and death threats. After **CARNIVORE XP–386759–493879–988321**

As more flags appeared in our neighborhoods, Chicano/Latino and grassroots organizations throughout the country were cowardly tagged with jingoistic statements by anonymous "patriots." In San Diego, the legendary murals of Chicano Park were defaced by white supremacists. In San Francisco, the windows and digital murals of the Galería de la Raza were tagged with anti-immigrant and antigay

Miss Amerika.
Alexis McKee. Re:Group performance salon, San Francisco, 2003. Photo: Lou Dematteis.

phrases. One night, a passing car shot a bullet into the Galería window. It felt like the 1970s in Central America.

The word "terrorist" surreptitiously expanded to signify, at first, all radical Muslims, then all Arabs and Southeast Asians and finally all Arab-looking people including Latino immigrants—documented or not. Since 9/11, US-based Latino artists who travel abroad regularly, including myself, have been systematically detained at airport checkpoints, body-searched and interrogated. Many of our art materials, props, and costumes have been confiscated without an explanation or an apology. We have slowly learned to endure the post-9/11 humiliation rituals at airport security checkpoints. We are all slowly learning to live with ethnic profiling and racial paranoia as official culture.

The drastic measurements of the Homeland Security Office and the Patriot Act which turned the country into the largest neighborhood watch program ever, paired with the tightening of borders and the new immigration and travel restrictions began to affect international cultural exchange. Visas were denied or indefinitely postponed. And foreign artists from countries on Bush's ever-expanding black list were no longer allowed in the land of freedom and democracy. Unfortunately many myopic cultural institutions from Europe, Asia, and Latin America have responded by "boycotting" US artists, as if this would hurt the Bush administration at **CARNIVORE XP–386759–493879–988321**

As expected, the de-funding of the arts soon followed. The budget priorities of the new Republican junta were clearly national security, law enforcement, and the military. As the attention of the country focused on a myriad of threats (some real, most mythical), a fictional "Axis of Evil," and the much-touted "weapons of mass distraction," Bush and cronies managed to covertly dismantle the funding sources of all progressive communities and grassroots organizations, including the alternative and experimental art worlds.

In this climate of manufactured hysteria, art was sent from the back seat of the funding bus straight out the back door. The unspoken yet pervasive narrative stated: "Who needs art when we are fighting international terrorists?" In California alone, the Arts Council lost $19 million out of its $20-million budget. Today, California, the fifth largest economy of the world, holds a pitiful continental record worthy of *Ripley's Believe it or Not*: The second smallest per capita budget allocated to the arts after . . . Bolivia: Three cents per person per year.

The fear of losing one's funding or one's job created a more insidious problem: Self-censorship. Throughout academia and the art world, with a few exceptions, we were all in silence. We were scared of not knowing the exact placement of the new borders of tolerance. Our European and Latin American colleagues kept asking us the same unpleasant question: How come the artists and intellectuals in the USA are not speaking up and putting up a good fight? When are you guys going to break the silence? All we could do was raise our shoulders in total disbelief. "What irony," I wrote to one of my publishers late last year (2002), "Mexico, my original homeland, is clumsily learning to live with the new dangers of freedom and democracy; while we here in the US, my new homeland, are learning to live without freedom." Breaking the silen**CARNIVORE XP–386759–493879–988321**

CARNIVORE XP–386759–493879–988321

II

The Bush administration contributed to the repoliticization of art. Why? All the values and principles they chose to target were at the core of art practice including: Freedom of speech, civil liberties, cultural diversity and tolerance, the right to dissent and criticize power, and the right to geographical mobility.

Since most institutional spaces were closed to critical art, virtual space became the de-facto territory of contestation. A new anonymous political-arts movement began to emerge as unsigned posters, hilarious political cartoons and outrageous Photoshop images and QuickTime movies critical of Bush and his few "international" collaborators (or rather scared followers) circulated in virtual space.

After a group of poets rejected a Faustian invitation by the First Lady to read their poetry in the White House, a huge antiwar poetry website came to fruition. For a while, it was the most visited literary website ever.

By early 2003, as we approached the irrational invasion of Iraq, sectors in the intellectual community and even the pop music and Hollywood establishments began to finally "break the silence." It warmed our hearts to hear celebrities like Susan Sarandon, Harry Belafonte, Martin Sheen, Peter Coyote, Sean Penn, and the Dixie Chicks speak their minds. There was a new unspoken agreement amongst all of us: "Let's live as if the Patriot Act didn't exist. Let's conquer this fear. Let's finally speak up and see what happens. Let's **CARNIVORE XP–386759–493879–988321**

In mid-February (2003) over twenty million people across the globe demonstrated energetically against the war. Many artists, students, and intellectuals who normally don't walk the political streets were there, along with myriad unlikely colleagues including housewives, senior citizens, war veterans, and even apolitical citizens who had recently lost their jobs due to Bush's narrowminded politics. Most demonstrations were peaceful and quite imaginative in terms of their performance strategies, visual languages, and poetic slogans. A window of hope seemed to temporarily open up in the smoky horizon.

III

Artists, arts administrators, curators, and producers are now facing many predicaments. Due to the drastic funding cuts, cultural institutions have had to trim down considerably their programs and staff, and most grassroots institutions and alternative art spaces face probable extinction within the next two years. Every week, we hear of yet another arts organization, museum department, or community center that just lost its funding, of yet another arts administrator, or artist colleague who was just fired. Commissions and tours are being canceled left and right. Our organization, La Pocha Nostra, has lost ten large commissions since 9/11 and (as of November of 2003), 70 percent of our budget is coming from our international touring.

The toll that the Bush era is taking on people's mental and physical health is immense. Understandably, we are exhausted, poor, overworked, and scared shitless of the immediate future. The amount of unemployed artists in the US is comparable to any "Third World" country; our cultural institutions are sinking; our communities are all in disarray; and we don't even have a political project at hand to envision an alternative. It is no coincidence that in the past two years personal illness, divorce, and suicide, against a backdrop of social, racial, and military violence, have all increased exponentially. Understandably, our bodies and psyches are internalizing the pain of the larger sociopolitical body and the confusion, fear, and despair of the collective psyche.

These dramatic conditions are forcing our frail arts communities to engage in serious soul-searching and tough questioning. Across art spaces, galleries, theaters, bohemian cafés, recording and rehearsal studios, we are all expressing our perplexity and asking similar questions: What are our new roles as artists and intellectuals in this cartography of terror and despair? How do we restore the mirror of critical culture for society to see, once again, its own ethical reflection? Are critical artists an endangered species in the US? Do we wish to live in a country without museums, galleries, theaters, cultural centers, literary journals, film festivals, and an alternative press? If America continues to follow this path and chooses to become a closed society and a cultural wasteland, will we be able to tolerate living here as complete outcasts or will we be forced to become expatriates in Europe, Canada, or Mexico?

What concrete actions can we realistically undertake as a sector (and not as disenfranchised individuals), to reclaim our stolen civic self and our legitimate right to create and articulate our artistic visions? How to keep these questions alive, discuss survival strategies with our local and national communities, and present our case coherently to the press and to members of the political class? Is it possible to **CARNIVORE XP–386759–493879–988321** the FBI is already knocking at the door of several artists and intellectuals including **CARNIVORE XP–386759–493879–988321**

IV

Since 9/11, I have had this recurring dream. I dream of a faraway country in which artists are respected in the same way pop celebrities, military men, and sportsmen are respected in our country. Artists receive a decent salary, own their homes and cars, enjoy vacations, and have medical insurance.

The media and the political class value their opinions. Writers, philosophers, and performance artists appear daily on national television and radio. They perform multiple social roles as social critics, chroniclers, and advisers, intercultural diplomats, community brokers, and spiritual leaders.

In this *sui generis* society, one can actually purchase poetry books and art magazines in convenience stores, museums are free, and every neighborhood has a cultural center designed and run by artists. In this most unusual society, even corporations, city councils, school districts, and hospitals hire artists as advisers and *animateurs*. In this imaginary society, artists don't have to write texts like this one.

track two

PEDAGOGY

A useful guide to the Pocha method

Gómez-Peña's critical essays and chronicles in Track I contextualize the following exploration of La Pocha Nostra's performance methodologies and pedagogy. Gómez-Peña and his la Pocha Nostra colleagues comprehensively document the micro- and macrologistics of performance praxis in "Cross Contamination: The performance activism and oppositional art of La Pocha Nostra." This manifesto is followed by "La Pocha Nostra's Basic Methodology," a handbook that details the evolution of their performance methods from rehearsal to opening night, from the "bare minimum" to "advanced jamming exercises." These two texts comprise years of exploring the process of performance. For this reason, it is La Pocha Nostra's most important contribution.

With the exception of the introduction by Gómez-Peña, this manuscript was prepared collaboratively by Guillermo Gómez-Peña, British La Pocha Nostra associate Rachel Rogers, and other Pocha members. Due to its explicit emphasis on pedagogy, it couldn't have been written any other way.

Elaine Peña

The Pocha cartel.
Standing (left to right): Kari Hensley, Guillermo Galindo, Juan Ybarra, Emiko Lewis, Roberto Sifuentes, and Guillermo Gómez-Peña. Kneeling (left to right): Monica Lleó and Michelle Ceballos. San Francisco, 2003. Photo: Jarda Brych.

5

Crosscontamination

The performance activism and oppositional art of La Pocha Nostra

(Manifesto, 2004)

Guillermo Gómez-Peña, with Rachel Rogers, Kari Hensley, Elaine Peña, Roberto Sifuentes, and Michelle Ceballos

In 1993, Guillermo Gómez-Peña, Roberto Sifuentes, and Nola Mariano founded La Pocha Nostra in Los Angeles, California. The objective was to formally conceptualize Gómez-Peña's collaborations with performance artists such as Sifuentes, James Luna, and Sara Shelton Mann. In 1995, La Pocha Nostra moved to San Francisco's Mission District where it has been based for the past nine years. In late 2001, La Pocha Nostra completed the process of incorporation and became a nonprofit organization. As of June of 2004, members include performance artists Guillermo Gómez-Peña, Emiko R. Lewis, Michelle Ceballos, Violeta Luna, Juan Ybarra, and over thirty associates worldwide. Projects range from performance solos and duets to large-scale performance installations using video, DVD, photography, audio, and cyberart. This text attempts to articulate the complexities of this most unusual "organization." We truly hope to inspire our colleagues across disciplines to develop similar models and methods. Feel free to pirate any of the following ideas.

I La Pocha Nostra: An ever-evolving manifesto

La Pocha Nostra is an ever-morphing "transdisciplinary arts organization" based in San Francisco with branches and factions in many other cities and countries. As stated in our mission statement, "We provide a base for a loose network and forum of rebel artists from various disciplines, generations, and ethnic backgrounds." If there is a common denominator, it is our desire to cross and erase dangerous borders between art and politics, practice and theory, artist and spectator. We strive to eradicate myths of purity and dissolve borders surrounding culture, ethnicity, gender, language, and métier.

La Pocha Nostra is neither an ensemble nor a troupe. We are more of a conceptual "laboratory"—a loose association of rebel artists thinking together, exchanging ideas/aspirations, and jumping into "the abyss" together.

La Pocha Nostra has died and been resurrected dozens of times. It has manifested itself as a garage performance troupe, an experimental sideshow, an interactive living museum and curiosity cabinet, and a politicized fashion show. It has expressed itself as a "performance clinic," a town meeting, an "intelligent" rave, and a virtual resource center. La Pocha Nostra is frequently a Trojan horse: Two or three artists may be invited by a major institution but we bring ten to twenty others and involve them all in the process.

La Pocha Nostra is a virtual *maquiladora* (assembly plant) that produces brand-new metaphors, symbols, images, and words to explain the complexities of our times. The Spanglish neologism *Pocha Nostra* translates as either "our impurities" or "the cartel of cultural bastards." We love this poetic ambiguity. It reveals an attitude toward art and society: "Crossracial, poly-gendered, experi-mental, *¿y qué*?"

La Pocha Nostra challenges the traditional art-world mythologies of the *artiste* as a suffering bohemian and misunderstood genius. La Pocha Nostra artists are social critics and chroniclers, intercultural diplomats, translators/mistranslators, informal ombudsmen, media pirates, information architects, reverse anthropologists, experimental linguists, and radical pedagogues. To us, the artist is, above all, an active citizen immersed in the great debates of our times. Our place is the world and not just the "art world."

La Pocha Nostra is, by nature, antiessentialist and antinationalist. We claim an extremely unpopular position in the US: "No homeland; no fear; no borders; no patriotism; no nation-state; no ideology; no censorship." We are committed to presenting a polycultural and diversified "America"—an internationalist, humanist, and progressive perspective which has nothing to do with US unilateralism, the Bush doctrine, or the Patriot Act.

La Pocha Nostra collaborates across national borders, race, gender, and generations as an act of citizen diplomacy and as a means to create "ephemeral communities" of like-minded rebels. The basic premise of these collaborations is founded on the ideal "If we learn to cross borders on stage, we may learn how to do so in larger social spheres." We hope others will be challenged to do the same.

La Pocha Nostra is an ever-changing community. Depending on who is sitting at the table at any given moment, Pocha can be two people or fifty. We create regenerative sources of labor built from concentric and overlapping circles. The inner circle comprises six to eight artists and scholars whose membership is determined by their degree of commitment and time. The next circle includes performance artists, musicians, filmmakers, and designers working part-time on several Pocha projects. There is also a series of outer and overlapping circles of artist associates, theorists, and producers who live around the world. They may collaborate on a project if the time and place are right. Members and associates can move from one circle to another. The constant change of membership inevitably alters the nature of the work and contributes to the permanent process of reinvention.

La Pocha Nostra functions through an open belief system. We strongly trust in the idea that consciousness is stimulated through nontraditional presentational formats. Therefore, we view performance as an effective catalyst for thought and debate. Through *sui generis* combinations of artistic languages, media, and spontaneous performative formats, we explore the interface of globalization, migration, hybrid identities, border culture, and technology. Our rehearsals and workshops, weekly staff meetings, and quarterly board meetings always involve intense discussions of hot issues. We foreground the theoretical and methodological possibilities of performance to address these issues and the changing role of the artist in society.

La Pocha Nostra encourages public dialogue. We hope our performative-ritual formats are less authoritarian and static than those we see in academia, religion, pop culture, and politics. We constantly challenge theorists to be more performative and artists to explore intellectual avenues. It works most of the time. Every now and then we engender a monster, and that's also fine.

La Pocha Nostra was created out of our necessity to survive as Chicano/Latino artists in a racist art world. The fact is that Chicanos and other "artists of color" don't have the funding support enjoyed by the Anglo avant-garde. We must respond with complexity and imagination to this endemic lack of funds and access.

La Pocha Nostra's performance pedagogy performs a major role in our political praxis. Why? It challenges authoritarian hierarchies and specialized knowledge by creating temporary utopian spaces where interdisciplinary dialogue and imagination can flourish. These utopian spaces are framed by, but not contained within, a pentagon-shape of radical ideas whose vertices are community, education, activist politics, new technologies, and experimental esthetics.

La Pocha Nostra is a unique esthetic. Our "robo-baroque" and "ethno-techno-cannibal esthetic" samples and devours everything we encounter: Border and Chicano pop culture, TV, film, rock and roll, hip hop, comics, journalism, anthropology, pornography, religious imagery, and, of course, the history of the visual and performing arts. We crossreference this information, "embody" it, and then reinterpret it for a live audience, thereby refracting fetishized constructs of otherness through the spectacle of our "heightened" bodies on display. We are a live crossover jam culture.

La Pocha Nostra's esthetic praxis involves ethnic- and gender-bending, cultural transvestism, and power inversions. Many of our images show women and people "of color" in control. In our world, cultural borders have moved to center stage while the alleged mainstream is pushed to the margins and treated as exotic and unfamiliar. We place the audience member/viewer in the position of a "foreigner" or a "minority." It sounds "heavy" but it's actually a lot of fun.

La Pocha Nostra crosses dangerous esthetic borders. We cede both our will and the stage to the audience. We invite them to cocreate the piece and to participate in our "extreme performance games" riddled with postcolonial implications.[1] These games are integral aspects of our work.

La Pocha Nostra has an ever-growing archive comprising thousands of photographs, videos, books, magazines, soundtracks, documents, props, and costumes. We are permanently searching for interns to help us to organize a functional working archive. Sadly, we have never had enough hands, space, or filing cabinets to complete this task. We are currently in the process of turning our performance video archives into an educational DVD series. The first one of the series is already available.

La Pocha Nostra is an informal service organization. In addition to providing ethno-techno body language, imagery, and poetics, we offer new ways of thinking about art and community, multicommunity outreach, and new audience development. It's part of the "Pocha package."

La Pocha Nostra is, above all, a utopian idea. Our "Utopia" is a marker in the political distance, a philosophical direction, and a path we often lose. Unfortunately, our frail egos and financial hardships occasionally cause us to fall into personal voids and temporarily forget our goals. One La Pocha Nostra responsibility is to inspire each other to recapture strength and clarity.

La Pocha Nostra is committed to a permanent process of reinvention. This means La Pocha Nostra's membership and projects may have changed when this "open text" is finally published. Unfortunately permanent reinvention and ever shifting

1 See "Pocha Live," pp. 81–5.

multidimensionality hinder sustainability. This is one of our systemic problems. How do we solve this dilemma? We still don't know but we are willing to accept suggestions (<http://www.pochanostra.com>).

II Pocha live: A crosscultural poltergeist

Over the past years, perhaps our most significant contribution to the field has been in our hybrid realm of performance/installation. We create interactive "living museums" that parody various colonial practices of representation. This often includes the ethnographic diorama (as found in museums of natural history), the freak show, the Indian trading post, the border "curio shop," the sex shop/strip joint window display, and their contemporary equivalents in global media and corporate entertainment. We "exhibit" our highly decorated bodies sometimes as "specimens" from an endangered tribe or "border saints" from a persecuted religion. We surrender our will to the audience and assume composite identities dictated by the fears and desires of museum visitors and Internet users.

The composite identities of our "ethnocyborg" personae are manufactured with the following formula in mind: One-quarter stereotype, one-quarter audience projection, one-quarter esthetic artifact, and one-quarter unpredictable personal/social monster. These "artificial savages" are cultural projections of First World desire/fear of its surrounding subcultures and the so-called "Third World Other." The live performance becomes the process via which we reveal the morphology of intercultural fetishes and the mechanisms propelling the behavior of both our "savages" and our audiences.

The audience steps into a "total" environment. Our ethnocyborg personae are displayed on platforms of varying heights and sizes for three to four hours a night, sometimes over a three-day period. Live and prerecorded music, multiple video projections and slides, fog, cinematic lighting, embalmed animals, old-fashioned medical figurines and "ethnokitsch" design motifs all help to enhance our "ethno-techno" and "robo-baroque" esthetic and create a "heightened state" for the spectator/participant.

The experience is purely voyeuristic in the first hour of the performance. The ethnocyborgs create slow-motion emblematic *tableaux vivants*. A catwalk connecting two platforms becomes a revolving stage for short performances by local artists commenting on fashion, gender, and ethnicity. All action happens simultaneously. This ritualized action samples and mixes radical political imagery, religious iconography, "extreme" pop culture, sports, racially orientated fashion, and theatricalized sexuality. Symbolic sexuality is everywhere. Some performers feel inclined to eroticize political violence and even war while others utilize performative sexuality as syntax to gel religion and politics. Creating symbolic sexuality is also a means to invert power relations and media images of demonized "Otherness." These ever-morphing *tableaux vivants* overlap with each other creating surprising juxtapositions and fleeting glances of unique third meanings, which develop above and beyond our original intentions.

The performative structure is open and noncoercive. Audience members walk around the dioramas designing their own journey. They can stay for as long as they wish, come in and out of the space, return hours later, or even the following day. They can participate in our performance games or simply watch. No one is ever judged.

As the evening evolves, what began as a purely voyeuristic experience becomes increasingly participatory. We begin to make ourselves available for audience members to "explore" and play with us. They can touch us, smell us, even hand-feed us. They can tag (spray-paint) us, braid our hair, change our make-up and props, and try different wigs and headdresses on us. In other words, they get to use the performers as "human dolls." They can point guns at us to experience the feeling of having another human surrender at their feet. Some spectators even put dog leashes around our necks and engage in consensual power games with us. Audience members sometimes suggest combinations we've not attempted before, in which case we have to try and respond to their challenge. The "menu" of possible performance interactions changes from site to site.

We often set up a diorama station where audience members can choose a "temporary ethnic identity" and become "their favorite cultural Other" using make-up and costumes. They are encouraged to integrate themselves into our living dioramas once their "instant identity change" takes place. Audiences love this part. Almost everyone is willing to escape their ethnicity and gender as long as there are no physical or social repercussions. Again, we don't exercise judgment on anyone.

We also give audience members the option to take off their clothes and *symbolically* perform their interracial sexual fantasies. We are always surprised by the number of people willing to be sexually performative in public. This even happens when we are performing in conservative cities or in countries not used to performance art or experimental theater. (We can't stress enough that the nature of this play is strictly symbolic and never crosses over to include actual sexual acts. Sometimes it becomes necessary to point this out repeatedly to the audience.)

Occasionally we incorporate an open mike in the center of the space to allow audience members to speak up or talk back. They can read their own poetry, voice their opinion on the proceedings, express an outrageous fantasy or desire, or give commands to the performers. We politely persuade them to hand the mike to others if their performance is uninteresting or too long.

Audience member combs Guillermo Gómez-Peña's hair during a performance of *El Mexterminator Project.*
New York, 1998. Photo: Karl Peterson.

Both audience members and performers are continuously making esthetic, political, and ethical decisions. The subtext of these performance games seems to read: "We are all racist and sexist; we are all horny, tender, playful, and violent; it's human nature; we are all implicated in this madness. Let's figure it out together. Let's cross each other's borders and see what happens." It is precisely in these raw interstices of tolerance/intolerance that we can really further a dialogue on intercultural relations. We try to avoid hollow gestures of sympathy and "empathy" that superficially transform human relations. Challenging the audience to choose whether or not to participate in this or that performance game means it becomes necessary for them to exercise their civic muscles and political intelligence. We strongly believe that performance furthers dialogue by creating various pathways, trajectories, and unsuspected intersections which are mostly discovered/learned through the body and later circulated through language and action. This is precisely where the true political power of the work lies.

In the last hour of the performance we reverse the gaze and step out of our dioramas. We then create *tableaux vivants* with the most responsive and audacious audience members. We manipulate their personae by sculpting their bodies or by adding or subtracting costumes and props. The distance between performer and audience is completely erased. This is our favorite part of the performance.

Inspired by director Richard Gough, we sometimes set up a "food station" in the performance space where a local chef cooks their favorite dishes. These delicious food snacks are sold with names invented by us to suit the atmosphere of the event. We place the audience member in the uncomfortable position of being a cultural tourist by situating the food station right in front of the catwalk (where an extreme fashion show takes place). We also set up a bar inside the performance space. This encourages a carnival atmosphere throughout the experience. The behavior of the audience changes as they become dramatically less inhibited during and after the ingestion of tropical cocktails or shots of strong liquor. This scenario allows for a more "revealing" performance for both performers and audience members. We are fully aware that this scenario is dangerous, particularly during the last hour when we frequently give up total control of our dioramas. We often find that postcolonial demons are dancing all around us.

Unless we detect the potential for real physical harm, we let all this happen. Why? Our objective (at least the conscious one) is to unleash the millennial demons, not

Performance action by Guillermo Gómez-Peña and audience members.
La Capella, Barcelona, 1999. Photo: La Capella.

to pontificate. As performance artists we wish to understand our new role and place in this culture of extreme spectacle. We believe that these bizarre millennial rituals and games trigger a long-term process of reflexivity in the psyche of the viewer. We hope this leads to deeper ethical and political questions. This heightened awareness allows spectators to look at and accept images they would usually reject as impossible, distasteful, or unrealistic. Later on, the audience will recall them and will have to deal with their own memories in the "cold light of day." This allows them to critically question what they have seen and their feelings toward such imagery.

What the live audience ends up experiencing is a stylized anthropomorphization of their/our own postcolonial demons and hallucinations—a kind of crosscultural poltergeist. The space between self and other, us and them, fear and desire, becomes blurred and unspecific. It becomes ground zero in intercultural relations. In this sense, the performance/installation functions both as a bizarre set design for a contemporary enactment of "cultural pathologies" and as a ceremonial space for people to reflect on their attitudes toward other cultures.

For the moment, our job is merely to open the Pandora's box of our times and let the demons loose, to open the infected border wound, so to speak. Others (academics and activists) will have to help us understand those demons.

III Producing Pocha

Producing a large-scale performance by La Pocha Nostra is an exciting pain in the ass. The performance begins to take shape when our eccentric "tech-rider" arrives. An old-fashioned barbers' or dentists' chair, taxidermied animals, realistic-looking weapons, raw meat, prosthetics, and braces are just a few of the items necessary to produce the performance.

The prop list of "local ethnic kitsch and motifs of problematic depictions of Other cultures" is always the most challenging. The "local" prop list brings together a range of unpredictable elements that will depend on the locality, the resources available to the host producers, and their willingness to search for these arcane, site-specific items.

The producer will need to designate someone from their institution/team to lead the scavenger hunt for props, costumes, and design motifs. It may be one person or a group, a "pop-archeological brigade." This individual or group of people will have an enormous influence over the look of the final piece. Their local knowledge and connections are essential.

Ideally (for a major project), two other teams will be created alongside the prop team. The technical team (who must understand our esthetic praxis), and the performance team (these people actually take the workshop and perform) are formed a few weeks before La Pocha Nostra members arrive at the venue. Once we arrive in town, and our jet lag has worn off, we begin to consolidate these teams and their labor at the first production meeting. We go over our technical needs, get to know the local artists (or students) who will be working with us over the next few weeks, and check the status of props and costumes that have been collected and those that are still to be found.

At a typical meeting or rehearsal, we'll have good food, some wine (and rum if we're lucky), and lots of strong coffee. Conversations about war, immigration, globalization, and new technologies are interwoven with contemporary art theory and practice. Current affairs and politics are considered in nearly every esthetic discussion and decision. There is always a lot of laughter. A strong feeling of community quickly develops. Rudeness and disrespect are simply not tolerated within the group. Our aim is to avoid, at all costs, the self-destructive existential malaise of the alternative art world—spiritual exhaustion, political quarreling, and cannibalism.

Every performance project we undertake is "site-," "time-," and "theme-"specific. Each piece is framed by a different metafiction congruent with the cultural and political specificity of the site and the overall project. Whether the metafiction is some kind of "expo," "a futuristic museum of ethnography," a "Chicano cyber-punk religion," a "multimedia opera," an "extreme fashion show," or an "intelligent rave," it permeates the overall esthetics of the installation, the performative strategies of each participant, and the advertising campaign.

AN EXAMPLE OF A POCHA META-FICTION

For the production of* Ex-Centris *at Tate Modern, 2003), written by US performance theorist Leigh Clemmons

A message from our corporate sponsors

This has been a time of unprecedented global cultural expansion for Ex-Centris, a subsidiary of HysTerra Mimetics, Ltd., PLC. As the originators of the now-obsolete World Wide Web of the twentieth century, we have now expanded into the far reaches of the world, dominating ethnic fashion, ethnic-specific "real sex" websites, discount shopping, gourmet coffee, fossil-fuel dispersion and the international art market.

Ex-Centris realizes HysTerra's dream of the Experimental Prototype Collective-Unconscious Community of Tomorrow (Epcot).

HysTerra, in this case, turned the idea of Epcot into a fantastic theme park showcasing the world's cultural diversity. Now we bring the spirit of Epcot-Futura to the global market, satisfying your desires for intercultural fetishes, stylized violence, and tastes of culture more crumbly than the cheapest Cornish pasty. Our favorite component in the HysTerra Ethnographic Showcase, Ex-Centris offers its answer to the Magic Kingdom's "Este es un Mundo Pequeño." "The Global Adventure" captures the soul, so to speak, of this wondrous planet and brings it to life with stirring performances by ethnocyborg symbionts in their authentically simulated environments. You can enjoy the chance to "interact" with them and opportunities abound for you to enjoy the full pantheon of authentic cultural experiences: From transforming into your ethnicity of choice and engaging in fun S&M "power games," to firing a machine gun at a live Mexican. The heart of the Panethnic Showcase and home to one of the most incredible ethnocyborg symbiont shows in HysTerra-y is the Altar to World Religion, featuring the Self-Crucifixion Center, where various ethnocyborg symbionts will stretch their bodies into culturally dictated religious positions. Finally, you will find assorted educational films to enhance your "total audiovisual experience." Ex-Centris is by far the most "adult" of all the theme parks, but don't be fooled; there is plenty to see and do here and fun for all. We are glad that you have decided to spend a few hours in our world. Neutralizing identity has many challenges. HysTerra will not deny; we will not ignore; we will not pass along our problems to other generations. We will confront them with focus, and clarity, and courage. And we will prevail. Have a nice day!

Mora Leikmee,

Official Quotacon, HysTerra, Ltd.

Disclaimer: No ethnocyborg simbionts were harmed or exploited in this showcase. After the mandatory six-week quarantine period, all have tested negative for HIV and tuberculosis.

La Pocha Nostra's specific performance marketing techniques are very creative. We regard our marketing campaign as part of the actual performance project. Some of the techniques we have used in the past include: Creating fake posters of alleged conservative groups objecting to us being in town, contacting diverse media outlets, community organizations, activist groups, and assorted underground club communities. Our email campaigns are written in performance mode and are intended to create some hype before the piece opens.

AN EXAMPLE OF POCHA'S MARKETING METHODS

For a touring project titled *The Museum of Fetishized Identities*, we utilized the following promotional email:

```
Subject: FW: THE MUSEUM OF FETISHIZED IDENTITIES
▶ Attachments: chellista56790.jpg
>POCHA ANNOUNCES FIRST IN A NEW LINE OF "ETHNO-CYBORGS" DELIVERED TO YOUR
>LOCAL ART VENUE
>
>Is your cultural institution currently suffering from a lack of audience
>attendance and/or funds, or post-9/11 philosophical direction?
>
>La Pocha Nostra is launching the first in a new line of "ethno-cyborgs,"
>designed to revive arts institutions and performance spaces. All La Pocha
>Nostra Latino performance cyborgs made in Taiwan.
>
>Named "La Cyborg Chellista No. 56790" (and shown here as a jpeg
>attachment) she comes complete with range of settings from "empathy" to
>"search and seizure." She provides you with a wide variety of tools to
>improve:
>
>multi-culti audience development
>identification of new receptive funding sources and
>Design of high-tech performative events catering to multiple communities.
>
>For the latest 2003 designs, look out for fall cyber-catalog!
>
>For orders and bookings, please call Teknola Mariano at 1-800-ETHNOCYBORG
>or
>email her at teknola@ethnocyborg.com
>
```

Physically piecing together all the staging elements of a large-scale La Pocha Nostra performance/installation takes between two and three days and involves a minimum of three techs, an onsite producer, between four and eight stagehands, and the performers. All this happens in dialogue with the two or three La Pocha Nostra artists on site.

The La Pocha Nostra members' performances are already developed to a certain extent (around 60 percent) before we get to the site. (We already have a catalogue of personae we can choose to perform. During the workshop we will decide which personae we feel most appropriate for that particular performance.) However, if time permits, we may develop new material for a persona during a workshop. We will usually have a rough idea of the structure for our individual performances before the final stages of the workshop. For example, we will have thought about the order we might perform the personae, which actions might work better toward the beginning of the piece as more static images, and which would work better near the end, so we can involve the audience. We will have decided what tasks we will ask the audience to perform, and the type of audience member we are looking for to carry out specific actions. The final structure is always unique to the particular site and will emerge organically from the workshop.

Generally, we find the participants and their material need to be poured into our preexisting mold in order for the event to come together over such a short period of time. Given a longer residency, three or more weeks, participants are able to work on and develop new material and may also come up with ideas that might change the structure. However, given our regular two-week time frame, we have to have a tight structure. There is enough flexibility for individuals to find unique performative actions and to create settings for their personae.

The most fixed element is the physical staging of the performance. We work with platforms and a catwalk in the vast majority of our performances. Any successful rehearsal-performance process needs a structure. Structure is the most important element, particularly when the workshop involves so many unknowns. Each performance is unique and individual because of these "unknowns," but we need something to guide us before we (as a group) find our own way. Again, over a longer period of time, we may come up with a different structure that could work better in a particular site or with a certain group of performers.

The day before the performance we should have everything in place: Video, slides, music, costumes, transitions, audience interactions. There may be unexpected last-minute performers and elements that are integrated into the performance. Some recent examples:

- In Chicago, a graffiti artist became part of the performance by working on a wall in the gallery. His participation was negotiated a couple of hours before we opened the doors.
- In Baton Rogue, we involved a real pig and its handler in the piece when we performed in a former rodeo arena called the Pig Palace. They decided to accept our eccentric invitation the day before the performance.
- In Zurich, we had six huge taxidermied animals, including a seven-foot lion, a mountain goat posed with the Swiss flag, and a monkey. They all arrived in the space on the day of the opening.
- In San Francisco, our hometown (as in Sydney, Australia), several local performance artists showed up at the last minute with very strong proposals. We chose to include them in addition to the troupe that had taken the workshop (clearly,

The Museum of Frozen Identities included both performance artists and human-size wax figures playing a chess game with Mexico's national identity over a three-day period.
Museo de la Ciudad de Mexico, 1997. Photo: Monica Naranjo.

not without consulting them first). We managed to find a suitable place for each of them on different nights.

Often, these surprise elements work so well, we retry them again in different contexts. An unexpected element can become the new standard for the next piece.

Up to the rehearsal before opening, we continuously ask ourselves: How can we make it more complex, more layered? At the same time, how can we make it more clear and succinct? How can we push the outer limits of the piece just 10 percent more? Early on opening day, the final, *final* decisions have to be made. This is the point where we say "OK, now we *have* to stop adding props, costumes, movements, videos, and parachuting performance artists, and stick with what we know works." However, since it is an interactive performance, there are more surprises, new juxtapositions, and unpredictable performative audience members who will change the course of the performance over the next three days. The performance will always look and feel different.

Opening night is always the most exciting and dangerous day. We usually meet four hours before call to apply make-up, put on our costumes, refurbish our props, tweak the final details of our "diorama" or individual installations, and warm up. An hour before the performance we stage photographs for a local photographer (preselected by us) and we ritually toast our ephemeral, but nonetheless solid, performance troupe. The second adventure begins when the doors open.[2]

By the end of the process, we have all become a part of the same dysfunctional family. Real bonds and true artistic, intellectual, and personal friendships are created. A few weeks later, we start the process all over again in another city or country with yet another incredible group of artists and troublemakers. The community grows larger as our health slowly deteriorates and our hearts continue to ache. It's beautiful and painful; what more can we say?

IV *Ex-Centris*: La Pocha Nostra's international cultural exchange as political praxis

> **"La Pocha was born out of the connections made by migrant artists encountering one another on the road. In this sense, Pocha is a way to formalize those connections and maintain an open global network of ongoing artistic and political communication and collaboration."**
>
> *Roberto Sifuentes*

La Pocha Nostra emphasizes the creation of intercultural, crossborder collaborations with performance artists from many countries. Why? It is a direct response to the ironic global phenomenon that immigrants of the "Third World" live within (and redefine the culture of) the much-touted First World (for many the very country responsible for the homeland's hardships). We have challenged ourselves to locate artists in other countries who are involved in the mapping of parallel artistic territories. We seek out artists who occupy the space between "homeland" and host country, between cultural memory and present politics, between troubling notions of gender and race. We named our networking project "an *Ex-Centris* (out of center) internationalism."

Our fundamental objective has been to bypass hegemonic centers of cultural power by drafting an ever-evolving cartography that interconnects nomadic, immigrant, hybrid, and "subaltern" rebel artists from various countries. We are interested in the cultures generated by the millions of uprooted peoples—the exiles and migrants from so-called Third World countries, the orphans of crumbling nations and

2 Please refer to the second section of "Crosscontaminations," pp. 81–5 which describes a live performance.

states who are moving North and West in search of the source of their despair. In the process, these "orphans of the developing world" are creating a new fusion of high/low culture, which is anticolonial, oppositional, and experimental. We are interested in their meeting places. In this imaginary cartography, Chicanos and other US Latinos are closer to British Pakistanis, French Algerians, and German Turks than to New York City, and the US–Mexico border extends to the Eastern European borders. In this cartography, East LA may be closer to Ramalla, or the São Paolo favelas than to Santa Monica.

The result has been a series of long-term collaborative performance projects between individuals deemed "artists of color" in the USA and artists from the UK (London, Birmingham, and Wales), Spain (Barcelona, Cantabria, and the Canary Islands), Indigenous Canada, Germany, Poland, Australia, Brazil, Cuba, Peru, and Mexico, among other countries. We seek to articulate another kind of global culture. Emerging from grassroots communities, this hybrid culture often resists, consciously or unconsciously, the "legitimate" forces of globalization. In this sense, we are part of the "Other Global Project." With these concepts in mind, we create collaborative artworks involving between two and fifteen artists from our host country (depending on the time spent in each location and what is possible financially) and three to four La Pocha Nostra artists. The workshop and rehearsal process prior to the presentation of the performance searches for thematic connections and an esthetic common ground.

Once the performance takes place, the next goal is to give continuity to the project. We challenge ourselves to complete the circle by bringing a version of the piece to the USA. We have to face the provincialism of US funding boards every time we bring one of our international collaborations home. They simply don't understand the political importance of international cultural exchange. We often end up funding and producing the "international" project ourselves. No biggie. *Estados Unidos esta muy tapado.* It's just the way it is.

V Ten questions we haven't yet found answers for

1. What is our new place and role as performance artists in the new century?
2. What are the future possible formats for performance art?
3. What do words like "radical," "transgressive," "rebellious," and "oppositional" mean after 9/11?
4. Where are the new borders we must cross?
5. What are the new reasons for sitting at the table together, so to speak, in a time where all progressive political projects seem to be bankrupt?
6. What binds *our* otherwise extremely diverse ethnic identities, esthetics and community concerns? Is it perhaps the search for "radical" tolerance and for a new way of presenting and distributing important ideas? . . . Or the need to find a new spirituality emerging out of the debris of our recently fallen world?
7. Are we able to recuperate the possibility of change in a society like ours, in which all changes implode or are instantly commodified?
8. Is it possible to make politically pertinent art (not "political art") in the face of globalization gone wrong, government censorship, panic culture, mindless interactivity, Reality TV, and the general passivity of the citizenry?
9. How can we continue to deal with extremely sensitive issues without sounding self-righteous or scaring away our audiences?
10. Can we get our audiences to cocreate the work with us?

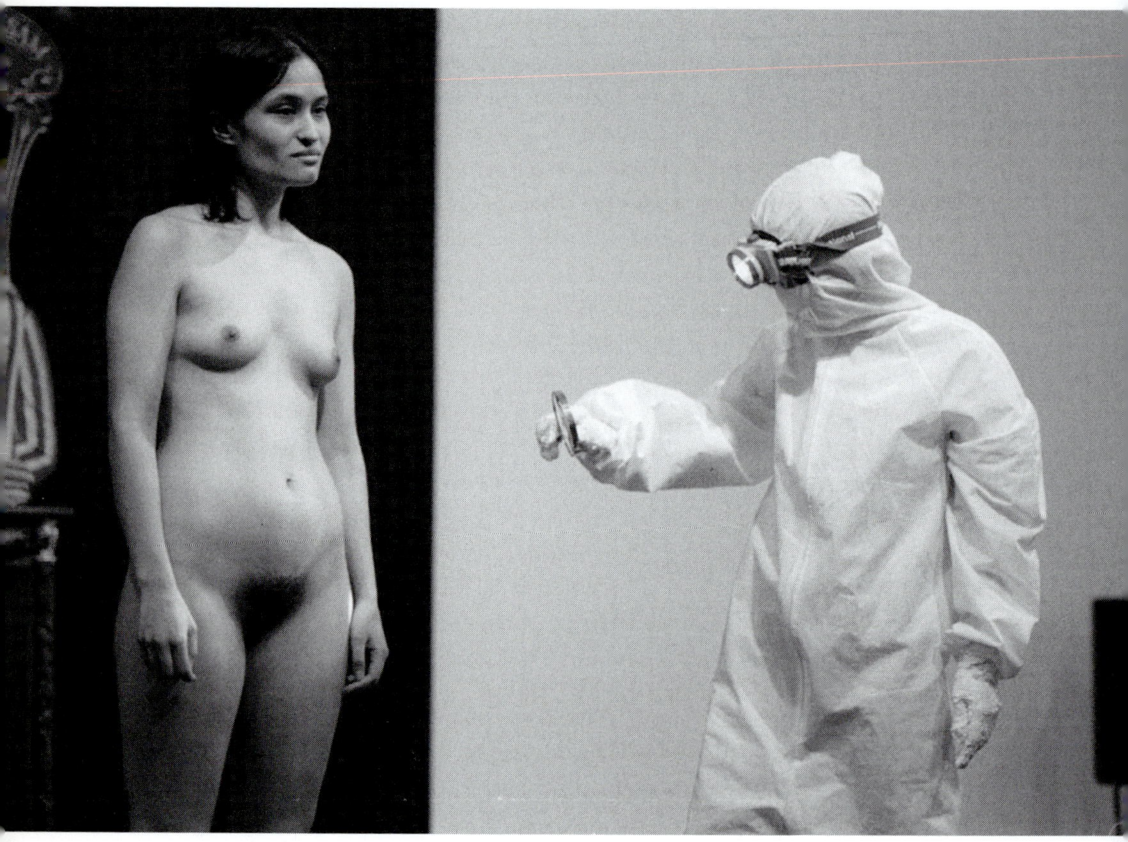

Ex-Centris.
Kazuko Hohki and Rajni Shah. Tate Modern, 2003. Photo: Hugo Glendinning.

6

La Pocha Nostra's basic methodology

(Handbook, 2004)

Guillermo Gómez-Peña and Rachel Rogers

Performance as radical pedagogy

For years I held on to the romantic ideal that as an artist my place was out in the world and not interred within the university system. I always perceived colleges and universities to be solipsistic and divorced from social reality.

I was prejudiced.

I regarded them as "reservoirs for thought" rather than laboratories for social action. I viewed tenure as the kiss of death for an artist. Besides, I was determined to prove that it was possible for a Chicano performance artist to remain independent and survive, against all odds, in a racist art world. This long struggle spanned over twenty years. It resulted in permanent financial debt and a few visits to the hospital—but hell, weren't these just symptoms of living under ruthless, capitalist regimes?

During the mid-1990s, my collaborators and I experienced a serious "philosophical vertigo."

We were faced with:

- the collapse of real socialism and the consequent triumph of the backlash;
- the cult of new technologies and rabid globalization;
- the increasing disregard for art and the voice of the artist by the new technocrats ruling the global project.

These factors contributed to generalized skepticism, pervasive spiritual emptiness, and political despair within the art world and academia.[1] Race, nationality, gender, and ideology were no longer the main reasons people collaborated. It became clear that our new artistic project had to find the new intersections between performance, theory, community, and activist politics. Performance pedagogy gave us the clues we were looking for.

I began to accept temporary "teaching gigs." I thought: If I could only turn the classroom or workshop-studio into a performance and rehearsal space, reconcile my theory and praxis, and utilize my performance techniques to teach, I may be able to find a temporary utopian space within an educational context. I saw the potential of the classroom and workshop space. It could become an extension of both the performance space and the social world, a kind of demilitarized zone and nerve center for progressive thought and action. This temporary space of utopian possibilities had to be highly politicized, antiauthoritarian, interdisciplinary, (preferably) multiracial, and, ultimately, a safe place for students and workshop participants to really experiment. With these elements, students could push the boundaries of their fields and identities, take necessary risks, talk back, and be heard. If performance is a form of radical democracy then performance artists must learn to hear others and teach others to hear.

During my sporadic incursions into academia at institutions such as MIT, UCLA, UNAM (Mexico City), University of Michigan (Ann Arbor), CCA and the Art Institute in San Francisco, I encountered a new generation of students. They are extremely sophisticated and hyperaware of gender and racial politics. They have grown up with computers, global media, and interactive technologies. They are fluent in international pop culture and Reality TV and therefore feel at ease with social interactivity and role-playing—two of the main obsessions in contemporary performance art. Sampling, pastiche, abrupt juxtapositions, and hypertextual thinking are a "given." Having been groomed by "extreme culture," they are not shocked by anything my generation considers racy or sensitive.

These students are "progressive," but in a somewhat abstract way. They do not have formal political alliances or "cojones" ("spunk" or "chutzpah"). "Progressive politics" is more of an existential attitude connected to the spectacle and hype of alternative pop culture. Environmentalism, multiculturalism, and antiglobalization are "lifestyles." They distrust all corporations, nation-states, geopolitical borders, and politicians. They love geographic mobility and enjoy "participating" in big experiential art events. They are a new generation of "enlightened slackers," multicultural samplers, and designer anarchists. Their shortcomings are fixed firmly in the territories

1 See "*Culturas-in-Extremis*," pp. 45–64.

of commitment, consistency, and ethics—particularly ethics. They regard ethics as passé, an obsession belonging only to their parents and teachers.

The challenge: How to talk about ethics and commitment to a generation profoundly (and rightfully) distrustful of adults, without sounding like a self-righteous old fart? Could I be a hip adult and still discuss ethical matters without sounding like I was defending traditional community, religious, or family values? Could I find a way to imply ethics and not state it? Above all, how do I create pedagogic praxis that is "fun," "cool," and highly performative?

To me, one of the most radical and hopeful aspects of performance is precisely its transformational dimension. Students and young artists can discover the political, poetic, sensual, and spiritual possibilities of performance as well as its intricate connection to both their everyday lives and to the civic realm.

The following text faces the aforementioned challenges. It describes, in very simple terms, how La Pocha Nostra coordinates and carries out a workshop. My colleagues and I have included the most useful exercises we have utilized in the past ten years. Many of these exercises are an intrinsic part of our performance pedagogy. Our eclectic methodology includes performance exercises, rituals, and games which have been borrowed, "cut-and-pasted," and excerpted from several disciplines and cultures. Our interdisciplinary methods engage from experimental theater, Suzuki training, dance, contact improvisation, and ritual performance to shamanic practices, performance art, and everywhere in between. We have tried to cross every possible methodological border. In this process, new exercises specific to the ethos and performance work of La Pocha Nostra have been discovered and developed.

In this La Pocha Nostra "handbook" we have included three types of exercises:

1. "hands-on" or physical performance exercises to help participants reconnect with their bodies, operate in "performance mode," and develop original performance material;
2. perceptual exercises to help them sharpen their senses;
3. "conceptual exercises" to help sharpen their analytical and rhetorical skills.

All of the exercises help develop a strong sense of community, if only for the duration of the workshop. In this manuscript, just as in our workshops, these different types of exercises are intertwined.

All the La Pocha Nostra workshop/performances involve at least two (if not three) company members in order to reflect the polyvocal and decentered nature of our pedagogy. For this reason, this manuscript was (and had to be) prepared collaboratively. My main accomplice in this endeavor is my beloved British sister Rachel Rogers (from the Center of Performance Research, Aberystwyth, Wales).

This is why the language intermittently jumps from "Chicano-English" to "British-English" and back again. There has also been much input from my editor, Elaine Peña, and from other La Pocha Nostra members and associates. In order to reflect this collaborative spirit, I will shift voice from "I" to "we." "We" truly hope the ideas, suggestions, and wild exercises articulated in this manuscript will be useful and enjoyable tools for the reader. In the spirit of La Pocha Nostra, we say: Do it now—"de ya!" Don't wait. Just gather a handful of colleagues and props and try these exercises. *Comenzamos . . .*

AIMS AND OBJECTIVES OF A PERFORMANCE WORKSHOP[2]

- **To groom emerging artists and inquisitive students, helping them to develop and sharpen their performance and analytical skills in dialogue with likeminded cultural rebels.**
- **To create a temporary space in which tolerance and reflection are respected and used to build an ephemeral community of young rebels and critical artists.**
- **To develop new models for relationships between artists and communities, mentor and apprentice, which are neither colonial nor condescending.**
- **To find new modes of being and relating laterally to "the Other" in a direct and unmediated way, bypassing the myriad borders imposed by our professional institutions, our religious and political beliefs, and pop-cultural affiliations.**
- **To discover new ways of relating to our own bodies. Firstly, decolonizing them, then repoliticizing them as sites for pleasure and penance, for memory and reinvention, for action and refraction.**
- **To seek a new esthetic, truly reflective of the spirit and tribulations of our times, and of the concerns of each participant.**
- **To make performance art pertinent to a new generation of potential activist-artists who may eventually have to save us from the very monsters and pitfalls that we, their arrogant forefathers, have created.**

2 Quoted from a La Pocha Nostra document.

Convocatory and preparations for the workshop

Coordinating a "performance methodologies" workshop is often part and parcel of producing a La Pocha Nostra performance. Our crossdisciplinary, crossracial, and crossgenerational workshops involve students from various schools of study, as well as local performance artists, actors, dancers, and spoken-word poets. Over a period of up to five weeks, for five to seven hours each day (often longer), we expose the participants to our performance techniques. We challenge the participants to develop a "hybrid persona" based on their own complex identities, personal esthetics, and political tribulations. The workshop slowly morphs into a rehearsal process, then into a performance where we perform alongside our new colleagues. The objective of this text is to explain how we go about doing this.

If the workshop takes place at a university, we always aim to integrate students from the departments of art, media, theater, dance, anthropology, Chicano/Latino studies, performance studies, and English and Spanish literature. We strive to build the most interdisciplinary group possible. It never hurts if they already have some physical training. It also helps if the participants are familiar with our work and with the performance-art field. If some of them are not, we encourage them to read up on La Pocha Nostra's work. We refer them to books, videos, and journal articles we've developed, or to our website.

If the workshop involves local artists, the host institution will need to preselect them (in many cities we already know artists who put us in touch with possible collaborators). If not, selection of potential collaborating artists is usually done according to the level of esthetic kinship with our work. We never really conduct "auditions" in the traditional theater sense. If the host organization (whether a museum, a theater, a festival, or a university) feels unsure about these criteria, they will often send us biographies, letters of intent, and videos from interested artists. We make our final selections based on this information. We do not necessarily choose the most highly trained candidates or the most popular or handsome individuals, but rather those with the most interesting ideas and complex personalities. This selection process usually works, though every now and then one or two of the chosen students/artists will end up being a real problem, and we have to let them go as soon and as politely as possible. Why does this happen? We speculate that some people may wish to join the workshop because they have a mythical notion of our practice. When they realize it involves hard work, they become passive-aggressive. Others may realize a few days into the process that their political or esthetic beliefs are incompatible with ours. Others may have extremely challenging personalities or they may not feel comfortable collaborating. We are not therapists. We feel it is better for the wellbeing of the whole group to let these students go as soon as this problem arises. This can be difficult both for the individuals concerned and for the group, but we have not yet found a satisfactory resolution.

The ideal number of participants is between eight and fifteen people, preferably eighteen years of age or older. Workshops can last from three days to five weeks (this will depend on the budget of the overall project, the availability of the participants, and the space). Sessions usually start around noon. We always try and tailor the schedule to meet the needs of the majority of participants, but we never start before noon. If the workshop involves the making of a collaborative performance it must be at least a week in length.

Participating in the workshop does not necessarily guarantee participation in the actual performance. The final decision of who will perform is decided by members of La Pocha Nostra. However, if people are passionate and committed it is most likely that they will find a role in the piece.

In more interdisciplinary contexts, it's important to note that not all participants need be involved as performers. Some participants may develop specific tasks: Work on a short film or video project, create a bank of slides or still images, design the program, or compose original music. In other words, we can create a small parallel group of visual-media and sound artists who contribute tremendously to the performance workshop. We negotiate the overlapping of the two groups in the following manner: All participants work together during the first week in order to develop a sense of community. In the following week(s) the groups meet up in the evenings to discuss problems and share progress.

The group also sets aside time, often at the end of a working session, to theoretically analyze the creative process. We openly discuss the project's esthetic currency, cultural impact, and political pertinence. Issues, arguments, points of tension, and resolutions raised will differ from group to group. It is important that both participants and La Pocha Nostra members are given space to voice their thoughts and concerns about the material. This allows the group to develop its own sense of identity and esthetic clarity in a very short period of time. The goal is to empower them as individuals and civic-minded artists; to make them be part of the total experience of constructing a large-scale performance piece which can have a strong impact in the artistic, academic, and activist milieux.

The bare minimum

Space and lighting are extremely important workshop elements. Ideally, the room must be approximately eight to ten meters squared with wooden floors, large mirrors, and the option of soft lighting. The windows must have curtains or blinds to control the level of daylight. Electric lighting is acceptable as long as it can be dimmed. Fluorescent overhead lighting, as found in many institutions, is unworkable. It kills any atmosphere, drains the energy in the room, and is not at all versatile. Black-box theaters and empty gallery spaces can work well as long as we have continuous and exclusive access. An adjacent room or a nearby office for us to store our props, costumes, and equipment is also important. There should always be a good-quality sound system with a CD player. A microphone (to allow individuals to experiment with voice) is also very useful but not absolutely necessary.

Not to sound frivolous but a coffee-maker with good strong coffee, milk, sugar, fruit, and bottles of water make the workshop more pleasant.

With the exception of certain exercises that demand complete silence, there will always be music playing during the workshop. Music performs multiple functions in this context. Besides creating mindscapes and "charging" performance imagery with culturally specific content, music can also help to manipulate the mood and sentiments of the creative process. The music La Pocha Nostra utilizes is an eclectic fusion of drum and bass, classical, rock *en español*, rap, and electronica. Sometimes we stick with one genre for a whole day. Other times we mix it up to create abrupt mood and content changes. Participants are also encouraged to bring their favorite CDs to feed this combination of styles.

It is fine if theorists, journalists, filmmakers, or other performance colleagues wish to pay us a visit. They are always welcome (that is, by prior appointment). We encourage all visitors to take part in some sections of the workshop. Why? Constantly shifting the gaze between action, contemplation, and reflection is an intrinsic part of La Pocha Nostra's methodology. Besides, the foreign energy of an occasional visitor forces participants to expect critical responses and to avoid thinking of our temporary community as a precious or privileged "secret society."

Initial notes to the workshop participants

When we meet the participants for the first time, right before starting the workshop exercises, it is important to give them some basic notes.

First, we stress the significance of keeping a diary of their thoughts, and, most importantly, of the images and ritual actions they discover during the process. They should find a way to clearly record/score some of the surprising images that emerge during the process. This documentation can be in note form or through drawings. It is very likely that some of these images will find their way into the final performance.

Although we assume that most people are familiar with the work, every now and then participants are shocked or scared by the intense and explicit nature of images generated during the workshop. If anyone objects to physical proximity, esthetic irreverence, or politically and sexually charged work, they are probably in the wrong workshop. Any discomfort must be discussed straight away.

Often the group will be extremely eclectic. It is important to emphasize the challenge of the workshop as a great anthropological experiment. How *do* we find common ground for fifteen people, speaking several languages and coming from different countries, generations, gender preferences, and artistic backgrounds?

It's crucial to stress the importance of autonomy as a performance goal. Division of labor in performance (as opposed to theater) is addressed on the first day. We seek egalitarian and multitask models of production as opposed to hierarchical production processes. La Pocha Nostra can provide participants with some conceptual parameters but we are not here to "direct" them. Rather, we allow them to assume responsibility for themselves and find their own place within the world we all are creating together.

It is also crucial to stress that the workshop is not therapy. These exercises allow individuals to confront certain artistic, ethical, or political issues; sensitive personal issues should be left outside the room. Participants must learn to differentiate between legitimate complaints ("I'm having a crisis with the lack of direction" or "my image is not clear [or complex] enough yet") and those complaints belonging to the order of social or cultural privilege, private confession, or lack of experience ("I don't like my props" or "I can't work today 'cause I just broke up with my girlfriend"). This is where democracy becomes thorny. We believe that democracy is not something you think about but something you do every day. It's not about complaining, but about decision-making and creating each day. Although we understand that participants have personal problems outside of the performance space, we ask that complete focus be given to the issues and exercises at hand. La Pocha Nostra is here to help students cross new borders, not to console or pamper them.

Participants also need to understand that although the workshop is an enjoyable experience and humor is a vital element in our work, they must take the work and the process seriously. Participants must commit to arriving consistently and on time to all sessions. Unfortunately, many people still see performance art as a recreational activity (some time off "real work" where they can go wild). We are extremely polite and accessible, but we don't allow this kind of dilettantism during our process. Fostering punctuality and commitment helps develop a strong sense of group responsibility. This development creates a safe and secure environment and will allow the group to truly trust each other in performance. Potentially, there is nothing more dangerous than to go onstage with a group of people one does not trust.

It is important to "demagnetize"—to talk about our experiences at the end of the day. Sometimes this happens naturally. We may debrief after a break whilst in the rehearsal room, or over coffee or drinks at a bar or café. It is important for us to "connect" in a more informal way with the group. Some of the most interesting ideas and reflections on the work emerge from these gatherings.

Having said this, we can begin to work. *Agarrense*!

Performance exercises, rituals, and games

All exercises have a definite structure and follow a natural line of progression from one to another. Some exercises are repeated and developed daily, others only once or twice throughout the duration of the workshop. To those using the La Pocha Nostra method for the first time, I would recommend using the first four exercises daily as a point of departure to building a strong sense of community and purpose. Some groups may need to spend more time getting to know one another whilst other groups gel instantly. The instructors can make these decisions when they have spent a little time with the group.

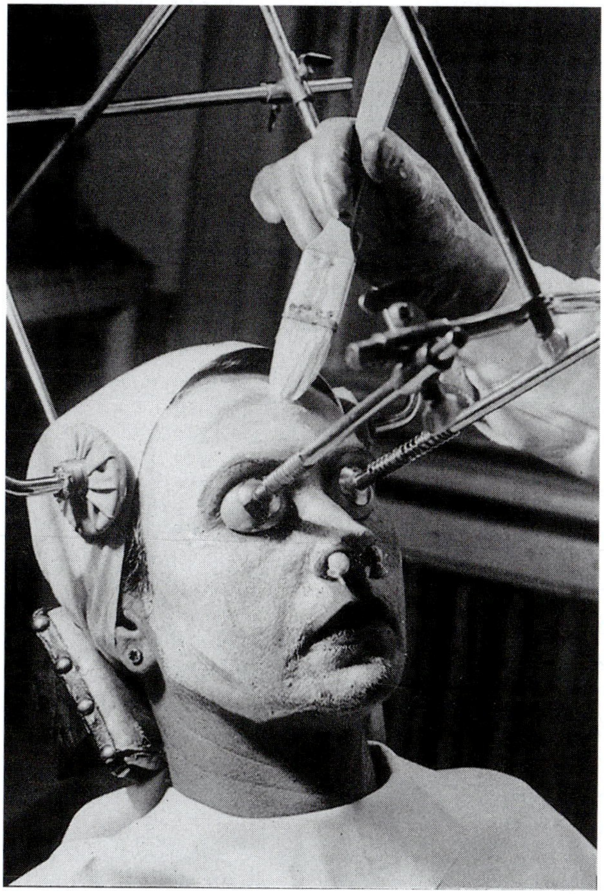

At the identity morphing booth.
Archival photo.

Warming up, stretching, and breathing

The first twenty minutes of each day involve basic warm-up and stretching exercises borrowed from dance and theater traditions. The most common warm-up and stretching exercises will serve the purpose. The point is for participants to get their blood and energy flowing, to sweat, and to stimulate endorphins in the body. Warming up and stretching also help individuals reconnect with their bodies, to "reterritorialize" themselves inside the space, and concentrate on the tasks at hand. Participants should be able to make the transition from the outside world into the performance arena (or sanctuary). At the end of the warm-up, we usually include ten to fifteen minutes of breathing exercises borrowed from yoga and martial arts traditions. This also helps increase focus within the group.

Today's question

Once we are warmed up and sweating, we often begin the session by asking a rhetorical question. We want to trigger the imagination and transport participants to a critical mental landscape. We try to pose a different question every day such as:

- Why are you really "here"?
- Which border do you wish to cross today?
- What is the most profound source of your performance material, or where exactly does your performance material come from?
- What issues have been obsessing you lately?
- What metaphor would you like to use today to describe the state of affairs in the world?
- Is there an image or a persona you always wanted to create but were unable to?
- Why performance as supposed to theater or dance?
- When you hear the word "community," how many people do you think of?
- Are you willing to die defending your ideas? Why?
- Do you trust your government? Do you trust this institution?

These questions are intended to create a critical backdrop for the session, not necessarily to be answered.

The Walk in the Darkness

This exercise is completed in silence. We ask participants to walk in a circle, counterclockwise, trying to keep the same distance between the people in front and behind them. We encourage them to keep the circle as perfect as possible. As they walk, we ask them to look only at the feet of the person in front and to try and keep in step with them—walking on the same foot and at the same pace. We try out different speeds, gain momentum until we reach a trot, then finally we begin to slow down until we are walking at a very slow pace.

Next, we ask participants to close their eyes and continue walking in the darkness. We encourage people to make their own journey, to break from the circle and walk randomly in the space. They must proceed with caution, as the space will be new to the majority of them. Participants should be aware of potential spatial dangers such as chairs, tables, steps, and walls. Individuals are also encouraged to recognize other participants without relying on sight or voice. When people bump into one another (and they will), they should be careful not to overreact. It is important that they do not open their eyes at all throughout the entire exercise. The instructors need to be looking out for any potential crashes that could possibly hurt a student and do their best to stop them from occurring. It is very helpful (but not mandatory) to have more than one instructor.

Conclusions: The aim for the group is to learn to negotiate between caution and trust, to be adventurous but hyperaware of their surroundings. The ultimate goal of this exercise is to "conquer" a new space by making it totally familiar. Generally, we are accustomed to using our eyes to assess space and situation, to assist with balance and identification. This exercise will force the participants to listen, feel, smell, and touch. We challenge participants to develop these senses to equal their sense of sight.

Variations: With eyes closed, utilize the entire body to move around the space (some participants may choose to crawl, roll, or slide). Participants may respond more creatively to the objects and textures of the space as well as to other bodies if they alter their levels of physical being.

Forming Communities in the Darkness

At the end of "The Walk in the Darkness," we encourage people (still with eyes closed and in silence) to team up with someone else. They may tag along holding someone's arm or hand for a while or they may part and seek someone else in a completely different location. After five minutes of walking in pairs, they can begin to form temporary communities of three, four, and then five people—each time joining up for a while, then breaking free. Eventually, they should form one single large community. We ask them to begin "compressing the community" into one compact entity (please make sure they don't squash those standing in the center). The goal is to end up with a human conglomerate in which each and every participant's body parts are interconnected. We ask them to feel the vibration and temperature of the bodies around them, to listen to the breath of others, to lose their sense of self a bit. The feelings they experience may vary from profound tenderness and a strong sense of belonging to disgust and repulsion by the smell of sweaty bodies.

At this point we ask the group to hum together. Starting in the same pitch and tone, participants are instructed to slowly raise the volume until the sound of humming fills the room and the vibration can be physically felt. We then ask them to deviate from this single track of humming, to experiment with variations of tonal patterns, structures, and volumes until they lose themselves in a trance-like experience. After some time, we encourage them to be really creative with their sound patterns—to add words or phrases in different languages, animal sounds, or to speak in tongues.

After repeating this exercise on several consecutive days, participants can begin to give voice to solos, duets, or trios. Their vocal collaborations can become a tiny, intimate shamanic opera.

After about ten minutes, we ask participants to slowly lower the volume until they reach total silence. After this intense period of humming and lexicological chant poetry, the return to silence can be overwhelming if it is not controlled. Before we allow them to open their eyes, we ask them to imagine whereabouts they are placed in the human conglomerate. Who are they standing beside? Who are they touching? We encourage them to use their sense of smell and touch as well as their intuition. When they do open their eyes, they are quite surprised as their imagination often betrays them.

Running Blind

La Pocha Nostra member Juan Ybarra developed the following exercise which focuses on the relationship between trust and limits. We ask participants to form a line at one end of the room. The objective is to use the longest part of the room as a conceptual "running corridor." Two La Pocha Nostra instructors wait directly opposite them. On the count of three ("1-2-3-go!"), the participant at the front of the line closes their eyes and runs as fast as possible toward the two instructors waiting at the other end of the room. We ask them to imagine an important journey in their lives (crossing the border, escaping the past, confronting one's destiny, etc.) before they embark on this uncertain journey. One instructor will clap their hands to signal that the runner should slow down and stop. If the participant should run too fast, the instructors will always be there to physically stop them before they reach the wall.

Conclusions: This is a quintessential exercise in trust and valor reminiscent of warrior-training in tribal societies. It can tell us a lot about the state of our inner selves and our fears. Often, participants who appear very extroverted or tough in everyday life will not be as brave in this exercise and vice versa. It's quite scary, but it can be lots of fun, and is definitely a great icebreaker.

Falling Down

Argentinian director Roberto Gutierrez Varea taught La Pocha Nostra this trust exercise. We adapted it to suit our unique brand of border-art practice. It complements the previous exercise very well.

We ask participants to begin walking randomly around the room (eyes open this time), to vary their speed, and to describe their travel patterns aloud. Each time you pass someone you make direct eye contact. One aim is to repeatedly change direction at speed without colliding with other participants. At a certain point, we ask them to call out their own names clearly, slowly, and one at a time. They should fall to the ground immediately after shouting their name. Those around them must respond instantly, must catch their colleagues before they hit the floor. There should be no prescribed order for calling out names. Some participants may not get to fall because they don't yet have the courage to trust their colleagues. Others may try several times, having either a very trusting nature or enjoying the risk of a fall. Participants need to understand that though this is an exercise in trusting others, they must also take responsibility for themselves. For example, they must shout their name loudly and clearly and only when there are others around to catch them!

Variation: Michelle Ceballos often prefers participants to work in pairs. One person stands with their back to the other person and falls directly into their arms.

The Spectrum

Mexican performance artist and intercultural mediator Leticia Nieto taught us a great conceptual exercise that helps negotiate extreme difference within a widely eclectic group or between two quarreling factions. My colleagues and I adapted it to the needs and conceptual parameters of La Pocha Nostra.

"The Spectrum" is another effective way to break the ice on the first day of a workshop. It works especially well with people of diverse ages, ethnic, national, and professional backgrounds who are meeting one another for the first time. The more eclectic the group, the better the exercise works.

Before starting, it is important to explain that the exercise is, first and foremost, about "the subjectivity and fluidity of notions of identity and community." They must also understand that the exercise is about self-identification and self-perception and not about imposed identity.

We ask participants to imagine a line or "spectrum" on the floor ranging from one to ten. The exact positions of the two extremes are established. We then begin to present the group with a rhetorical series of "binary opposites" or hypothetical extreme positions. The aim is for participants to take a stand, to physically position themselves along the line of the spectrum according to their own subjectivity.

Some of the binary categories we utilize include:

- culturally, artistically traditional/total iconoclast
- monoracial/multiracial (blood from more than four different racial origins running though their veins)
- 100 percent apolitical/100 percent politically minded or "militant"
- individually minded/community-minded
- religious (whether formal or alternative)/atheistic or agnostic
- 100 percent gay/100 percent heterosexual
- racist/absolutely nonracist or "postracist"
- sexist/absolutely nonsexist (whether men or women)
- patriotic and respectful of your political class and nationality/anarchist: you simply don't believe in the nation-state or in any form of government
- totally puritan/sexually obsessed.

From this point on, the categories and topics become increasingly specific, emotional, and subjective. We ask participants to notice how their positions within the groups and on the spectrum shift constantly and how community alliances change as well. The categories continue:

- close our borders/open up all the borders
- anti-immigrant (immigrants in your country are fucking everything up)/ pro-immigrant (immigrants are the salvation of our country)
- total support for the War on Terror/we should get out of the Middle East once and for all

- never been censored/systematically censored since 9/11
- death penalty for major criminals/abolish the penitentiary system as it is and replace it with more enlightened programs of resocialization
- anti-abortion/pro-abortion
- support your country's education system/your country's educational system is completely dysfunctional and should be abolished and reimagined
- art has political and social transformative power/art is just a stylistic exercise and philosophical reflection for the enlightened and educated.

Once each category is stated and participants have taken their positions along the imaginary line, we ask one person standing at each extreme and one person in the center to articulate their number (on the scale of one to ten) and to explain their position.

Toward the end of the exercise we turn the tables and ask participants to create their own binary opposites. At this point La Pocha Nostra members join the spectrum.

Conclusions/reflections: This exercise has multiple functions. It helps our new collaborators, especially the younger ones, to understand that we are all members of multiple communities at different times and for different reasons. It physically illustrates the idea that our identities are fluid and constantly changing. More importantly, they realize that we are all complicated individuals. This realization helps participants build a more complex picture of their new colleagues, especially those who are dramatically different from them in terms of race, class, age, métier, or subcultural affiliation.

If the exercise is conducted carefully, it can get people to discuss extremely sensitive issues. This can be a crucial component to finding common ground and building community. If the workshop lasts more than a week, it is recommended that the exercise be repeated on the last day to see how people's spectrum positions have shifted during the workshop process.

Discovering the other "Others"

This exercise is one of the oldest and most basic shamanic exercises we know. It is very likely that the reader may have tried it out informally without realizing its implications. Kids, lovers, witches, and madmen do it all the time.

We begin by asking participants to walk randomly around the space. We ask them to think of someone they would like to partner with. This should be either someone they don't know very well, someone who is from a different racial background, or both.

Once the group has divided into pairs, we ask each pair to stand a foot apart and look into each other's eyes without blinking. It is very important that individuals get over nervous impulses—giggling, coughing, blinking, etc. Also, it is best if both people are about the same height. This exercise will last between five and ten minutes so participants must be able to maintain eye contact without straining their necks.

After a few minutes of intense staring, the features of your partner will start to morph and strange visual things will happen. First, you may see changing colors or auras around your partner's face. You may then see the faces of children, elderly people, and people from different races, cultures, or even historical periods. Participants often report that they saw animal features or mythological beings. The experience can be unnerving. Everyone should understand that they can break from the situation at any moment.

Variations: After five minutes, we may ask that the pairs hold on to one another, first with one hand and then with two. Their hands should be connected at the palms to create better energy transmission. Alternatively, we may ask participants to convey a feeling or an attitude to their partner. We would begin with a simple feeling, something like: "We are here together sharing a moment in life and art and we're both happy about it." Later on, we might ask the couples to express more complex feelings: Defiance, tenderness, seductiveness, and impenetrability. It's important that they try to do this without gesticulating, articulating, or staging their facial features.

Conclusions: This exercise helps develop a strong sense of *presence* over representation, of *being* as opposed to acting, and of being in the "here and now,"—the time and space of performance. Also, it can help participants in understanding the difference between ritual time and theatrical time. All these notions are crucial to the process of understanding the difference between performance art and, say, theater or dance. These notions will become very important later when developing actions for their hybrid performance personae.

Poetical ethnography

This poetical ethnographic approach was developed during rehearsal. It is possibly the most famous and risky La Pocha Nostra exercise. This exercise should be undertaken with extreme care and supervision. Any person who doesn't feel comfortable with their own bodies or with intimate contact, for whatever reason, should be advised not to participate. All participants are allowed to step out of the exercise at any moment either completely or just to take a break. Nonparticipatory observers should not be present during this exercise. Their gaze could destroy the necessary intimacy of this experiment.

We start by asking participants to walk around the space and designate a partner, preferably someone who is not their familiar. They should gravitate toward one person and intuitively assess if their desire to partner is reciprocated. If this is not the case, we ask them not to take it personally and to continue walking around looking for someone else.

Couples should stand in front of each other, two to three feet apart, and discuss their role within the experiment. One will be the "ethnographer" and the other is the "specimen." This verbal negotiation should be kept brief.

Certain basic rules must be established once the roles have been assigned. Ethnographers should always be compassionate, sensitive, and truly open. It is important to be adventurous but always respectful. They should *never* examine areas that may be considered taboo (breasts or genitals). The exercise *can* allow for more intimate examinations (usually later in the workshop process) but only if permission is given. If ethnographers examine areas which might still feel awkward or uncomfortable for the specimen (i.e. the feet, the inside of the mouth, the back of the ears, etc.), the specimen can give a hand signal. The ethnographer will understand the specimen is not happy and that they shouldn't "go there."

We now ask for questions or concerns. If none exists, the exercise can begin.

Specimens close their eyes. Ethnographers begin to examine their "objects" in stages. First, the ethnographer should try to find out as much as possible by examining the specimen from different perspectives, angles, and distances. After three minutes they can begin to include smell. They should (respectfully) smell their specimen's hair, face, hands, and clothes. Three minutes later they can begin to use touch. They should try to experience the texture of the other person's clothes and skin. They should look for interesting marks and idiosyncratic features (scars, pores, veins, tattoos, jewelry, the brand of their clothes, dyed hair, make-up, perfume, nail polish); any signs of specificity or difference they can find. Again, if the specimens feel awkward at any moment they can give a hand signal. After a few minutes more, the ethnographer can begin to "listen to their partner's body." They should try to hear their breathing, pulse, and digestion.

At this point both partners can take a break. The ethnographers should thank their specimens for ceding their will and sharing their most intimate secrets. Partners now exchange roles and reverse the gaze.

Once the couples have examined one another, we ask all participants to walk around the space in search of a new partner. Again, they should assess if their desire is reciprocated. The exercise is repeated once new partners are chosen. This time, participants take their exploration just a bit further.

After incorporating sight, smell, touch, and hearing, we ask the ethnographer to begin comparing their own limbs, height, skin color, hair texture, scars, clothing, etc. to that of their partner. A few minutes later they can begin to examine the bone and muscular structure of their specimens. They are now ready to "activate the other person's body and see how their joints work." We encourage them to look at weight and the effect of gravity on their partner's limbs and bodies. Where is their center of gravity? What happens if their center of gravity is shifted? (Ethnographers must be aware that if they are physically moving the other person, they must be able to support their weight at all times. If they don't feel able to do so, they should not shift their partner's weight. The specimen should never be in danger of falling.) When this intimate role-play comes to an end (usually after about ten to fifteen minutes) we ask them to gently bring their partner back to their original position. They swap roles and change the gaze. This exercise can be repeated with different partners up to four or five times during the first week of the workshop.

No matter how careful one is and how prepared the participants think they are, there are times when individuals may react strongly to this exercise. People have broken into uncontrollable laughter or tears and decided to leave the exercise abruptly. If this does happen, one of the La Pocha Nostra instructors should take the individual out of the workshop space and calm them down. We usually suggest deep breathing or a brief walk and let them have a break until they are ready to return. We have only experienced serious problems a few times. Once we paired a "Chola" (female gang member) with an upper-class Anglo woman in Los Angeles. This was a big mistake. In "street" body language, looking intensely into someone else's eyes is to challenge them to a fight. On this occasion the Chola accepted the challenge. We had to stop the entire exercise and "mediate."

Conclusions: This exercise helps negotiate the delicate borders between risk and consent, caution and adventure, self and other, artist and audience member. The location of these borders becomes a collaborative effort. Yet, the question of who is really in control is not always easy to answer. The exercise also helps us develop trust and compassion for others, helps us to further reconnect with our own bodies, and helps us become aware of the totality of our bodies as sites for performance. Pocha believes that the human body is the ultimate raw material, instrument, and worksite.

Homework #1: Developing our "pop archeology bank"

At this point in the process (usually at the end of Day 3), we give participants some ongoing homework. We ask them to gather artifacts that have specific cultural or spiritual meaning for them and that are strongly connected to their ideas and esthetics. These objects may belong to their "personal archeology," or simply be objects that evoke important chapters or moments in their life. Some examples: Figurines, talismans, fetishes, masks, wigs, hats, shoes, and pieces of clothing or fabric. Participants must be willing to share these objects with others. Practically speaking, they should not be too small or too large. We must be able to use them in the performance.

Some of these objects may become part of the individual's performance; other objects will supplement the workshop's "performance archeology bank." We must continually edit out objects that do not contribute to the performance.

Creating tableaux vivants

We begin by asking participants to walk around the space in search of a partner. Partners should stand three feet apart in front of one another. This time the role-playing is of a different nature. One person is "the performance artist" and the other one is the "raw material" or "human artifact." After deciding who will perform these roles, the human artifacts must close their eyes and become completely compliant with the wishes of the performance artists.

The core idea is as follows: The performance artist will utilize the whole body of their collaborator to create "an original image" based on their own material and esthetics. (The "raw material" or image should keep their eyes closed throughout the whole exercise.) As a point of departure, we ask them to try and create "an image they've never seen before," or "an image they would like to see in the world." Using this language encourages participants to think outside stereotypical associations. We always challenge participants to think beyond social or psychological realism, to access metaphoric and symbolic realms. The first couple of times this exercise is practiced, the "performance artists" should only utilize their partner's body and their accessories: Hats, jewelry, clothing, etc. Later on, the performance artist may incorporate objects and artifacts that have been collected by the group.

The only rules we insist on in this exercise are: (1) No clothing can be removed without the consent of the "raw material"; and (2) The "performance artist" should try at all costs to avoid the obvious and the simplistic, major clichés, stereotypes, and literal meanings. Everything else is allowed. The objective is to come up with extremely surprising and original images, living metaphors that articulate the complexities of our times.

When the performance artist feels that their images are complete, they can walk around and observe the creations of their colleagues. After a short time, they can intervene and minimally alter the other creations. Why? It is important to begin questioning the sacred notion of authorship and to establish collaborative and multicentric relationships with our partners in crime.

Once all the creations have been viewed, the "performance artists" must carefully bring their partners back to their original position and state of dress. It is important that this is done with a lot of tenderness: Massage their backs a little, thank them immensely, and then exchange roles.

Variations: Before starting the exercise, suggest a subject matter that is not too specific: Violence, religious fundamentalism, interracial fetishes, or celebrity culture. Alternatively, give participants two parameters to work with—say, fashion and race, or violence and spirituality.

After practicing this exercise a few times we suggest the "performance artist" give their creations a small enigmatic or contradictory action. This change may add other meanings or layers to the image. Notice how this alters the atmosphere, particularly when we stand back and view all the creations. We may also suggest the performance artists insert themselves into the final tableaux.

Homework #2: Marking, decorating, and tagging the body

We often ask participants to bring some make-up (particularly eyeliner, lipstick or water-based body paint) to the workshop the following day. The objective is to begin "marking," "decorating," and "tagging" the body.

Creating tableaux vivants *in groups*

We divide the workshop into groups of four and repeat the prior exercise. This time two people create an image using the other two as raw material. Again, we explain that the "material" includes clothing, the collected group objects, make-up, and markers. When the performance "diptych" is finished, we ask them to check out the other groups' creations. They may intervene a little if they feel the need. The roles within the groups are then reversed.

In this collaborative version, it is important to make several points clear to participants. When the two "performance artists" are manipulating their raw material, they must be sensitive to each other's esthetic decisions. It is fine to alter a decision made by the other, but every choice should transition toward something else, not negate the other's work.

This exercise can be repeated in future classes. We augment the number of participants in the collaborating team, first to six (three and three) then to eight (four and four) and so on until the entire group is divided into two collaborating teams. In addition to augmenting the number of collaborators, we may also introduce other ideas—such as the importance of choosing an interesting location within the space to position the image. Participants may incorporate the existing surroundings (walls, furniture, lighting fixtures, the proximity of other images, etc.) into their tableaux.

We increase the numbers on the collaborating teams so that participants become increasingly aware of the need to negotiate other people's esthetic and conceptual decisions. In other words, this exercise can, given a few attempts, actually teach people how to collaborate.

Introducing the discussion about the implications of documentation

At this point in the process (say Day 4) we reiterate the idea that we are constantly developing material and that each participant should be keeping a clear record of their most interesting images, ritualized actions, and conceptual ideas. Whatever the group feels "worked" might well end up in the final performance.

A discussion about the importance of and risks accompanying photographic and video documentation should be introduced as well. The crucial questions include: How should we incorporate documentation into the process? What does it mean to bring a digital photo or video camera into the process? Should everything we do be documented, or only the (sanctioned) results of the exercises? What are we going to do with this documentation—merely revise it as a visual diary or perhaps create a mini-documentary of the entire process (as we have done a few times)? This discussion is bound to recur several times during the process.

A camera is brought into the process only with the consent of the group. Besides matters of ownership and copyright, which are slippery in the interface between video and performance, the obvious risk is that the presence of a documentation device may alter the quality and intention of our performative behavior.

If the group decides to allow photo and video cameras to document aspects of the process, there should be some basic rules: This documentation is only for internal use within the workshop and cannot be uploaded to any website without written permission of La Pocha Nostra. Ideally, one or two participants should take turns using the camera. This documentation will act mostly as a digital diary. We can refer to this footage to search for interesting images and juxtapositions once we are shaping the final performance.

Building impromptu installations with our props and costumes

When participants have collected enough interesting artifacts from their own closets and personal collections (refer to Homework #1), we can begin constructing installations with these artifacts.

All the artifacts are arranged in a large circle on the floor in the center of the room. Usually this is a task we ask several of the participants to complete during a break or at the beginning of the day. We ask that these objects be arranged in a way that is both practical and esthetically compelling. The "performance circle" becomes a bizarre type of archeological installation. Sometimes this can be done using categories (all the wigs and headpieces in one section together, all the weapons in another, etc.). Any make-up can be placed on a separate table. The "circle of performance artifacts" should be simply lit (blinds/curtains drawn to block out daylight). It is important that participants understand that all objects must be handled carefully and with respect. A superfluous object should be placed thoughtfully back in the circle of objects as part of the collective installation.

We begin each day by creating a variation on this installation with props and costumes. It helps immensely if the same space can be used each day.

Learning to cede our will

We divide the group into two. Members of one group choose partners from the other group. Each couple must find a space in the room where they feel comfortable. The individuals who were "chosen" are instructed to surrender their will, to become raw matter for the next twenty minutes. Unless the final image they appear in requires them to have their eyes open, they must keep their eyes closed for the duration of the exercise.

First, the "creator" gets to costume their "matter" in any way they want, according to their own esthetic and conceptual concerns. Then they can add make-up or body paint. When they are satisfied with the complete image, they should position them in a symbolically charged or dramatically interesting mode. When the "matter" is in position, the "creator" can begin to create a mini-installation around them paying close attention to elements such as light, sound, and architecture.

Once everyone has finished and has seen the other creations, the fun can really begin! Creators can now outline a "performance script" for their creation. They give simple commands to carry out: Repeat an action that contradicts or complicates the image in a surprising way or perhaps repeat a short phrase. The end result is a performance in which the "passive collaborator" becomes a prosthetic extension of the "creator."

Homework #3: Impersonate your favorite subculture

This experiment should only be attempted if the workshop runs for at least two weeks. We ask participants to impersonate their favorite subculture for a day (usually a day when we have no workshop). The idea is for them to dress up according to their projections and fantasies of that particular subculture and to spend an entire day going about their daily business "in costume." We ask them not to "represent" or act out their chosen artificial identity, merely to inhabit it visually and reflect on the gaze of others. We do caution them against taking unnecessary or stupid risks. For example, it may not be a good idea for an upper-class Anglo student to dress as "gang member" and spend the day in South Central LA or for a Chicano to pay a visit to City Hall wearing a Mexican wrestling mask. Strategizing and discussing the nature and dimensions of risk is part of this exercise. We ask them to keep a diary of their experiences and share excerpts.

The results are amazing. Some examples: A female student from India, who had up to that point "felt invisible in Los Angeles," chose to dress up as a "perfect *National Geographic* traditional Indian woman" and spent the day riding public transport. Suddenly everybody was polite and helpful to her. Anglo men were particularly fascinated by her performed authenticity. Some treated her as an innocent infant, patronizing her with almost theatrical tenderness. Others treated her as a wise mother figure. They were relating to stereotypes, not to the human being. A Japanese-American "punked-out" student, tired of scaring Anglos, decided to become a Geisha for a day. This opened a Pandora's box of codified orientalist desire from the men she encountered. She received over fifty invitations for dinner. On another occasion, an incredibly arrogant white upper-class student decided to go to the Beverly Center dressed up like a Cholo (male gang member). Within minutes, he was accosted by security and forced to leave the premises. It was his first experience with racism. In another instance, a self-defined "superheterosexual" man decided to wear women's clothes and was systematically harassed by other men like him. He became self-reflexive about his own homophobia.

Conclusions: As one student put it in her diary, "One of the lessons [she] learned was that we are not 'straitjacketed' by our identities." Identities are cultural constructions, artificial constructs. They can be altered and reshaped at will through the conscious and strategic use of costumes, make-up, and props. Performance artists know this. Students and young artists discovering this become tremendously empowered.

Instant living museums

This is an advanced exercise that requires at least five days preparation and focused engagement with previous exercises.

We divide the workshop into two groups. One group will construct still images utilizing the other half of the group and then reverse roles. The objective is to create our first "living museums" of human artifacts or "artificial savages."

The whole process of creating a living museum should take no more than ten minutes. Before each experiment we suggest a different type of museum or subject matter. Some examples that have worked for us are:

"Let's create a . . .

museum of contradictions
museum of exoticized (or fetishized) identities
museum of fallen celebrities
museum of identity freaks or cultural monsters
museum of comic-book superheroes and super-villains
museum of religious kinkiness
museum of cultural tourism
museum of Western apocalypse."

Other suggestions from the group are also welcomed.

At the beginning of the exercise we advise each "creator" to work with only one person. First, they get to transform their chosen human artifact, utilizing two or three objects in addition to the subject's own clothes, hair, and make-up. Once the image is almost complete, they are asked to place it in the room in relation to the other created images. Finally, they should find an interesting, perhaps symbolic, position for their creation.[3] When everyone is satisfied with their individual creations and with the overall composition of exhibits in the room, the creators become the audience for one another's creations. As before, they may intervene a little to polish the other images if they feel it is necessary.

Occasionally, the entire group of "creators" can work on the subjects at once. However, great care should be taken as chaos can descend very quickly.[4]

3 **Participants should be aware of time and the possibility of discomfort for the creation. If the pose is difficult or uncomfortable, decide on the position, then allow the creation to hold a neutral position until the rest of the group is ready.**
4 **If this happens and the instructor feels the focus of an exercise is completely lost, we will ask everyone to stop, lie on their backs, close their eyes for five minutes, and breathe deeply. After this "time out," participants can stand up, walk around, and start over again.**

Inverting the social and racial pyramid

At this point in the workshop, La Pocha Nostra members conduct a "secret experiment" during a discussion. We discreetly invert the social, gender, and racial pyramid of workshop participants. For example, female students of color call the shots in the "inverted reality." They lead the discussions and determine who can speak, when, and how long. They also determine the direction and angle of the discussions.

Decision-making power and leadership is first handed to "women of color," then to white women, then men of color, homosexual white men, and finally, to heterosexual white men. Although we never discuss the nature of the experiment openly on that day, it slowly becomes clear to the whole workshop that something is different. Often at the end of the discussion, white men complain that they felt "inconsequential and invisible." This gives women (and the men of color) the opportunity to explain precisely how they feel every day.

Conclusions: With a few exceptions, almost everyone will be challenged and/or empowered by these social, racial, and gender inversions. On one occasion a couple of white men went directly to the Dean of "X" University to complain about the fact that "Professor Gómez treated [them] like minorities"—bless their hearts. In order not to lose trust within the group, it is of utmost importance that we tell the truth and explain the structure and reasoning behind the exercise. Simply, we are manipulating people's social reality. We generally find that focusing on these issues, even for a short period of time; the group develops sensitivity and awareness.

Creating human murals

This is probably the second most "famous" Pocha exercise. It is done best after the group has been working on *tableaux vivants* or living museums for at least an hour and a half. This exercise demands total privacy and extremely controlled conditions in order for it to work. Participants should not be walking in and out of the space during this exercise. It is important to light one area with a warm light (this space should be approximately twelve feet by six feet). We call this lit space the "performance area." We also light the "installation" of props and costumes. The rest of the room should be dark.

The ideal number of participants is twelve; the rest of the group can watch. If you are working with a larger group of twenty or more participants you could form two groups and work on opposite sides of the space.

Participants should begin by spending about five minutes silently walking around the circle/installation and reflecting on the props and costumes they might want to use during the exercise. When they have selected a few, they should carefully step inside the circle to retrieve them. Participants should never fight for artifacts or pieces of costume. This means a certain amount of silent or polite negotiation may be necessary to decide who can use which objects.

When everyone has a "set" of props or costumes (approximately three to five each), we ask them to stand in a semicircle facing the "performance area." Basic instructions are then given.

First, one person goes into the "performance area," places an object, and steps back. The next person goes in and places another object in relation to the one before and so on until we have a simple installation. Then we ask one or two people to step in and become objects themselves.

Next, we begin to complicate things! One person should step into the "performance area," place their own body in a symbolic position or individual tableau reflective of the subject matter, and then freeze. The next person could intervene and alter the image or position themselves in relation to this image. Each decision counts in terms of overall subject matter, composition, tension, originality, etc. The next person could alter both the images or position themselves in relation to the total composition. This should continue until there are at least seven people inside the "living mural."

At any moment, an individual in the mural may feel their image is no longer necessary or has lost energy, meaning, or presence. They can edit themselves out and become temporary audience members. Then, one by one, the observers join in. There should always be at least five people outside the mural. Their role is to be an outside eye, an impromptu audience. The aim is to sustain interesting visual and conceptual negotiations within the mural. If the mural loses clarity or energy, those outside should intervene immediately. It's a great way to think collectively and exercise our performance intelligence and esthetic criteria.

Every time someone steps out of the mural they should return their props and costumes to the circle and choose a few other props for their next intervention.

After the group has had some practice in creating living murals, we offer them specific subject matter. This suggestion could be as abstract as: "Construct a mural about fear or lust or hope or all of these." Some explicit suggestions include: "Construct a mural about your feelings vis-à-vis the current war in the Middle East," or "create an image that articulates the current culture of nationalism and paranoia permeating the West." Sometimes the suggestions are personal: "Represent a dysfunctional family," or "deal with your own interracial sexual fetishes and fears."

Diorama created by the audience during the performance of *Ex-Centris.*
Tate Modern, 2003. Photo: Hugo Glendinning.

Deconstructing/activating the living murals

After participants have worked together for a few days creating human murals, we complicate the exercise even more. We begin when the human mural has begun to develop its own internal logic, dynamics, and energy. We intervene and "direct" the mural in situ. Some examples:

- We ask participants inside the mural to change their positions on the count of three, "freeze!" and then "go!" It's a great way to begin deconstructing the images and making participants hyperaware of their position within the mural.
- Later, we might ask them to "add more tension to the image." We suggest: "Reverse the gender and power relations in the image." "Everyone freeze with the exception of [*name of one or two participants*]."
- Shift subject matter: "Hollywood gone-wrong" or "*National Geographic* on acid" or "An apocalyptic rave" or "Gilgamesh meets Popol Vuh on CNN" or "Send a postcard to the White House or to the Pope," etc.

The options are limitless. These moving tableaux are exciting for both the participants (who must think on their feet) and for those watching the creation of bizarre imagery. Unless these images are recorded, it can be very hard to retrieve or recall these improvisational exercises. Perhaps it is better that they remain ephemeral and unrepeatable.

Suggestions for different ways to "direct" a living mural

- Give commands with a megaphone, then pass the megaphone around and ask others to deliver their own instructions.
- Dramatically change the music and ask participants to allow it to influence their imagery and to "move to the music."
- "Conduct" the mural with a music baton as if it was an orchestra.

It is extremely important that those conducting the workshop occasionally reverse roles of leadership by involving themselves as participants.

Homework #4: Performance miniscripts

At this stage in the workshop we sometimes ask participants to bring a set of written instructions for a short performance, a sort of miniscript to be interpreted and carried out by others. The instructions must be very clear and extremely brief (not more than five lines) and should be anonymous.

We allocate one hour at the end of the next day to perform the instructions.

Everyone sits in a circle and places their instructions in a hat. One at a time participants choose a piece of paper, read the instructions silently, and carry them out in front of others. If the instructions involve other people, the main performer should secretly inform their colleagues of their participation. Of course, if any of the tasks are objectionable, people have the option to interpret them more loosely. This exercise encourages the group to think about interpretation and subjectivity.

Performative conflicts

This exercise was developed during a five-week residency at Dartmouth College. We use the same methods utilized in previous exercises to split the group into pairs. When paired up, we ask them to find two chairs and position them five feet apart. Each person should choose one prop, then sit in the chair facing their partner. The chairs should be distributed evenly around the room leaving plenty of space for movement around them.

Participants can start the exercise by gazing into each other's eyes. Each couple engages in a power game using precise symbolic actions, gestures, or moves to stake their claim to the territory (a conceptual and performative territory, that is). The aim is to overpower the other without being obviously aggressive. The only "weapon" they have is the prop they choose. This object can have any function they wish. Each participant's action should follow the pattern of a rising crescendo from subtlety and "aloofness" to overt conflict. This should build over five minutes.

Amazing things can happen in this exercise. Participants soon understand that "winning" has little or nothing to do with performing aggressive gestures or displaying physical strength. It's all about exercising our performance intelligence and "responding" to a specific challenge. One must learn to use the opponent's energy and actions to one's benefit. It is really a conceptual game, a combination of the dynamics of aikido and the strategy of chess.

After five minutes, we ask them to find a final image that encapsulates the nature of the conflict. We then ask them to walk around the space and look for another partner to team up with. We hand out different props to the new couples. We often repeat this exercise five or six times during a workshop as it always engenders new and surprising imagery.

Conclusions: Sometimes we discover that people who may not be very good at developing diorama material work exceptionally well in situations of conflict. This interaction can be the source of some truly interesting actions for a duet. Their interaction may be performed live or as a short video piece.

Human altars and mortuary dioramas

This is another postmodern interpretation of an ancient ritual performance practice in which the human body becomes the centerpiece for a collective altar. After creating the "circle of props and costumes," we ask for a volunteer. They should lie on their back in a lit area. The rest of the group will construct a "human altar" using this body as a centerpiece. First, the group should position the body and then cover/surround the "human altar" with artifacts. It is crucial to pay careful attention to the choice and syntax of the objects in relation to the body. This creates both a "human installation" and a ritual performance/installation.

In the past, we have used religious music to help enhance the experience. This can create strong emotional tension within the installation and between participants.

People should be particularly aware of the fact there are often too many people working in this archetypal "community art project." This means active participants

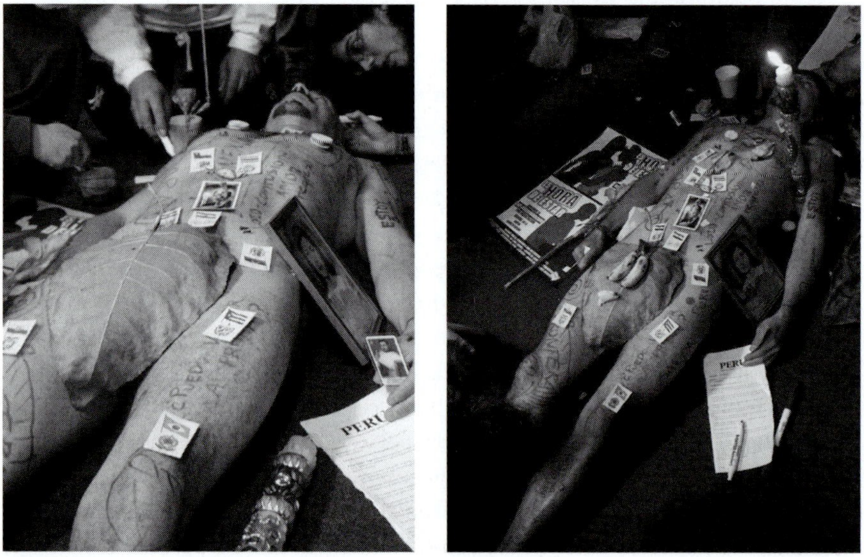

Juan Ybarra becomes the centerpiece for a human altar created collectively by one of the work groups at the Instituto Hemisferico gathering in Lima, Peru, 2000.
Photo: Marlene Cancio.

need to be precise, thoughtful, and swift in their interventions. Only three people may work on the human altar at once. Others should observe and wait. Silence is mandatory throughout.

When the image is finished and everyone is satisfied, the participants can alter the lighting to create a final "effect." Also, a few creators may want to position themselves within their altar installation in order to complicate the image.

The subject matter of the "altar" can vary. We suggest that the group create an altar to:

- the Madonna of border-crossings
- a dead US soldier in Iraq
- a fallen celebrity
- a migrant worker or an immigrant from a local diasporic community.

Variations:

- The volunteer lies on a table or coffin.
- Two volunteers lie next to each other to create a diptych.
- Three volunteers lie in different areas of the room while the entire group works on them simultaneously. Each altar can have a different subject matter.

Homework #5: Developing our first "artificial savage"

We ask the group to develop their first "artificial savage" personae using all the knowledge and experience they've acquired from the workshop. These personae should not be simply impersonations of popular or stereotypical characters, but rather a composite collage of each person's political, religious, social, and sexual concerns. The products should be "living metaphors" or "human artifacts," rather than biographical characters.

First, participants should design their persona using artifacts, costumes, and make-up. If they are planning to use an object or a costume belonging to someone else, they should ask for permission. Owners always have priority over their artifacts.

Next, they should decide on four or five physical actions for their personae and create a simple ritual structure to contain these movements. The piece shouldn't last more than five minutes. Although the subject matter varies from persona to persona, themes should be connected to the overall subject matter of the final performance.

The students may wish to add sound (a word, a phrase, or a melody). This is fine as long as it does not involve a lengthy script or memorization. Also, the relationship between language and action should not be obvious.

Some useful themes we have used for this homework assignment include:

- selling your culture (or identity) to a foreign audience;
- stylizing a problematic (or racist) representation of ethnicity (either your own or one you are very familiar with);
- creating an ethnic/gender-bending self-portrait (try to avoid biographical or confessional material);
- portraying a stylized version of a culture or subculture (other than your own) that you are particularly obsessed with or scared of;
- fetishizing your own cultural fear/desire.

These five-minute pieces are to be presented to the group the following day. At this point in the process, the workshop tends to slowly morph into a rehearsal (often without the participants even noticing).

"Fleshing out" and fine-tuning a persona

We begin to flesh out and fine-tune performance personae when participants bring the first draft of their "artificial savages" to the workshop. We start the day by warming up, constructing our installation, and doing some basic exercises to focus ourselves.

We then take a half-hour break and ask participants to fully prepare their personae by applying make-up, costumes, and accessories to their bodies as necessary. We stress the importance of being detail-oriented.

Participants and La Pocha Nostra members form a circle once we have decided to reconvene. One at a time, participants move to the center and model their persona. We offer brief, polite, but tough critiques of the visual persona based on the costume only. The objective of this critique is to tighten the images. Inevitably, some props or pieces of costume will be removed, added, or simply moved around. When everyone is satisfied with the "first draft," it's time to activate the persona.

We begin by asking participants to distribute themselves evenly across the room. Slowly, with eyes closed, they begin "to embody their personae." They should start with facial expressions. The whole persona should inhabit their face and only their face. After a few minutes, they should bring their persona to their necks, shoulders, and then slowly into their torsos and arms. At this point the body is active from the waist up. A few minutes later the participants should allow their persona to take over their legs and feet until the whole body is in "performance mode."

It is important that participants understand there is no separation between performers and audience in this genre of "diorama" performance. The audience will always be in close proximity. Every detail and every small gesture makes a big statement. Also, this proximity forces performers to move their performance energy in different directions. They are not on a proscenium stage.

Next, we begin giving instructions that allow participants to work the material at different speeds—to change the rhythm, to vary their intention, to distill their quality of movement, and to refine their style. A new instruction should be given approximately every two minutes. Some of the most useful instructions include (not necessarily in order):

- "Run through your material in real time, as you envisioned it."
- "Now, try it in ritual time, somewhere between real time and slow motion, with a strong sense of purpose and clarity."
- "Speed it up as if it was an old silent movie."
- "Begin to elongate and stylize each movement."
- "Go through your material as if you were a fashion model. Be aloof, precise, and self-consciously casual."
- "Compress the material to two square feet. Repeat everything but small; same energy and intentionality, but very small."

Carefully break down your actions into units. Each segment should last a count of three and have a clearly defined beginning, middle, and end. This will create a geometric structure to contain the material and enable you to jump from one point within "an action" to another. It will also give an angular, sharp-edged and architectural quality to the movement. Therefore this is both a spatial and a stylistic command.

Finally (after thirty minutes, or so), begin to sample your actions and shift commands or "performance modes" yourself.

We remind participants constantly to look for interesting and smooth transitions between their actions. The transitions are as important as the actions themselves. We also ask them to freeze for fifteen seconds each time they think they have (accidentally or consciously) discovered an interesting position.

Variations: We ask participants to continue running through their material but now in pairs, so that the gaze of a friendly audience member will begin to affect the material. After a few days doing this exercise alone, we ask participants to form a circle and sit on the floor. One at a time, each person should stand up and present a one-minute segment of their material. The others give commands (using the examples above) to alter the dynamics and style of the material.

Conclusions: The ultimate objective of this exercise is to look for a ritual structure capable of containing the flesh and bones of the emerging persona. This exercise should be repeated at least four or five times prior to the final performance. If the workshop leading to a performance is only a week long, then this should be the last exercise on the fourth day leading up to the show.

After "fleshing out" material for a couple of hours, it is crucial to have a critical discussion. We find it is best to break for about forty-five minutes and then meet up in a café or bar. This puts some time and space between the performance and the critique. This discussion serves multiple purposes:

- We begin to identify segments of action that should be included in the final performance.
- It becomes clearer who needs to concentrate on developing their material.
- We actively discuss the parameters of the final performance.

All discussions must be conducted with utter respect, making sure that the most extroverted participants don't monopolize the situation.

It must be understood that the exercises detailed above are intended to provide basic guidance for performance development. The details of specific performances will emerge from a combination of sources—charged moments in the exercises, relationships in the group, and between individuals and their personae, the political and esthetic concerns of group members, the location of the workshop, and many more.

Hybrid personae and ethnocyborgs

(Addressed to the workshop participants and local collaborators)

Dear colleagues,

The following images can be used as a point of departure or inspiration to construct your own personae while working with us in the next three weeks. Avoid naturalism at all cost; embrace ethnic- and gender-bending. Look for surprising juxtapositions. Bring in your own racial, gender and social contradictions into the mix.[5]

5 To complicate the images we sometimes stencil the names of corporations on to our bodies, for example: Chevron, ATT, Sprint, Prada, Taco Bell, Enron, Exxon, Halliburton, the Gap, HBO, Syntex, etc.

SINGLE IMAGES

- *Zapatista guerrilla or Indian shaman jumping rope or working out on exerciser or treadmill*
- *PLO or Zapatista supermodel*
- *Aztec drag queen boxing with hanging dead chicken*
- *Burning witch bound on a pole using black leather rope with ritual artifacts around them (Race can dramatically alter the reading of this image)*
- *Arab/Chicano homeboy in drag (Pendleton, turban, dark glasses, baggy pants and skirt)*
- *Blonde woman in full burkha doing strip tease*
- *Black woman in KKK outfit doing strip tease*
- *Baywatch refusé/Gringa neoprimitiva*
- *Intercultural fetish adverts (duets)*
- *Lesbian fetish seen through the male gaze*
- *Homoerotic images/actions performed by supermacho stereotypes, i.e. militia in drag*
- *Katakali punk dancer*
- *Inverted minstrel or full body minstrel*
- *Nude body on a surgical table with the words written on torso: "Occupied territories" (you may add one prop to frame the content culturally).*

INTERACTIVE IMAGES

- *"Asian bride in search of tender Anglo husband (write your phone number on my body and persuade me you are the one)"*
- *Authentic "African Queen" sitting on a throne while white men from the audience kneel and shine her boots*
- *Arm-wrestling between two symbolically opposite personae (whoever wins invites audience members to arm-wrestle)*
- *Female performer arm-wrestling with audience members (across race, gender, and class)*
- *Male/female playing strip poker with audience members*
- *Staging an Aztec sacrifice using a "gang member" instead of a priest (the "victim" is a blond audience member dressed by us as an American tourist visiting the Third World)*
- *Shooting booth: "Shoot the immigrant while crossing the border"*
- *Zapatista lap-dance on a blindfolded audience member.*

Determining the final roles of the workshop participants

About four days before the opening night is the time to "audition" the members of the workshop in order to find pertinent roles for each of them. The "auditions" are very casual and are never meant to judge, but simply to determine the nature of people's participation.[6]

Possible roles for participants:

- Those with more developed material can inhabit a full diorama (platform).
- Two or three performers whose material is thematically related can share or alternate a diorama.
- Others with shorter but compelling pieces can use the catwalk and develop actions to complement the theme of "extreme fashion."
- A few can perform on ground level with the audience. These performers have the freedom to involve the audience by giving certain individuals direct and specific commands, or perhaps they might choose to pose as conservative audience members objecting to the performance and generally causing trouble.
- Performing La Pocha Nostra members need "performance assistants" (usually one each). Workshop participants may help with complicated costume and prop changes during the actual performance (as all changes are made in the performance space). They should also help broker our complex interactions with the audience and help us find interesting audience members willing to participate in our interactive games.
- One artist, preferably someone good with words, needs to "manage" the open mike, where we allow audience members to talk back or give us commands. From this position they can also recruit audience members willing to recite poetry, sing, or do a short comedy skit (these parameters should be decided by the group in advance).

Notes: These initial roles are tentative and may change during the days prior to the performance. On the two last days, when we are finally in rehearsal mode, we advise that the participants be divided into two groups: (a) Those who have already found their image and actions (one of the Pocha artists will help them polish their material); and (b) those who are still in the process of developing an image or a set of actions. At this point in the process, the latter group will most likely perform secondary or supporting images directed by a Pocha member. In the morning, these groups will work separately, but during the second part of the day both groups should work together.

6 See "Pocha Live", pp. 81–5.

Advanced jamming sessions

"El Aquelarre" (the gathering of brujos)

If the workshop is running for two weeks or more, and if the conditions feel right, we schedule an evening jam session to which we may choose to invite a few local artists. These sessions are a composite blend of several exercises and they are meant to give participants and guests a sense of how it feels to take part in an actual La Pocha Nostra performance.

Each *aquelarre* follows roughly the same pattern. A few volunteers clean and prepare the space before the event begins. Those who arrive first start to prepare the space by placing props, costumes, and personal "archeological artifacts" in the center of the space.[7] They should also design a simple, practical lighting design. Two main areas should be lit—the circle of props and costumes and the ephemeral performance space. If possible, a couple of handheld lights should be available to increase lighting options.

People should begin to arrive at 7:00 P.M. and join in the preparation of the space. At 7:30 P.M. we commence the warm-up. We stretch and repeat a couple of basic performance exercises such as "Walk in the Darkness" or "Falling Down." At around 8:00 P.M., we choose our props and costumes for the evening and mark our bodies with make-up. This is done in complete silence. We also allow ourselves to alter other people's personae. We may take this opportunity to remind participants that their own bodies are sites of performance—decorated, marked, made up, and riddled with implications.

At 8:30 P.M. we begin our journey. One by one we insert ourselves into the second lit area or "ephemeral stage." We create an ever-evolving tableau of images with our bodies. We interact with one another without much spoken dialogue. We communicate through our props, costumes, body language, or occasional "Esperanto-like" vocalizations.

Each image, persona, and symbol complements or contradicts those around it. These juxtapositions within the mêlée create surprising secondary meanings: "Out of this world images" or perhaps "images we would *like* to see in our world."

Most tableaux slowly acquire movement and sound throughout the evening. At times, a single image may be "just too good"—perhaps one or two performers are creating an incredible image and the rest of the group is only witnessing the action. The group should hold back and watch the image change and develop. With time, the image will start to lose its power. A third performer should then take the stage and alter the image.

7 See "Building impromptu installations with our props and costumes", p. 116.

We should always be thinking of the next intervention. The idea is to constantly exercise our performance intelligence inside and outside of the performance event, in and out of "performance mode."

If there are any musicians or DJs in the group, we often ask them to create a parallel discourse by sampling from our eclectic soundbank. An open mike allows for the possibility of adding spoken-word poetry or vocals to the overall experiment. Around midnight, participants will begin to leave the exercise. A few may choose to continue experimenting with material and developing their personae.

Whatever happens at the end of the evening, there should be clear arrangements to clean the space. It is important to be able to work straight away the following day. This means some people may volunteer to stay late or arrive early the next morning to ensure this happens. This may sound petty, but it makes all the difference.

Conclusions: These sessions benefit all who are involved. It challenges them to change an atmosphere, up the pace, or leave the stage and allow others to take over. As with all exercises and sessions, it is important to find some time to discuss the evening's proceedings. In our experience, people sometimes don't know when to stop and let others continue in their stead. Some participants *always need* to be in the spotlight. If this is an issue in the group, we discuss the problem and possible solutions.

The Double Circle

The most difficult and most rewarding of all the Pocha "jamming" exercises was developed by La Pocha Nostra during a residency at Dartington College of Arts in the UK.

We define two stage areas. One is a circle about three meters in diameter preferably located in the center of the room. This circle is defined by the most interesting props. The second area is the performance stage. Once the session has begun, both spaces must be active at all times.

Each space operates independently from the other. The circle is an experimental performance space for one person, one image, and one prop. There should always be at least five people in the larger performance space creating ever-changing tableaux and living murals. Participants must practice "dual focus" at all times—keeping an eye on both performance spaces and making sure they are never left empty. Again the emphasis is on making quick but sophisticated performance decisions.

The Performance Salon

(For invited guests only, no more than twenty.)

The space is prepared in advance and divided up as follows:

- There should be four tables with props on the left side of the space:
  - hats, headdresses, masks, and wigs
  - clothing and costumes (jackets, dresses, shoes, etc.)
  - "weapons," sex toys and other miscellaneous props
  - make-up and a large mirror.
- There should be a platform in the center of the space and a catwalk (*pasarela*) joining this first platform to a second between four and six meters away.
- A video screen should display unedited images of past jamming sessions.
- A smaller "composer's station" is also set up to one side.

Simultaneous actions: After performers have tried out props, make-up, and costumes, four simultaneous actions begin to happen:

1. On the main platform: A series of five-minute solo pieces in ritual time (almost slow motion). This is a good way to develop and test individual pieces for the group.
2. On the *pasarela*: Each performer completes a three-minute "conceptual fashion show."
3. On the second platform: Two performers construct fetish characters using two other performers. When they have finished, they position the composite personae in a *tableau vivant* for five minutes.
4. At the composer's station: The DJ will continually mix a soundtrack for the exercise whilst also keeping video projections of previous sessions running.

Conclusions: The aim of the exercise is to combine spectacle and process. The exercise is informal yet intensely focused—there is no backstage. We often use this exercise to try out material if we are preparing for public performance. Whenever someone gets tired, they should step out of the experiment for a while. It is essential that someone film as much of this exercise as possible. The footage is a vital tool for final decision-making.

The Magical Chess Game

This "minijamming session" is quite versatile. There are only a few general provisions: Privacy, good light, good food, good energy, and a large table. We highly recommend playing/performing this game after having dinner together. The ideal number of participants is five or six. The game may become a bit chaotic and lose its focus if more than six people play. Extra guests have the option to watch in silence or possibly trade places with the players later in the game.

The requirements are very simple. Each "performance guest/player" should bring up to five small objects from their "personal archeology" collection. These could be small figurines, action figures, talismans, toys, or tourist souvenirs. The items need to be small, iconic, and not too precious (in case they break). People should also bring gambling gear (cards, dice, or a board from any game such as chess or Monopoly).

After dinner, we turn the dining table into the game board/performance stage.

1. We lay out all game boards. We think of the collage of game boards as an architectural structure or a mini-installation. To begin, we place some of our figurines on the installation/board. The idea is to find interesting symbolic connections between the figurines. This is not so different from what we are aiming for with our own physical bodies during other jam sessions.
2. Starting clockwise, each player will make a move. Each move can involve either changing the place of one or several of the figurines, adding or editing, or occasionally even changing the position of a game board. The next person must respond to the previous move until the game develops its own organic and magical logic. Eventually, gestures, sounds, short spoken texts, and small performative actions can be incorporated into the "move" each person makes. There are no performance limits to this game.
3. The game is over when we have all exhausted our imaginations (for the evening, of course). The game can take half an hour or go on all night depending on the imagination and energy of the participants. It's fun and very bizarre and there are no real "winners." It helps us stretch our imaginations and reflect on politics, poetics, spirituality, and art-making with friends and colleagues. It is a different way of conversing and relating to others.

Variations: Advanced groups can create a "human performance chess game" in which two teams of performance personae replace the figurines—a kind of philosophical "dungeons and dragons" riddled with cultural, political, and esthetic implications.

Workshop conclusions

Thinking of La Pocha Nostra as an ongoing form of radical pedagogy and not just as a set of finished performance projects has made us rethink our entire performance praxis. It is true that the performance itself carries a transformative seed, a seed that nests in the psyche of the audience in situ and grows in the weeks following the performance. However, the actual methodological process of developing original material (as outlined in this book) might be the most politically transgressive and hopeful aspect of the work. In other words, the process itself is actually becoming the ultimate "project" for us.

Why do we think this?

During the workshop, we often observe that:

1. extremely shy and self-involved students become artistically extroverted within a week;
2. racists and sexists open up to dialogue with the very Other they fear or distrust;
3. art dilettantes discover the passion and commitment necessary to create;
4. traditional artists discover other possibilities of creation and distribution of ideas and imagery.

Participants are given the time and space to theoretically and physically identify their own political and esthetic beliefs and differences. During this process La Pocha Nostra members and participants realize that we can negotiate political, racial, gender, esthetic, and spiritual differences. We cross borders we simply can't cross on a daily basis. This discovery is extremely empowering. Our process is carried on after the workshop and tends to spill into people's personal and professional lives.

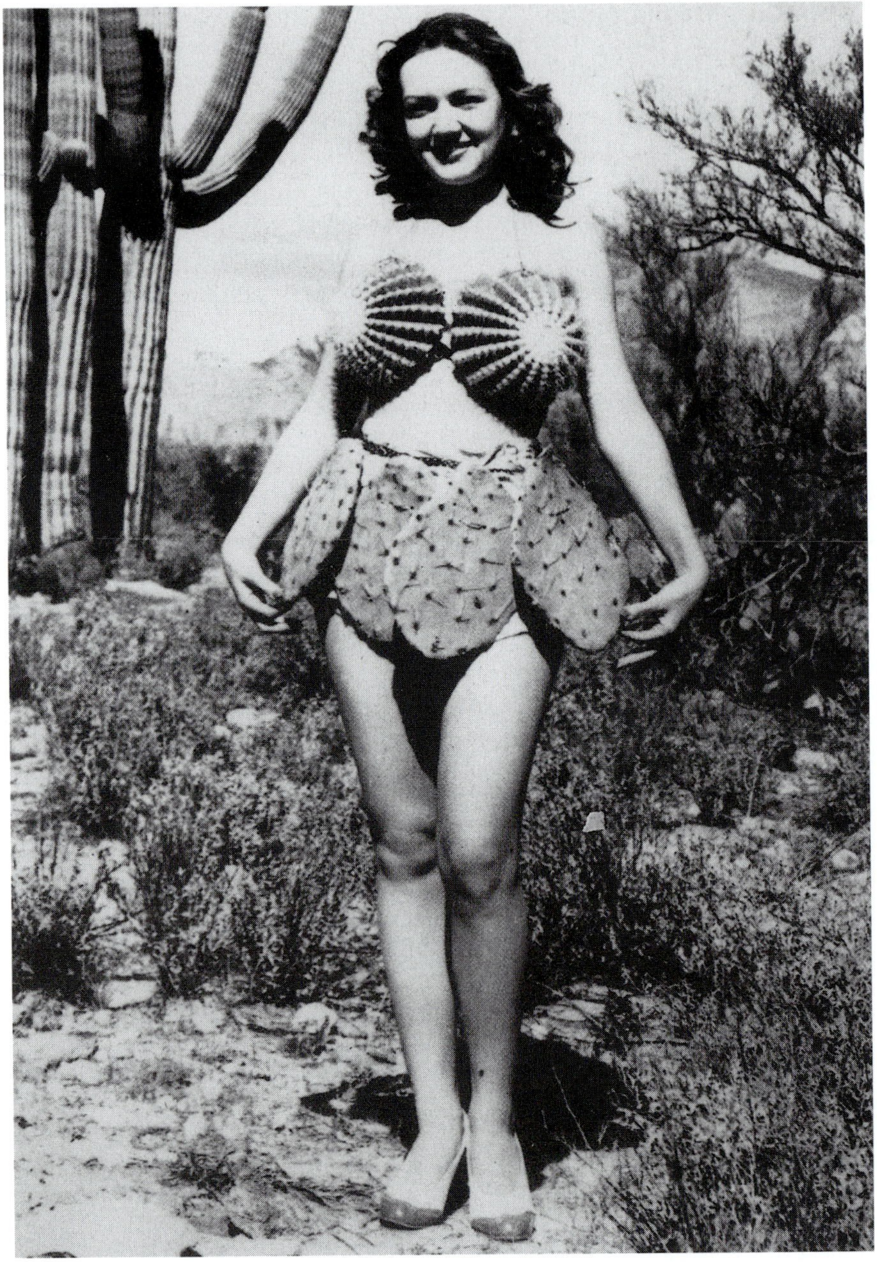

Pop culture imitates performance art. Señorita Cactus.
From a greeting card.

Performance art expropriates pop culture. La Superchicana 2. Isis Rodriguez performing one of her alter egos.
Isis Rodriguez. Photo: Eugenio Castro, 1998.

track three

PERFORMANCE RADIO

Guillermo Gómez-Peña has always been interested in looking for unorthodox ways to operate as a performance artist in the public sphere. This is particularly difficult in the USA, considering artists and intellectuals are often encouraged to operate exclusively in the "art world" or academia. Gómez-Peña admits his adventures into satellite TV and National Public Radio (NPR) are the closest he has ever gotten to the public sphere. He has worked with NPR since the mid-1980s, first on *Enfoque Nacional* and *Crossroads*, then on *All Things Considered* and *Latino USA* in the 1990s.

What follows is a recent selection of radio commentaries exploring various genres: Sci-fi, social chronicle, and what Gómez-Peña terms "performance letters." "On Dual Citizenship" and "Frida lite or Fat-free dah" were recorded for *Latino USA*. The remaining texts were showcased on *All Things Considered*. We included two pieces: "The Imaginary Effects of a Trans-American Free-Trade Zone" and "Postcards from Alaska: A chilling tale of performance artists in the snow" because both radio programs considered them simply "too far out" to air. With the exception of "Letter to an Unknown Thief," these radio texts have never been published.

Elaine Peña

7

Letter to an unknown thief

(Radio Chronicle, 1999)

*In 1998, my laptop containing the manuscript of my last book (*Dangerous Border Crossers*) was stolen. The thief had access to my email. What follows is the last desperate letter I wrote to the thief. It aired on National Public Radio a month after the incident.*

Dear Thief,

I am the melancholic man who left his laptop computer on seat 8A of United flight #17, coming from JFK into LA-X, on June 14th.

Remember?

It was the last day of a two-month-long tour. I had just completed two huge art projects: A performance/installation in Manhattan and a "Spanglish Lowrider Opera" in LA (which, by the way, opened that very day), and I was exhausted, *jodido.* I hadn't slept for at least three days. I walked out of the plane like a zombie and went straight to the baggage-claim area. Minutes later, I realized my precious laptop was missing. I ran back to the plane like an (ex-zombie) madman, but the computer was gone. It was never delivered to the lost-and-found desk. I don't know if you were a passenger who left after me, or a member of the cleaning crew, and I really don't care. In fact, I don't expect ever to recover my neo-Aztec high-tech control center. I just wish to make you aware of what you unknowingly did to my sense of self and identity, to my past, and to my ideas.

Ladrón: You stole my digital memories; years of literary work; at least five years' worth of poems, performance, film and radio scripts; essays and personal letters; and several chapters of my upcoming book. You have not the least idea of what this means to a Chicano intellectual who has been fighting the erasure of collective and personal memory. You may not even know what memory is. Luckily many texts from the first three years had already been published in books, magazines, and newspapers. But the last two years (OUCH!) are floating somewhere in virtual space, and only you (or whomever you sold my machine to) have access to them.

Yes, *cabrón*. You stole my parallel mind and memory.

Well, not entirely. I have found earlier versions of many documents, and I have spent the past two months engaged in the Proustian task of reconstructing fragments of my already-fractured memory through old discs, printed manuscripts, handwritten diaries—even napkins! And let me tell you, it's a pain, *ese*, but nonetheless a true Chicano Buddhist endeavor.

Maybe I will emerge from this nightmare a better writer with a stronger sense of self, like Mexico after the brutal conquistadores' burning of the Aztec and Mayan. (Excuse my epic tone but I am understandably pissed.)

By the way, how much did you get for my four-year-old laptop? Five hundred bucks? Seven hundred? Did you feel any guilt? Did you at least have the curiosity to investigate the mindscape of your victim, and read my love poems and political essays? The breakdown of my taxes perhaps? My most intimate secrets, the ones I never even intended to publish? Did you access my email, enter my cyberheart, and peek through hundreds of personal letters from friends, lovers, and family? Or did you throw everything in the virtual trash before you sold the machine?

You know, pinche thief, as I write this letter I am realizing that I don't really hate you. In fact, I am beginning to feel strangely thankful, for you have forced me to so many harsh realizations: (a) MY LIFE cannot be trusted to high technology; (b) airports are not less dangerous than, say, South Central Los Angeles; and (c) I must always (always!) be prepared to reconstruct the puzzle of my already fragmented self. So . . . *gracias, ladrón*.

But this philosophical realization won't absolve you from divine justice. The crucial question still is: What will your punishment be? If you believe in karma, you are in deep trouble. For doing what you did, you might end up reincarnated as a stone or an oyster in your next life. If you are agnostic, your punishment will be even worse. One day in the immediate future (the future nowadays is always immediate) some nerd in Silicon Valley will invent a tiny device or a program to track down lost computers. And I will buy one immediately. I will then show up at your doorstep with my homeboys, costumed as one of my most scary performance personae: "El Mexterminator," the super-immigrant hero defender of migrant-worker rights and archenemy of racist politicians . . . and now of computer thieves. We'll rough you up, believe me.

Sincerely, your *pinche* victim

Guillermo Gómez-Peña
Performance artist in despair

8

HSAC-TV: The Home-Shopping Art Channel

(Radio Chronicle, 2001)

In the past months, I have heard a lot of daring proposals to develop an alternative self-sustaining arts-funding system capable of outliving the Bush administration. I would like to put forth my own modest proposal: What about the creation of a "home-shopping art channel"?

A national consortium of art spaces could purchase ten hours a day of national cable TV airtime to sell "affordable contemporary art" to the average citizen. From small paintings and sculptures, to conceptual, video, and computer art, the viewer would be exposed daily to samples of the most innovative work produced by American artists, and could buy them, right there, in front of his TV. The most expensive item would be under $300.

An ever-changing team of curators would choose the artwork, and a revolving pool of spoken-word poets and performance artists would write the TV scripts and do the pitching. In other words, the actual selling of the art objects would also be an art piece. Special programs would include conceptual infomercials and experimental talk shows. Every month, a different independent filmmaker would be in charge of the overall "look" and style of the programming, making the other home-shopping channels look like amateur TV.

Let's imagine a typical evening of our utopian project:

Say we turn on the TV at 6:00 P.M., and the Kronos Quartet is performing short pieces by new composers while a repertoire of amazing audio CDs is for sale. Maestro Andrei Coudrescu selling rare poetry books with his vampiric charm follows

Kronos. At 7:00 P.M., performance artist James Luna advertises conceptual Indian art while delivering a monologue on "life on the res." Then, Chicana writer Sandra Cisneros and performance artist Karen Finley sell "wearable art" and artist-made dresses in between monologues, followed by the Culture Clash Chicano comedy troupe offering the viewer racy low-rider and "pinto" artwork. By 10:00 P.M., an eccentric art critic presents a selection of gorgeous photographic prints dealing with "the posthuman body," body-modification surgery, and female bodybuilders. Later on, hip computer impresario Bill Joy pitches CD-ROMs and DVDs designed by artists at, say, $40 each. At midnight, sex radical Annie Sprinkle will sell erotic art aided by two topless drag queen/spoken-word artists. From 1:00 to 2:00 A.M., we can enjoy the daily festival of short video art and animation, each tape with its price and inventory number on the screen. Every day would be entirely different. Occasionally we could invite celebrities with brains to volunteer with the pitching: People like Tom Waits, Flaco Jimenez, Martin Sheen, Peter Coyote, or Pedro Almodóvar. If the project flies, we could then expand to an Internet shopping site for those in need of "retail therapy detoxing."

The benefits of HSAC-TV would be diverse and manifold. Our utopian programming would expose new audiences to a wide repertoire of ideas and art imagery, turning the average US citizen into a potential art collector and connoisseur. We would be employing artists, both to produce the program and produce work for the program. And of course there would be substantial proceeds from the sales, a percentage of which would go to the art-makers, a percentage toward paying for more airtime, and a percentage toward the much-needed national arts fund. This fund would in turn distribute grants to visionary artists who create works in all disciplines that truly speak to our contemporary experiences and dilemmas. Since we are talking about an entirely private enterprise, both the TV program and the art fund would be off-limits from the scrutiny of narrowminded politicians who believe, or rather pretend to believe, that contemporary art is obscene, elitist, and un-American. When searching with the remote control, the HSAC-TV channel would look like a fairly decent civic-minded endeavor next to Howard Stern, *Jack Ass*, or *X-treme Sports*. The worst criticism we could get is that we are trivializing the sacred art experience. And that we can live with, no?

9

The imaginary effects of a Trans-American Free-Trade Zone

(Radio Chronicle, 2001. Banned by NPR)

NPR announcer: In Quebec City, Canada, on April 20, 2001, the heads of thirty-four governments of North, South, Central America, and the Caribbean met in secret with hundreds of corporations to negotiate the terms for the creation of a "Free-Trade Agreement of the Americas." Performance artist Guillermo Gómez-Peña speculates about its possible repercussions.

Gómez-Peña:

Dear listener,

I ask you to close your eyes, and imagine a fully globalized American continent unified by free trade, "global" media, and communication technologies.

It's 2004, "the Year of the Stalking Fox" according to the Mayan calendar. This trans-American free-trade zone is controlled by fifty macrocorporations with an executive board made up of nameless officers from the World Bank, the WTO, the pan-Asian community and of course, the US President. "Governments" function as representatives of the executive board and politicians as local managers. The official currency is the "Ameri-Dollar," and the lingua franca is "Fusion English," spiced with "Corporate Spanglish," "Frangle," and "Cyber-Esperanto."

Corporate republics are popping up everywhere in the blink of an eye. Hong Kong has relocated to Baja California to establish the powerful Baja-Kong, the international leader in cyberporn and tourist kitsch production. The twin cities of San Diego and "Tiawana" (a prior merge of Tijuana and Taiwan) have united to form The Mac/quiladora Republic of San Diejuana, the center of an intricate black-market spider web. The cities of Lost Angeles and Tokyo are now united under the corporate governance of the Japangeles Corporation, which oversees all the financial operations of the Pacific Rim. The old city of San Francisco is now "Chilicon Valley," a Latino-Bohemian "entertainment city" co-produced by Sony-Metreon and Dreamworks. (Curiously, the neighboring Republik of Berkeley is the only Marxist-Leninist nation left on the globe.)

On the northeastern coast, things aren't any simpler. The US–Canadian border is an ever-fading memory. All the Caribbean microrepublics, including Nuyo Rico and Cuba York, have merged to form the Great Pan-Carib Nation, sponsored by Goya Products and Telemundo. They willingly accept refugees from Haiti and Miami. Florida and Cuba now share a corporate junta with the cryptic name Lenin, Mas Canosa Jr. & Associates. The motto on their flag reads: "Gambling, Tourism, and Erotica will set us free."

South of the new San Diego–Brownsville canal, the geopolitical changes triggered by the FTAA sound like a Chicano sci-fi B-movie script. To name a few: The nation-city of Mexico, DF, is presently negotiating its independence from V. Fox Entertainment, a merger of Bush, Fox & Associates. The Zona Autonomica

Anglo nomadic minorities illegally crossing the border into Mexico.
From a "Fiesta in Baja" surfer poster.

Zapatista, a division of MARCOS Oil, is separated from the rest of old Mexico by the Tehuantepec Isthmus canal, which in 2003 replaced the quaint Panama Canal—remember?

As the old nation-states topple under their own weight and get instantly reshaped into hybrid corporate entities, we witness the logical resurgence of ultra-nationalist movements. Puerto Rico, Quebec, the Labrador Peninsula, Montana, Texas, the US southwest, Yucatán, Chiapas, and all the Indian Nations are understandably the first ones to secede, followed by Mississippi, Georgia, Louisiana, and Alabama, which comprise a loose coalition of nationalist states known as Africa Nova. The new Liberation Armies are in charge of expelling anyone who is unable to show DNA proof of ethnic origin spanning at least ten generations.

Atavistic fights over matters of nano-sovereignty and bioregional identity resurface with an uncontrollable passion. These quarrels are complicated by disagreements over the exact placement of the new borders. The Balkanization of the Americas poses all kinds of challenges to our traditional notions of personal and national identity, race, community, and language.

For the moment, everyone seems to be agonizing over the following question: Which language should we use to communicate our mortal disagreements? Does the now-official "Fusion English" (as used in this text) surpass our lingua mater? Should we invent a postcolonial "Robo-Esperanto," inspired by the European experience?[1]

1 Examples of this invented "Robo-Esperanto" can be found in *Brownout 2*, pp. 175–214 below.

10

A sad postcard from San Francisco, Chilicon Valley

(Radio Chronicle, 1999)

[*Latino lounge music mixed with sounds of crowds*]

I'm sitting in a bar in San Francisco's fashionable Mission District. Less than a year ago this place was a Mexican cantina for local *winitos* and brown blue-collar workers; now it's a shi-shi lounge club jam-packed with upper-class hipsters in their twenties wearing gothic tattoos, retro hairdos, swing jackets, and "vintage" 1970s clothes. From the old décor, all that's left are two Mexican murals in the back wall. The bartenders are two blonde female bodybuilders with designer bodies and minds. There are no Latino customers other than myself, but the music coming from the original jukebox is pure Latino 1950s lounge, including Esquivel, Perez Prado, Acerina, and Javier Cugat. Occasionally we hear a tune by Herb Alpert and the Tijuana Brass who, as far as I'm concerned, are honorary Latinos. I wait for my friend, *City Lights* editor Elaine Katzenberger, while sipping Myers rum.

Suddenly in the middle of this typical Bay Area vignette, the door opens abruptly and an old Mexican homeless man pulling a shopping cart enters, holding what appears to be a sharpened stick. He begins to scream in Spanglish at the crowd: "I'm tired of all of you, yuppies *del carajo*!" He begins to theatrically threaten some customers with his handmade "weapon." He is clearly acting out, but the Femme Nikita bartenders have a different opinion. They grab baseball bats from behind the counter and go for the man's head. I cannot believe my eyes. I instinctively jump in between them and manage to persuade Las Animé Amazons that, "I'll take care of the situation." They back off reluctantly. I grab the old man's arm, take him outside and tell him in Spanish, "Life's a drag, *ese*. You must be real tired, *¿qué no*?" The man nods affirmatively. "So am I." I try to commiserate with him. He gives me a hug and begins to cry. "*Carnal*," he says, "All I need is a little *pinche* attention. I've been walking these streets forever, but since last year, no one looks at me anymore. These kids are arrogant and selfish. They can't even imagine this was my 'hood just a few months ago."

He's clearly referring to the rapid gentrification that has transformed the Mission from a laid-back Latino *barrio* to "one of the hippest 'hoods in the country," according to *Vanity Fair* and the *Utne Reader*.

I grab his hand very firmly.

"Man, this is the last chapter of a very old story: The conquest of the West."

"Yes, *ese*," he agrees. "They are the cowboys and we are the Indians."

Though I am not quite sure which category I fall into as a Mexican *mestizo*, I answer:

"True, but there's not much we can do about it, other than keep the flame of our rage alive."

After a long pause, a very sad one, I tell him:

"*Ese*, we gotta move on."

The old man grabs his cart and begins to walk away toward Market Street. I can see the distant lights of the financial district framing the fading silhouette of the homeless *veterano*. I go back to the bar, crestfallen. A lounge hipster comes to my table and offers to buy me a drink. I politely reject it.

"Thank you man," he says. "You handled the situation real smooth. It was like a scene from a spaghetti western."

The recurrent references to frontier iconography make me even more depressed. I walk out of the bar to wait for my friend. What I have experienced is clearly a new version of a very old western movie.

Elaine finally arrives. I suggest that we go to another bar, and that we please not talk about gentrification at all.

11

Postcards from Alaska

A chilling tale of performance artists in the snow

(Radio Chronicle, 2002)

Guillermo Gómez-Peña and Silvana Straw

Gómez-Peña: In February 2002, I was invited to perform in Anchorage, Alaska along with two of my troublemaking colleagues—Mexican performance artist Juan Ybarra and Washington DC performance poet Silvana Straw. I must confess we were allured by our mythical ignorance . . .

Straw: Will we be devoured by The Eternal Darkness—never to be seen again? Will we find anything to eat besides seal tacos? Will we be performing for audiences made up of bearded mountain-men in fur hats on their way back from ice-fishing? Maybe I should just listen to my mother and stay home . . . "*Silvana, don't go to Alaska with two Mexicans . . . The only reason Guillermo asked you to go to Alaska is because you are the only Italian-American performance poet with multiple phobias he could find to go with him. Listen to me, don't go to Alaska in February . . . the only thing you're going to find there are icy runways and one moose half-eaten alive by a Sasquatch.*"

Gómez-Peña: Our host was Out North, the only experimental theater in Anchorage, sandwiched between two churches, whose clergy live in chronic fear of the "demonic rituals" taking place next door. Although, we found out that one of the churches has its own form of performance art going on . . .

Straw: Every Halloween, in an effort to save pagan theatergoers, clergy members dressed as devils drop by Out North and invite them to their "Hell House"—an annual event where clergy and churchgoers do skits about the Seven Deadly Sins—a sort of right-wing Christian performance art—if you will.

Gómez-Peña: Titled "Apocalypse Manaña," our show was a reflection on what it means to be an artist and our search for our bearings in post-9/11 America. While Silvana and I engaged in a poetical conversation, Juan interpreted our dialogue through a series of ritual dances, his nude body painted with tribal motifs, as he performed on and around a huge block of ice.

Straw: We ended each show by passing out felt markers to our eclectic audiences—grandmothers, the pierced and tattooed, public officials, soccer moms, professors, students, and bohemians—asking them to write their feelings about the show on Juan's body. And—against all of our predictions—they went for it.

Gómez-Peña: Soon, half of our stereotypes about Alaska toppled by their own weight and the other half intensified exponentially. Stereotype #1: Anchorage is a scary place. True. According to a local journalist—"murder, suicide, and rape are six times higher than anywhere else in the country."

Straw: According to the FBI *Crime Rates Report*, in the year 2000, Alaska ranked #1 for the highest incidents of rape in the country. Prior to the establishment of the Alaska Native Women Sexual Assault Committee, "Alaska Native women accounted for 50 percent of reported sexual assaults in the Anchorage area even though they represent only 3.5 percent of the city's total population."

Gómez-Peña: Alaska is a sort of colony for the disenfranchised and a mythical paradise for lone wolves, misanthropes, and people running from the law or their inner Sasquatch. Despite the horror stories we heard from the locals, we found the kindness and hospitality of the people to be heartwarming.

Straw: Everyone was eager to be our tour guide—they took us to Flat-Top Mountain, on a mush-dog sled ride, and to a diner where we ate reindeer stew. When our car got stuck in the snow on our way up the mountain, another car stopped and a very polite man offered to help. When we told him we were visiting artists, he said, "Oh! I'm an artist too! Most people wouldn't think of me as an artist since I'm a mortician, but a mortician is an artist you know—you should see what I can do when I go into the back room."

Gómez-Peña: We abandoned the car and decided to hike the rest of the way. Juan, being a physical artist, was ten kilometers ahead, while Silvana and I lagged behind—our worst Alaskan phobias coming to life as we imagined ourselves frozen by the time we got to the top, Juan surviving despite the loss of his limbs and continuing to perform every night with Silvana and I entombed in ice-coffins with our prerecorded dialogue piped into the theater—a sort of Chicano John Waters meets Fellini in Alaska.

Straw: Everywhere we went, people gave us presents—tequila, homemade bread, and three lovingly hand-painted and costumed Barbie dolls designed to resemble each of us in the show—Guillermo in his Mad-Mex-Hopi Fancy Dancer regalia, Juan, the naked robo-warrior, and me with my "Italian mother talking" monster mask.

Gómez-Peña: Eccentricity rules in polar America. At our cast party, our gracious hostess shared photos of herself in her vagina costume, then showed us the giant bear mounted on her living-room wall. She told us how she shot and skinned him herself, revealing the scope-kiss of the rifle above her left eye as evidence.

Straw: Afterward, she invited us to her backyard, where we found several naked guests sitting in a hot tub surrounded by snow. Upon seeing us, they stopped their conversation about environmental policy and the benefits of sex on mental health and invited us to take a dip and make snow angels. We politely declined.

Gómez-Peña: Stereotype #2: The mistreatment of indigenous people is worse in Alaska than in other parts of the country. True. Our new friend Yupic artist Susie Silook showed us a famous historical photograph taken by an admiral of a nude and visibly frightened preadolescent Eskimo girl with a fur draped over her shoulder—unbearably performing the admiral's colonial fantasies. On the other hand, the powerful spirituality of Native Alaskans permeates everything—the collective psyche, the beautiful landscape, and all the artwork and literature.

Straw: Stereotype #3: There are no Mexicans in Alaska. False. There are in fact almost as many Mexicans in Alaska as there are Eskimos. We learned that there are 30,000 Mexkimos—most of whom work for canneries and the fishing industry. Their job is classified as "the most dangerous job in the US" by the Department of Labor. Due to extreme weather conditions, many of them lose their fingers or limbs to frostbite.

Gómez-Peña: Being in Alaska is like being without a context—and not just because we were performance artists in the snow. Everyone in Alaska is out of context, period . . . with the exception of the Natives. There are no cardinal points, no clear geographical markers, no metahorizons. You have the sense that you are on the edge of something—an ultra-periphery where everything seems up for grabs and anything can happen. And this perhaps allows for a very particular form of eccentricity, unlike any I have ever encountered—a sort of American magical realism.

Straw: One morning, when leaving the house, we saw a moose the size of a refrigerator jump our next-door neighbor's fence. No big deal. That same morning, on the front page of the paper was a photo of a baby moose that had fallen through the roof of someone's house and gotten stuck—the caption read "Moose Dropping." The two-page article ran side by side with an article entitled, "US Puts Saddam Hussein in Cross Hairs."

Gómez-Peña: One night, when returning home, we saw a huge animal track in the snow right in front of our door—a three-toed footprint, not two-toed like a moose track. And the most bizarre part was that there was only "one" footprint. We didn't sleep all night—partly because of the footprint and partly because of the fact that someone or some "thing" was ringing our doorbell all night and running away.

Straw: Was this some sort of parrot-headed, one-legged oviraptor that had emerged hungry after being trapped inside a glacier for too long and was ringing our doorbell with its toothless beak? Was this some sort of Midnight Moose Prankster with an extra toe? And the worst of our fears. . . . Could it be the Dreaded Winter Chupacabra?

Gómez-Peña: These incidents have become images in the strange film of the Alaskan bizarre. Perhaps the strongest feeling I had visiting the "last frontier" was that we were actually returning. Susie Silook articulated my confusing sensation. "This is not the Last Frontier," she said, "this is the original one. Twenty-thousand years ago, the first inhabitants of the continent entered via the Bering Straight and the Aleutian Chain." So perhaps this explains everything: The eccentricity, the footprint, the artist-mortician, and the migration north of 30,000 Mexicans—which, strangely enough, is a reverse migration back to our origins—back to the first frontier.

Straw: *Aca*, Straw and Gómez-Peña, looking for a new language to connect . . .

Gómez-Peña: . . . performance, geography, memory, and literature.

12

Touring in times of war

(Radio Chronicle, 2001)

I am a brown-skinned Latino performance artist, and I've been told many times in recent weeks that I happen to "look Arab." Since 9/11, my neverending tour to the outskirts of Western civilization has been bumpy to say the least. When the tragic attacks occurred I was in northern Spain, paradoxically performing a piece on the violent side effects of globalization. After a nerve-wracking week of waiting for airspace to reopen, my wife and I finally made our journey back home, and that's when an unprecedented adventure began for me.

It started at JFK airport in New York. After going through the final security checkpoint, my exhausted wife hugged me with relief. "Ahh, we made it back, *amor mio*," she whispered into my ear, sliding her hands into the pockets of my pants. We were immediately surrounded by five screaming policemen: "What did you put inside his pocket?" "*Cariñito*," she responded, meaning "a little tenderness." They were more than serious. We raised our hands like surrendering Hollywood bandits. One cop made me empty the contents of my pockets with the ferocious certainty I would produce a weapon. I complied in extreme slow motion. The sole, pitiful item—a snotty handkerchief—made them feel embarrassed. But to save face they sent me to secondary inspection. There I experienced the longest ethnographic inspection of my identity ever: A bizarre initiation ritual to the other "war on terror," the one Americans are fighting inside their psyche.

As a migrant artist and a Chicano veteran of "mistaken identity," I have to deal with new fears of TWAL (traveling while Arab-looking). I am not scared so much of

Muslim fundamentalists or airplanes. I'm more afraid of the entire country becoming a huge "neighborhood watch program" where anyone who looks or acts different comes to be seen as suspicious in the name of "high security." During my next trip, my fears were confirmed: At the Raleigh-Durham airport, I was singled out, along with a young Pakistani couple. The airline agent tried to persuade the three brown passengers that we "simply had no reservations." After showing him my tickets—and explaining that Mexico was not in the Middle East—I was finally allowed on the plane. But the other passengers looked visibly scared of me. In their fearful eyes, I probably looked like the lead singer of Oh Sammy Bien Latin & the Tali-Vatos.

Clearly my new dilemma was how to avoid ethnic-profiling on the road. Performance provided me with an expedient semiotic solution: I would simply intensify some of the friendly stereotypes Americans already have about Latinos. I developed three traveling looks: The gallant mariachi with my sombrero in hand, the Tex-Mex rocker, and the Native dandy.

It didn't help much. Five times during the next eight trips I was "coincidentally" chosen for "random security checks." And as my tour progressed, the contents of my trunks (mainly "ethno-techno" props and "robo-Mexican" costumes) began to diminish: Some, like my nineteenth-century Sevillian dagger and hi-Aztec mask, I took out myself. Others, including theatrical prosthetics and sci-fi sex toys, were confiscated by airport security and customs agents. And, understandably, they had no time to listen to a lecture on pop archeology and performance art. A couple of times, the agents scrutinized my scripts, books, and slides, which made me realize they were actually looking for "content." I congratulated them on their forensic sophistication.

Are all these incidents a mere preview of my new, exciting life as a permanent suspect? I keep trying to understand what politicians mean when they tell us to "go back to our normal lives." I guess performance artists have to redefine what "normalcy" means for us. Perhaps I should get a nine-to-five job, shave my mustache, and start wearing three-piece suits. Or maybe to be congruent with my art, I should travel with a sign hanging from my neck stating: "Nomadic Chicano artist, intense-looking but inoffensive, has no Arab blood, no political affiliations. Works mostly in galleries, museums, and universities. Please, cut him some slack. He is just trying to be normal."

13

On dual citizenship

(Radio Chronicle, 2000)

It's late December, 1999, and my wife, Carolina, and I are sitting at the San Francisco INS office, waiting for my turn to be interviewed for citizenship. My "resident alien card" was recently invalidated by a border patrolman who couldn't deal with an uppity Mexican, but luckily for the first time ever Mexico and the USA have agreed to accept "dual citizenship." So my lawyer has suggested that instead of applying for another green card (which it may take me up to two and a half years to receive), I should apply directly for citizenship.

It suddenly dawns on me: After twenty years of living in America, I'm gambling with everything I've got, including my family and friends, my art projects, even my voice on National Public Radio.

I hear my name in the loudspeaker: "Guermo Comes Pennis." I enter a nondescript office and my heart is pounding. A Chinese-American INS officer welcomes me with a huge smile, as if I were some kind of undocumented celebrity.

"Aren't you . . . Gómez-Peña . . . the performance artist!?"

No puedo creerlo, ya me cacharon coño! [Untranslatable.] "Well . . . yes." I try not to express my surprise.

"I . . . I . . . love your . . . your book, *The New World Border*," she tells me.

"I didn't know that INS officers actually . . . read," I say. I truly don't know what else to respond.

"In fact," she tells me, "I am a writer myself. I've got two books out on Chinese-American diasporic literature."

"What are you doing here? Researching the source of our immigrant pathos?" I ask her.

She cracks up, suddenly nervous, and then answers apologetically, "Well, there are not that many jobs available in academia."

It's one of those cases in which reality is much stranger than any of my writings.

Ten minutes later I walk out of the INS office with my brand-new dual citizenship. In a sense, I just exchanged my green card for the gold one. I give a humungous kiss to Carolina. Our kiss is heard throughout the entire INS building.

14

My evil twin

(Radio Chronicle, 2002)

NPR announcer: Reporting from the edges of Homeland Security, self-styled migrant performance artist Guillermo Gómez-Peña speaks of his recently discovered "evil twin."

Gómez-Peña: For twenty years I was a US "resident alien" and the fact that I was one of the best-known Latino performance artists in the country didn't exonerate me from having "to show my stinking badges" every time I returned from performing abroad. But I learned to be extremely cool and to not mistake racism for personal humiliation. Three years ago when I finally became a US citizen, I thought my bordercrossing nightmares would disappear, and they did for a while. I was able to enjoy the privileges of having a US passport. Then came 9/11 and, along with several million brown men with foreign-sounding names, I became a generic "suspect."

In the new era ruled by high security, enforced patriotism, and cultural paranoia, there was nothing romantic about being a nomadic performance artist. In fact, my misadventures at US airports became so frequent that I started dreading the mere thought of touring. I knew that seven out of ten times I was going to be "randomly" checked or "randomly" interrogated along with a few scared Pakistanis and Arabs. Missing connecting flights became normal and so did being sent to secondary inspection, having my suitcases thoroughly inspected and having my strangest props confiscated without an explanation.

One day things got much more serious. Coming back from Europe after a long tour, the immigration officer asked me several unusual questions including my social-security number, my mother's maiden name, and the year I had obtained my citizenship. When I asked him why I was being so thoroughly interrogated, he volunteered some shocking information: According to the computer there was "another Guillermo Gómez-Peña with a criminal past, someone apparently connected to drug dealing." I was finally allowed in, but something, a tiny Mexican bug, stayed in the computer forever.

From that day on, every time I leave or return to the USA, I have to go through the same ritual of mistaken identity. There is this other self I carry along, a ghost with my exact same name, allegedly a drug dealer, and we are condemned to travel together, to carry our identities on each other's shoulders, to bear with each other's fate, and whatever he does, knock on wood, will reflect on my official identity. It's like performing in an episode of the Chicano "twilight zone." "But officer," I usually reply after the exact same interrogation, "can't you take a photo of me, fingerprint me, or add to my computer file some additional information on my idiosyncratic looks?" *Nada.* The glitch is there and I just have to learn to live with it.

The last time I returned from Mexico, after explaining my case one more time to an INS supervisor, he told me boldly: "Sorry Mister Goumezz: There's nothing you can do until we catch 'him'." This, of course, assumes my evil twin does exist . . . but what if he doesn't?

When I started telling my story to other Latinos, I discovered I wasn't the only one with an evil twin. Several artists from Mexico have had their visas denied under a similar allegation. In fact, my experience is so common that I'm beginning to wonder if it isn't a new conceptual strategy of the Homeland Security Office to add yet another immigration filter to their already-thick process? An immigration lawyer friend of mine believes that the problem may be much less sophisticated: Their newly consolidated megacomputer system is probably crossreferencing too much unnecessary data or perhaps even the wrong data.

Whatever the reasons, the fact is that thousands of Latinos, not to mention Arabs and Southeast Asians, will have to continue enduring a systematic humiliation ritual in the name of national security. The word "terrorist" has mysteriously expanded to signify first radical Muslims, then all Arabs and Southeast Asians, and finally all Arab-looking people including Chicano performance artists and probably many perplexed migrant workers who, at this very moment, are incommunicado in one of those clandestine detention centers where all the people who fall in the cracks between high security, racism, and ignorance end up. I just hope with all my heart that one day some impatient INS bureaucrat does not decide to make one phone call and send my mythical evil twin there as well, along with myself, number one. If Mr. Ashcroft or Mr. Ridge could hear me right now, I'd like to ask them, vehemently, "Señores, are you aware of the fact that whenever there are too many exceptions to the rule of law, we are venturing into the slippery territory of fascism?"

15

Saddam in Hollywood

(Radio Chronicle, 2003)

I grew up in Mexico City watching US films and TV shows. Strangely, "the good guys" were always white, clean-cut, and tall, whereas their seditious dark-skinned enemies looked like my relatives and me. I was ethically confused to say the least. I simply couldn't understand why I always sided emotionally with the greasy "bandito," the savage "red skin," the Arab thief, and the hysterical Chinese gangster. Now in retrospect I know why: They looked like guys I knew in my neighborhood. And despite their exaggerated moral ills, their flamboyant personalities were more appealing to me than the simplistic values and benign colonial behavior of Batman, Ivanhoe, Tarzan, the Lone Ranger, or any of the myriad cowboys impersonated by John Wayne. The "good guys" actually looked like tourists to me.

When I began to read history, I learned that since its foundation the US needed to invent formidable mythical enemies, and that it was in the process of opposing them that one became an American. Then, as I became politicized, I learned that Hollywood was America's imaginary history. From Crazy Horse and Geronimo to General Santa Ana, and from the Battle of Little Horn to El Alamo, a complete rewriting of history had taken place. In Hollywood's version, white America always won. Even when it didn't. In Hollywood's Vietnam for example, Rambo exclaimed: "This time, we'll win!" Panama, Grenada, the Gulf War, and, later on, Afghanistan were successfully rewritten as miniseries by the electronic media in collaboration with the White House.

I am convinced that American patriotism has more to do with Hollywood and TV than with real history, and the script is always the same, give and take: A barbaric and unscrupulous enemy threatens the destiny of innocent American civilians or cities. "Freedom" and "democracy" are at stake. A single individual, a true American hero, with the help of a handful of civic-minded accomplices, ends up exterminating all the "bad guys" and restoring the American dream. Problem solved. Civilization and progress continue to unfold, until the next episode or movie.

In reality, with the exception of the ex-Soviet menace, our "formidable" enemies have been mostly tiny little nations with raggedy armies or bands of disenfranchised "villains." And it's been fairly easy to win over them and broadcast our version of the facts. In reality, as in film, knowing the truth does not seem to be that important. The point is the symbolic triumph, the restoration of our frail national identity and mythical might, to prove, over and over again, that we are the best, the strongest, and the most democratic.

In this imperial ritual of national-identity renewal, the enemy is personalized in a tyrant representing the current source of all evil: Whether Crazy Horse, Santa Ana, Fidel, Noriega, Qaddafi or the Taliban Honcho, there is always someone "out there" devoted full-time to the destruction of our Utopia, someone who has strangely been created and nurtured by us, by our own fears and weapons. And, sadly, this enemy, a lunatic brown man with a thick accent, always looks like one of my uncles. In a sense it is the same guy wearing different masks.

When Bin Laden, a real danger, evaporated, he mysteriously morphed into Saddam Hussein, the latest incarnation of the evil Other. No one really can explain to us why he is such a threat to America, other than the fact that Iraq, like fifty other countries including the USA, "may have" weapons of mass destruction. This time, President Bush is Buffalo Bill, David Crocket, Batman and Robocop all in one, but with an extremely original performance persona, a sort of theologically driven cowboy who addresses "the American people" as if we were children. He has descended from the Hollywood Hills and the Texan prairie to rid the entire world of generic "evil," in a most bizarre spaghetti western. In doing so, he is diverting our attention from another, less popular movie script: One about our inability as a nation to come to terms with our own fears and ghosts, with our own intolerance and authoritarian tendencies. In this other movie, there are many scary subplots. One of them goes as follows: An extremely aggressive America, with the greatest military ever assembled abroad, is desperate for oil and will do whatever it takes to obtain it, even if this means antagonizing and therefore radicalizing the entire Muslim world. The outcome might be extremely dangerous, but hell, our theological cowboy hero is a man of simple thoughts and neither history nor international diplomacy is his thing.

Reanímese con Coca-Cola.
1950s ad.

16

Frida lite or Fat-free dah

(Radio Chronicle, 2003)

Dear Listener,

When you see the movie *Frida*, you are meant to have an epiphany: Frida is Mexico; Mexico is tortured, sexy, and colorful; Salma Hayek is Frida; and therefore Salma is . . . Mexico.

Frida is a film about Salma, not Frida, a journey through the Mexico you always wanted to see, a mindscape located in . . . Hollywood, Mexilandia Inc. It's Lite Magical Realism catering to the demanding desires of the romantic gringo *flâneur*.

In the fantastic and rrooomantic Mexico of *Frida*, the film, not the painter, you can experience the colorful and eroticized ego of Salma Hayek, an ex-soap-opera actress who, after being stereotyped over and over again as a posmo-spitfire, herself had an epiphany: Frida is Mexico; Mexico is tortured, sexy, and colorful; *yo soy Frida*; *Salma es Mexico, amén*.

In Salma's Mexico, you will witness everything you've ever seen in Frida's paintings come to life, but "enhanced" and "improved" by special effects, computer animation, and Dolby sound, plus everything you've ever seen in the frescos of your local Chicano *barrio* and in the menus of your favorite nouvelle Mexican restaurant, all compressed and animated. It's visual high cuisine for the demanding global cultural tourist.

If you come to *Frida*'s Mexico you'll experience a two-hour 3D ride through the mindscape and erotic fantasies of Frida, I mean Salma, a jam-packed border fantasia

Rock Nacional

with lots of desperado style, a universe populated by (choose from the following menu) talking skeletons, devil piñatas, burning beds, more food than in *Like Water for Chocolate*, and, of course, Salma's designer breasts and special-effects scars entrapped in Cronenbergian desire, all dancing to the beat of tango-flamenco, huapango-pop and jarochabily. And if this weren't enough, you will peep through the window of the decadent period fiestas of the Mexican intelligentsia where gorgeous bisexual communist women discuss the political fate of the country and drink tequila with temperamental bohemians and fiery revolutionaries. *Si damas y caballeros*, enchiladas and burritos. It's magical realism made in Hollywood, MTV *teatro campesino*, a high-resolution projection of gringo desire, a drunken *turista* dream in Saint Michael de Allende, *puro* tequila fever, *ajua*! It's . . . it's definitely the hippest south-of-the-border . . . nightclub. And, for your own comfort, all political texts and unpleasant socialist propaganda have been erased by Salma's Department of Binational Tourism.

In 2003, amidst the War on Terror and the tightening of the US–Mexico border, the viewer/voyeur can still dream of a Mexico without Zapatistas, migrant workers, drug dealers, way before NAFTA, McDonald's, and techno music spoiled the party, and, in the process, get lots of ideas to decorate your house just like the Mexotic Coyoacan mansion you always wanted to have.

Last December I went to the Mexican premiere of *Frida* in Mexico City. It was in English but with suave Mexican accents like mine. Next morning the Mexican press said, "After all these years, Frida returns to *Bellas Artes* en inglés." But hell, we have to give it to "Salmita" . . . Her ego is much larger than Frida's. Though I wasn't too convinced by her pathos and bisexuality. Salma is just too, too, cute, contrived, and artificial for my dark taste. But Julie Taymor knows her craft, no doubt. Luckily Antonio Banderas just appeared for less than five minutes to add cachet to the venerable list of pan-Latino credits. My nephew told me: "Tio, Banderas performing Siqueiros is like Bruce Willis performing Subcomandante Marcos, ¿qué no?"

My mom loved it. After listening to my harsh criticism, she asked me what I would do if I were offered to direct a Frida movie. I answered: "Well, I would have a Kabouki Frida and a Sumo Diego, and invite Nagishi Oshima to direct it." Sorry. At this point I see no other way to redeem *a la pobre Frida Sufrida*!

Neither Diego nor Frida.
Guillermo Gómez-Peña and Violeta Luna during a photo shoot in Gómez-Peña's home. Mexico City, 2003. Photo: Miguel Velasco.

track four

PERFORMANCE LITERATURE

For the stage and cyberspace

Brownout 2, a solo performance script, was written while recovering from illness in a Mexico City hospital. This text is perhaps Guillermo Gómez-Peña's most ambitious and complex solo piece to date. *Brownout 2*, like all of his spoken-word performance texts, is always in process. The published version is "just an instance in the life of these works."

"America's Most Wanted Inner Demon" is an excerpt from a larger work in progress. It was written in direct response to ethnic-profiling and the culture of fear enforced by the Department of Homeland Security. The piece humorously traces sources perpetuating fear of "brown people" and how demonizing mythologies surrounding Mexicans and Latinos in the USA were instantly "transferred" to Arabs and Arab-looking people after 9/11.

"A Declaration of Poetic Disobedience from the New Border" is "part chant poetry and part political exorcism." This performance text pays homage to Martin Luther King, José Martí, and the beat poets. Gómez-Peña suggests "it can be performed with a live cellist, an opera singer, or a DJ. It also works as a solo piece or as a call/response with the audience."

The "cyber-*placazos*" were written for the Internet as part of the current virtual "global" movement of borderless literature, art, and journalism. Gómez-Peña stresses: "Once these *placazos* are released into the *terra ignota* of the net, they have no copyright. They can be used in any way the Internauta wishes as long as they are not decontextualized and keep their literary and conceptual integrity."

Elaine Peña

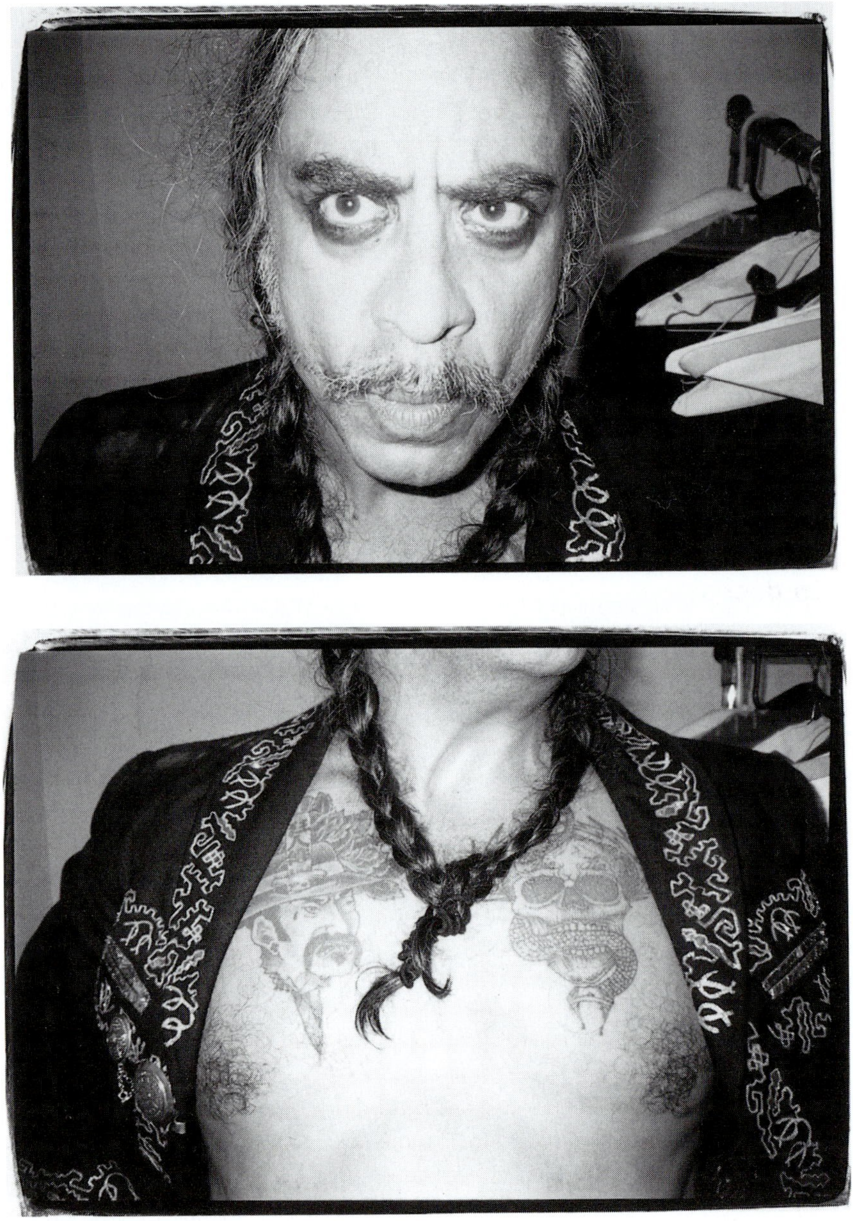

Guillermo Gómez-Peña experiencing an acute identity crisis.
Post-performance portrait (in two parts), 2001. Photo: La Pocha Nostra archives.

17

Brownout 2

(Performance Script, 2000–3)

Introduction

Elaine Katzenberger

In the summer of 2000, Guillermo Gómez-Peña suffered a health crisis that landed him in hospital in Mexico City for a month. The journey that led from Brazil, where he first became ill while on tour, to San Francisco, through the labyrinth of the US healthcare industry, to finally, in serious crisis, Mexico City, is a story in itself. Suffice to say that upon arriving in Mexico, Guillermo was, as far as he and those who loved him could tell, close to death. He was incapacitated for weeks, hooked up to various machines, poked and prodded each day, semidelirious and semiconscious, tethered to life by the determined refusal of his family and friends to let him go, but most of all by the unlimited and implacable love of his compañera, Carolina. He was spared, only to face what the doctors pronounced would be a severely altered future: One without touring, one without performance.

Luckily for all of us, that's not how it turned out. Although it took time and was initially only a frail hope, he was ultimately able to fully reclaim his health and has since returned to his usual Herculean level of activity and production.

Brownout 2 is only one of myriad projects he has developed since that crisis, but it is unique—the only one that draws its content from that tenuous period of grave illness and slow recovery. As we sat together revising the texts a year after it all happened, I was struck by the fact that the piece could be developed and staged as a sort of hospital-bed soliloquy, a meditation from the edge of death on the meaning of life and the possibilities of art. Gómez-Peña was completely taken with the idea and we set to work in our usual fashion, throwing ideas back and forth and trying things out for each other; by the end of the night we had the first draft.

Many of the first-person texts that ultimately came together in the script for *Brownout 2* were written in the hospital and in the months afterward, a time when Gómez-Peña was slowly and painfully regaining his strength, faced with the possibility of having to adjust permanently to what seemed like a puritanically disciplined and bland existence. It was a period of difficult questions, about the past, about the future. What, after all, does a performance artist who has spent over twenty years as a peripatetic provocateur do if he can't travel or perform? How had he arrived at this crossroads? If his years of efforts and experiments were now being framed as a "lifestyle" that his body would no longer tolerate, what were the possibilities for any kind of compelling or rewarding work? And how does one calibrate the effects and the effectiveness of a life lived through art? Were the issues and events that fueled the work really the right ones after all and had the work actually had enough impact? The texts were like semidelirious journal entries, a solitary, unmapped journey through the upside-down landscape of a life interrupted.

Performance is, by definition, a body-based art, so what happens when a performer is faced with the loss of this medium as a means for expression? What might be the inner dialogue that ensues? In this way, *Brownout 2* is about a crisis of the body—the artist's body, the body politic, a body of knowledge, a way of knowing and exploring and challenging. *Brownout 2* is an existential howl, a musing on the meaning of an artist's life, the place of art in society, the body's role in consciousness, the effects of years of cultural transpositioning, on family love, on relationships, on the nature of self. It is a polyphonic, multilingual rant, a *loquito*'s cry in the wilderness of facing the future, facing the past, facing death, and bracing for life. It is the summation of Gómez-Peña's twenty-plus years of being a crossborder ombudsman, an intellectual provocateur, a weathervane for the storms blowing through the cultural divide between "high" and "low," Mexicano and Chicano, art and theory, esthetics and politics, self and Other. And, mostly, it is a determined leap of faith into the future, with an affectionate nod to La Pelona (the Mexican death) whose embrace awaits us all, but not quite yet.

Type of space
Ideally a small to medium-size black-box theater. However, the performance can be adapted for galleries, auditoriums, and TV and radio studios.

Basic requirements
A lectern; a table covered with a black cloth for props; good sound equipment and a high-quality boom mike. A dressing room with soft-light, big mirrors, and good espresso is desirable. An SPX-sound effect machine is optional but desirable. A minimum of four hours prior to the event with two personable technicians to prepare the space and design sound and lights is necessary.

Costumes
Complete attire of either "El Traveling Medicine Vato," "El S/M Zorro" or one of my shaman-personas in drag.

Props to bring
Techno-glasses, rubber heart, robotic hand, bandana, stetson hat, tourist "Indian" headdress, "supermojado" wrestler mask, Spanish dagger, scissors, and a handful of "lowrider" prosthetics and braces.

Props to be provided by the producer
Battery-operated megaphone, hospital mask, realistic-looking handgun, "Mr. Clean" bottle filled with blue Gatorade, deodorant "blessing" spray can, and a bottle of Myers rum.

Border blessing

[*To be printed on the hand program*]

Norte:
Dear son, my only candle left,
I promise I'll protect you from those *norteño* gangs.
Remember: I am analog—you told me,
which means, I still know how to use my fists . . . and my legs.

Sur:
Dear mother, my historical womb and genetic code,
I promise I will clean up my act before I die
Clean up my house *de paso*.

Este:
Carolina, *mon amour*, I promise I'll be beside you
Catering to your most minute desires
Licking your knees and palms
Until globalization derails
And the Popocatepetl ceases to smoke.

Oeste:
Dear *clica*, *familia espiritual*, I ask for your forgiveness.
My absence was clearly a survival strategy.
How else was I supposed to outlive the backlash,
the INS, the IRS and the formalist art critics?
How else was I supposed to finish this script?

Dear criminals, *pochos*, *locas y destrampados*
"Life without you all, my nomadic tribe,
is virtual *horror vacui en gringolandia*."

These words are for you, about you.
My job tonight is to shatter the world
with the word, my only weapon left.
Am I delusional carnales?

The script

An audio CD plays as the audience walks in and sits down. I walk onstage and position myself behind the lectern. The table where my props lie is behind me; I bless the space with my "sacred spray," then I drink from the Mr. Clean bottle and spit it out on the audience.

INTRO

Dear audience/listener/viewer,
Tonight from my multiple repertoires of hybrid personae,
I have chosen to come as
the embodied psyche of an existentialist *mojado*
and it's quite a challenge, my dear friends,
for I've been stripped by airport security
of all my robo-baroque paraphernalia,
my ethno-technobilia *ye-ye*,
which means,
no more handmade lowrider prosthetics,
no mariachi robotic bodywear,
no cheesy fog machines,
no hanging dead chickens, nothing,
not even a voice-effect processor
to help me get rid of my accent.
Just one costume
and a bit of make-up
to protect myself.
O sea, back to the basics of performance.
It's Chicano minimalism,
a contradiction in terms,
but hell, I am a walking contradiction
and so are you . . .
So, dear foreign audience:
Welcome to my conceptual set.
Welcome to my performance universe.

Welcome to my delirious psyche.
Welcome to my border zone,
to the cities and jungles of my language
las del ingles y las del español
kick back,
light up your conceptual cigarette . . .
a prop
[*I light up a cigarette and inhale*]
and breathe in, breathe out,
breathe in, breathe out,
rreelllaaaxxxx.
Now, reach over,
grab the crotch of your neighbor
and massage,
yes . . .
this is the basic exercise of Chicano tantra
[*I snap my fingers/blackout*]

DAY 1

[*In a nasal voice*]
My neverending tour to the outposts of Chicanismo
finally crashed into the limits of my body
while touring Brazil last year.
Two weeks later, I was flat on my back
in a Mexico City hospital bed
hooked up to some retro sci-fi-looking *maquina*
staring down my own death, *la pelona*,
this time, she looked serious.
I laid there in a freefall through my psyche,
the digital *mapa mundi* of my *vida loca*.
I saw a bizarre infomercial.
In it I was a cheesy blond actor
announcing some unspecific product.

Inner Infomercial (en Gringoñol)

I love . . . Galapagos—I said
[*Mispronounce*]
I mean, Galapenos, digo
Gala-pennis
Jala-penis
Jala-pedos
Jala-peños perdoun
Io soy hapre-hendiendo
Un poquitou di español
Castillian, I mean
Perro io soy solo
Un gringou loco de amorrr
Per una chic-ana calienti
De Mission Street
Me mirra
Como flourrecita de
Chincuo Tamalo, digou
Chingo di Malo, I mean
Sink-oh diMaggio
Translation please?
Viva Coors culeros!
Welcome to the colonized territory of your psyche
Spanglish poltergeist, y que?

Mojado Existentialism

[*Donald Duck speak*]
This is the way English sounded to me when I was a kid
[*Indian tongues*]
This is the way my voice sounds when I'm onstage
[*French tongues*]
This is the way my voice sounds when I attempt to be comedic
un échec absolu
Testing, testing . . .
[*Telemundo announcer*]

En el proximo capitulo de El Malparido
un Chicano se enfrenta a los demonios de la lengua
Testing, testing . . .
This is the way my voice sounds when I'm rehearsing
Testing, testing . . . the limits of my identity . . . testing
This is not my real voice, *probando, probando* . . .
This is clearly not my real voice, *probando* . . .
This is one of my many official costumes
"El Narco Mariachi"
I wear it at least twice a week
'cause I am unable to discern
between myself and my performance personae
between art and life
The dream of last century's avant-garde
finally came true thanks to a Mexican . . .
Not bad, but not true, either.

[*soft rap*]
This is [*name of the theater*],
a place in [*name of city*]
and this is America, a state of mind,
a way of being while forgetting,
a certain pain, a strange malaise,
a cultural pathology,
an intercultural purgatory.
America,
my stage is your purgatory.
This stage is our battlefield:
Robocop vs. *the Global Evil Other.*
This script is my uncertain fate,
my tongue, my compass, your unbearable headache
[*Chanting*]
per ipsum, ecu nipsum, eti nipsum
et TV video patri omni impotenti
per omnia saecula saeculeros . . .

Ay!, *qué* Catholic I sound!
Delete!

[*In a nasal voice*]
True. It was a Catholic hospital
and the sisters, bless their hearts,
were so totally weirded out by my tattoos,
and pluri-flamboyant personality
***que la madre superiora* kept coming to my room**
to offer me confession
"Confiesa hijo de puta!" she thought,
as if my death were imminent.
[*I open my jacket to reveal tattoos*]
"Madre," I said
"these are my tattoos
they are like . . . *heridas estéticas*
insects in the page,
countries in my biographical map.
My tattoos are like
scripted words
as opposed to my scars
which are like unscripted sentences
in the open book of my body.
My forty-six-year-old brown body,
densely covered with Spanglish poetry
unedited still . . ."

Excuse me sir/miss: [*To an audience member*]
Can you read in Spanish?
No? . . . No big deal.
It's just that I'm obsessed with . . .
attempting to establish some basic connections
between body, word, and destiny,
between the politics of language
and the physiology of politics
verbi gratia:

Casa, my head
Cuello, going North
Lengua, looking for your lips
Pecho, I wish I had humungous freckled breasts
Panza, my wisdom shows
Pito, *ñonga*, the untranslatable place
Chocho, *coño*, volcano
Where all *Vatos* come from,
way before the Bering Straight
way before Europeans first set foot on this continent.
Piernas, the journey north continues
Pies, migrating in reverse
Espalda, wetback
back to the origins, *memoria*
ombligo, *video* . . .
Coño, my writing is getting real obscure
I wonder if it's the medicine or premature dementia . . .

DAY 2

[*In a nasal voice*]
I am surrounded by humungous doctors and nurses.
They've got this sound scanner up my rectum.
I tell you, *loca*,
health and dignity don't always mix very well . . .
[*Sounds of physical pain*]
If only I'd known before I parted
that California was not a movie,
that this psychotropical paradise sponsored by white hands
was actually maintained by brown hands,
precisely with their undocumented fingers
deep inside America's sphincter.
[*Guttural sounds of sexual pleasure*]
"My fingers, your sphincter," I said on Public Radio
and I lost my job for the third time.

Performance memory: *The CruXi-fiction Project.*
Guillermo Gómez-Peña, as a mariachi, crucifies himself in protest of US immigration policy, 1994. Photo: Neph Nevas.

[*To an audience member*]
You know, the best hamburgers in town
are cooked by Mexican chefs
precisely with their undocumented fingers.
Ese, do you feel them when you eat?
Can you smell them right now?
Are my undocumented words vivid enough *o que*?

Dear audience,
I've got forty-five scars accounted for
half of them produced by art
and this is not a metaphor.
My artistic obsession has led me to carry out
some flagrantly stupid acts of transgression
including:
Living inside a cage as a Mexican Frankenstein
Crucifying myself as a mariachi to protest immigration policy
Crashing the Met as El Mad Mex led on a leash by a Spanish dominatrix.
I mean, you want me to be more specific than, say,
drinking Mr. Clean to exorcize my colonial demons,
or handing a dagger to an audience member and offering her my plexus?
[*Pause*]
"Here . . . my colonized body"—I said
"My plexus . . . your madness"—I said
and she went for it
inflicting my forty-fifth scar.
She was only twenty, *boricua*
and did not know the difference between
performance, rock and roll and street life.
Bad phrase, delete. Script change.
But if only I was a radical geography professor . . .

Lección de Geografía Finisecular en Español Para Anglosajones Monolingues

Dear perplexed students,
repeat with me out loud:

México es California
Marruecos es Madrid
Pakistan es Londres
Argelia es París
Cambodia es San Francisco
Turquía es Frankfurt
Puerto Rico es Nueva York
Centroamérica es Los Angeles
Honduras es New Orleans
Argentina es París
Beijing es San Francisco
Haití es Nueva York
Nicaragua es Miami
Quebec es Euskadi
Chiapas es Irlanda
Ramallah es East LA

Your house is also mine
Your language mine as well
And your heart will be ours,
one of these nights.
[*I drink blood from my pulsating rubber heart*]

[*In a nasal voice*]
A crosseyed nurse asks me to please be quiet.
Other patients are losing their patience
with my Spanglish poetry. *Carajo*!
I need a smoke real bad!

Intercut: [*Drunk-like/misspelled gringoñol*]
After the seventh margarita [*hiccups*]

after the twelfth margarita [*hiccups*]
the drunk tourist approaches a sexy señorrita
at "El Faisan" Club, in Merida, Yucatán:
"*oie prrecíosa*, my Mayan queen
tu estarr muchio muy bela
con tu ancient *fire en la piel*
parra que io queme mis bony fingers
mi pájarra belísima
io comprou tu amor con mía mastercard"
She answers in terrible French:
"Ne me dérangez plus ou je vous arraches les yeux!"

DAY 3

[*In a nasal voice*]
I've been in and out of consciousness all day
writing and sleeping, or rather,
writing while sleeping and vice versa
writing shit like:

Poema en Robo-Esperanto

"Ladies and gentlemen,
enchiladas y burritos,
bagels and croissants,
let's imagine for a moment
a postcolonial robo-baroque Esperanto
composed of five European languages
plus Latin, Nahuatl and Chicano slang.
What would it sound like?
Alo? Alo Fortress Europa
Yestem Mexicainskim arteston.
Asken siquieren jodersen.
I wonder que would happen if,
wenn du open your computero,

finde eine message
in esta lingua poluta et disoluta?
No est Englando, no est Germano,
nor Espano; tampoco Franzo;
not even Spanglish ese.
No est keine known lingua aber du understande!
Coño, merde, wat happen zo!
Habe your computero eine virus catched?
Habe du sudden BSE gedeveloped o que?
No, du esse lezendo la neue europese lingua de Europanto
Uno cyber-melangio mas
avec la Chicanoization del mondo
[*Pausa dramatica*]

[*Gringoñol accent*]
In the Americas,
things are even more complicated
regarding l'identité
[*Stereotypical Vato Loco accent*]
. . . y es que la neta escueta
we just don't know where exactly
are the new borders located . . .
Tijuana, Baghdad . . .
plus au moins?
Texas, Kabul . . .
aqui o alla?
Earthlink, Yahoo . . .
ceci, cela?
que esto/que aquello
ici/là-bas
que tu/que yo,
I mean
not really wanting to decide yet
'cause
for the moment, machín
aujourd'hui

tlacanácatl el mío
Il corpo pecaminoso
hurts un chingo
especially my feet
íkchitl
pero también otras partes del cuerpo-
po-po-ca, capiscas guey?
tenepantla tinemi
y es que la pisca existencial esta ka-ka.
so drop your cuete mujer
et fiche-moi la paix
y hagamos la paz
con la lengua babe,
ici, dans la voiture sacrée,
en la mera rrranfla
my toyota flamígero . . .
toyó-tl
la salle du sexe transculturel
my lowrider sanctuary
tlatoani
I say
je n'ai rien à déclarer:
"El arte nunca será suficiente"
Translation:
Art is just a pretext for . . . for . . . for . . .
[*I scream*]

"Enough pretentious language poetry GP"
—Myself #12 scolds Myself #7
"Get back to script #1 *ese*
and face the hard facts":

[*In a nasal voice*]
Hospital de Santa Catalina, Ciudad de México, 10:00 A.M. . . .
I wake up sweating.
The IVs are clogged again.
My left arm's the size of my thigh.
I ring the emergency bell

As I wait for the *pinche* nurse
I write to Arthur Krocker on a napkin:
"Estimado señor K.:
The posthuman body is not exactly sexy.
Saludos desde la frontera del Mictlán.
Signed: Mex-terminated"

Dwelling in Unnecessary Wounds

But if only I was a good actor
the bastard son of Klaus Kinski and Sophia Loren
or the border twin of Nicholas Cage
none of this would have ever happened.
If only bad acting equalled good performance art or vice versa,
as mediocre theater directors tend to believe,
this performance would have never taken place.
Que weird thought!
If only I was a furious rocker . . . no.
A trendy painter? . . . no,
I'm bored with art magazines and openings.
A sharp comedian . . . ? Maybe, no, not really,
performance and comedy don't mix very well:
The result is often a joke that no one understands.
If only I had had the guts to join the Zapatistas for good,
the guts to fight the *migra* in situ, with my bare hands,
the guts to tell my family I am truly sorry for all the pain
my sudden departure caused them twenty-two years ago,
when I was young and handsome
and still had no audience whatsoever.
But I was a coward.
I ended up making a twenty-two-year-long performance piece
to justify my original departure, *el pecado original.*
But if only I had never left in the first place
what would have been of my life?
It would be considerably simpler, perhaps
I'd be less *loco* perhaps, less angry, less . . . Chicano.

Awkward phrase, insensitive, sorry, delete!
But if only I didn't have to worry about my audience.
Entertaining them with stupid gadgets and jokes,
Entertaining you to pay my bills,
to avoid prison, deportation, and mental hospitals,
to justify intellectually my sociopathic tendencies.
If only I didn't have to perform to exercise my freedoms
for I could do it every day, everywhere,
but that's the subject matter of an essay, not a performance.
Besides, you did not come here to witness
a radical political mind at work.
Or did you?
Do you wish to experience a radical political mind at work?
Politics as performance art or vice versa?

Exercise in Political Imagination #18

[*Either beeping or subvocalizing the "censored" parts*]
OK, I politely ask you to close your eyes
and imagine a faraway country
controlled by far-right politicians in their seventies.
They are supported by religious fundamentalists
oil tycoons and gun manufacturers. . . . Just imagine
they believe (or rather pretend to believe)
that "the liberal media" and experimental art
have thoroughly destroyed our social fabric,
our moral and family values, our national unity,
and they are determined to restore them at any cost.
Under the pretext of national security
they have decided to carefully scrutinize everything
that goes on radio, TV, printed journalism, the Internet,
performance art, including this very **[beep]**.
So, from **[beep]** to sitcoms,
and from news **[beep]** to **[beep]** programming,
they have digital censors which can detect key words
that trigger ideological or **[beep]** difference.

Since it is practically impossible to monitor everything,
they have devised a mechanism via which **[beep]**
the syntactic and conceptual coherence of a thought is **[beep]**,
especially when dealing with conflicting opin**[beep]**.
So, when it comes to expressing political di**[beep]**
most critical words have been **[beep]**.
And I mean, just words, such as **[beep]** or **[beep]** or **[beep]**
in order to ensure that *tende* **[beep]** information
does not pollute the minds of American patriots,
they have **[longer beep]**
forbidding also the use of terminology like **[beep]** or co-**[beep]**
or even an innocent term like **[beep]**.
In a world such as this, content would be restricted to **[beep]**
and the possibility to make intelligent civic choices
would be affecting our funda-**[beep]** to
[long beep intertwined with diptongues]
Imagine, what kind of a world would this be?
[*I grab the megaphone*]
Locos and *locas*, *perdonen*
but if I stop moving, performing, talking back . . .
I simply die.

DAY 4

[*In a nasal voice*]
Today I got to take a shower and write some emails:
"You won't believe it *tocayo* but
At first I couldn't retain any food or liquids
and then I started vomiting blood *bien Draculero*.
My lower body began to swell up
until I looked like some kind of medieval walrus.
The American doctors said it was a "tropical disease,"
a standard diagnosis for UMP (Unexplainable Mexican Phenomena)
at which point, in an act of desperation,

Performance memory: Guillermo Gómez-Peña boxing with his tortured alter ego, a hanging dead chicken.
Mexico City, 1991. Photo: Monica Naranjo.

I flew to Mexico City,
and put myself in the hands of the family doctor.
The tests revealed an alarming catalog of problems:
Parasites blocking circulation in my limbs,
my lungs, infested with scary-sounding bacteria,
and my liver, my liver had just about quit,
closed up shop, lights out, kaput.
Medical linguists and medieval poets call it "esteatosis,"
en latin
but in reality I was having a tête-à-tête with my own death.
She loves me so much
I could smell the Brazilian desire on her breath."
[*I brush my face and put on stetson hat*]

Border Love/Linguistic Misunderstandings

[*I sing*]
Kiss me, kiss me, my chuca
Como si fuera esta noche
The last *migra* raid
Kiss me, kiss me, *pachuca*
Que tengo miedo perderte
Somewhere in LA.

Ayyyy!
If only I had known the true motivations of my past lovers
when falling in love with El Charromantico or El Mariachi Liberacci
instead of myself #2, El Border Hamlet
me ama/no me ama
me caso/no me caso
me canso/no me canso
Chicano/Mexicano
que soy o me imagino
regreso o continúo

me mato/no me mato
en Mexico/in Califas
to write or to perform
en Inglés or in Spanish . . .
I hate you, no,
I forgive you, no,
I crave for you *locota*,
Where are you?
Are you still blonde?

[*In a nasal voice*]
It took me forty-three years to find her.
She's here tonight,
laying next to me
on this hospital bed,
her warm hand on my shivering plexus,
my right hand on her left breast,
blue fog covering the stage.
My memory wanders around
in the everglades of my laptop.

If only I had a decent command of English
when I got involved with my past lovers.
If only I had known the difference
between jerk around and jerk off,
between napkin and kidnap,
between prospect and suspect,
between embarrassed and *embarasada*.

If only I had known the difference
between desire and redemption
between political correctness and personal computers
between us and US
between humanity and mankind
We've only got one word for both in Spanish:
Humanidad, perdóname por ser tan bi-rollero

If only I had known the difference
between loneliness and solitude . . .
We've only got one word *en español*:
Soledad.
Forgive me for being so . . . pa-ra-dox-i-cal
soledad on stage, my flaming queen,
forgive me *chuca*
for spilling the beans
of my very spicy beanhood.

"He thinks like Octavio Paz,"
wrote the theater critic of the *Boston Globe*,
"but behaves like Geraldo Rivera on acid."
But if only I had known the gringo implications of
"*mi casa es su casa*"
meaning, *y tu pais también*
or "*Hasta la vista babe,*"
meaning, die fuckin' meskin
Or *vaya con dios vatous locous*,
meaning, deported back to the origins.
The South is always the origin
and crossing the border is the original sin.
Placazo:
Un emigrante mas equals un Mexicano menos . . .
Delete!

DAY 5

[*In a nasal voice*]
My friends and relatives are all here,
sitting around my bed.
I'm entertaining them
with a new performance text.
The tone is clearly much less personal and tortured.

Two months before election day,
The Third Party Chicano candidate addresses the Brown House:
Campaigning for the Brown House.
[*I put on dark glasses and bandana*]
Dear Chicanos and honorary Chicanos,
The historical mission of the USA is to put the world at risk
and then to save it from the very risks they created;
for example, to arm other countries,
and then to attack them for being armed;
to provide weapons and drugs to the youth of color
and then to imprison them for using them;
to endanger species and then to raise consciousness
and create programs to save them;
to evict the poor and then punish them for living on the streets;
to turn women and people of color into freaks
and then laugh at us for acting out accordingly.
The historical mission of the USA is very, very peculiar.
[*From now on I take off or put on glasses every time I shift voices*]

[*Bold lines delivered in normal voice/others in hyper-Chicano accent*]
Dear audience,
If I were a politician, would you vote for me?
Despite my outlaw looks, my obvious vices?
Despite my lack of theatrical training?
If this was, say, a presidential campaign
and not a performance-art piece,
what would I say? What should I say?

Imaginary political speech #5

[*Abrasive w/megaphone*]
Dear citizens of the millennial *barrio*,
We are faced with a very serious dilemma:
we have now entered the postdemocratic phase
of advanced capitalism,
and there's simply . . . no return.

Orale! Parezco Malcolm Mex.

We politicians have total disregard for human pain,
for the homeless, the migrants from the South,
our elders and teens,
the artists, the enfermed, the crazy ones, like you.
We have gotten used to living without seeing, without sharing.
For the moment all we share is . . . the moment.

No, no, no, that's a bad Daoist phrase.
I'll try imaginary political speech #7.

Imaginary political speech #7

[*I drop megaphone and raise my right fist*]
[*Grave voice*]
Dear orphans of the nation-state,
We now live . . .
we now live in a fully borderized world
composed of virtual nations,
transnational pop cultures, and hybrid races,
and all we share is fear and vertigo

[*To an audience member*] Hey, that's a great line

Fear?
Fear of the future, of war, love, and loneliness

And vertigo?

The feeling of standing on the edge of a new millennium.
Yessss!!
Pure *horror vacui*: Y2K, *y que*,
Apocalypse Mañana!
We feel it in our crotch
and it goes up our spine
and into our throat

and out of our nostrils and eyes
and it's fucking unbearable!!!!!

I'm overdoing it, I know,
but I see no other way to make my point.
Wait, there might be another way . . . a joint!

[*I light up a joint and smoke it*]

Imaginary Political Speech #12

[*Stoner voice*]
Dear generic American citizenry,
If you vote for me
I can assure you that as the first Mexican president of the USA,
I will fulfill your fears and desires like no other politician ever did,
and all your stereotypes will come true *carnales*, uufff!
I'll open all borders, legalize drugs,
create nude university campuses,
make daily sex mandatory,
make Spanglish the official language,
expropriate all TV stations and hand them over to poets,
abolish the police force and the national guard,
ban all weapons, from handguns to missiles,
deport Bush back to Texas
and Ashcroft back to his Episcopalian Inferno.

Orale, feels great to imagine . . .

[*I take out bandana and dark glasses. I drink from Mr. Clean bottle again*]

DAY 6

[*In a nasal voice*]
Since my liver can't tolerate the medicine
I need to fight the infections,

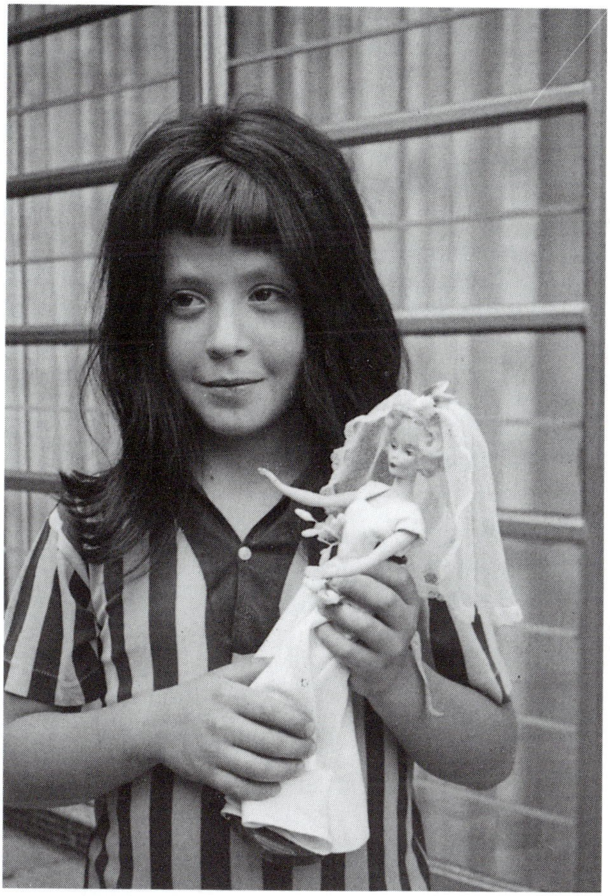

Early involuntary performance. Ten-year-old Guillermo Gómez-Peña in drag at his Mexico City home, 1965.

the doctors needed a way to simulate
its functions.
So, they connected me to a myriad more IVs
and made me look precisely like one
of my Mexi-cyborg performance characters,
like some kind of cheesy self-fulfilling prophecy
featured on the sci-fi channel *en español* . . .

[*Voice of sleazy Latino TV announcer*]
A continuación en Telemundo
Un emigrante asegura haber sido atacado por Migrasferatu
[*Normal voice*]
If only I had been more cautious when crossing the border
but, to tell you the truth, I'm glad I wasn't, 'cause
we are who we are,
because of every mistake we've made
and all the *locos* and *locas* we've met in the process
including the *pinche migra*
and every caress we've given and received
including those of our worst lover,
and if you want to get real He-ge-lian,
we are who we are
because of every performance we've done
and every performance we chose not to do.
Like tonight,
I chose not to do a lot of things. For example,
I chose not to make you laugh too much
so you wouldn't mistake me for a stand-up comedian.
I chose not to shock you unnecessarily
so you wouldn't get a bad impression of performance art.
I chose not to bring my gun
so you wouldn't think that all Mexicans are violent.
And precisely because I chose not to do all these things
I am who I am,
doing what I'm doing,
echando rollo profeta
chance-thinking as I go, go, Go-Mex.
I'm going,
we are all going
through the Biiiiiiiiiig Smoke,
[*Tongues*]
el in-ter-cul-tu-ral Poltergeist,
[*Tongues*]
driving along the information superhighway
[*Tongues*]

surfing the mindscape of the net
[*Tongues*]
the subconscious of America.
[*Tongues*]
It's scary,
but we are all writing this text as I speak.
I spik, you gringo . . . no
I speak, you listen.
Voice change; special effect #187:
[*Mute language for 30 secs*]

[*In a nasal voice*]
The nurse enters the room stage left.
She takes my performance temperature
and changes one of the IVs. Action:
Where is the pinche teleprompter I asked for?
I told you guys I was unable to memorize a full script.

The nurse does not understand my concern

I told you very clearly that this was not a theater monologue.
Hey Pancho, that light over there is too bright.
Can we put a blue gel
to add some artificial melancholy to my words?
Tonite, my words are my conceptual stage
And you, my dear audience,
you are my . . . hostage.
Nevermind!
Testing, testing, *probando*
"*Estoy muriendome en voz alta*
y nadie se da cuenta, probando . . ."
This mike sounds crappy ¿qué no?
Don't you guys have another one
That can actually improve my voice?
Make me sound more dignified,
sensual, compassionate, smart
I mean, isn't technology supposed to enhance humanity?

[*Pause*]
Nevermind!
Back to my main subject matter:
Mapping.
Mapping the immediate future
so you and I can walk on it
without falling inside the great faults of history.
You and I, verbally walking together,
You and I, an ephemeral community,
You and I, a tiny little nation-state,
You and I, a one-hour-long Utopia titled "You and I,"
Alone onstage,
Fighting together the World Bank,
the WTO, and the Bush Cartel.
Tu y yo, juntitos.
But who are you, really?
[*I powder my face and put on my stetson hat*]

[*In a nasal voice*]
After a week at the hospital,
I look at myself in the mirror
and see someone else,
a pale skinny man with a frail gaze,
I don't recognize myself,
and neither do my other selves.
I am the most other and fragmented I've ever been.
I'm literally talking to this Other self
on the other side of the mirror.

[*House lights*]
[*Addressing an audience member*]
Ese . . .
Where is the border between you and me?
Between my words and your mind?
Between my mouth and your fears?
Where exactly is this performance taking place?
Are we webcasting tonight?

Am I alone onstage?
Where are my dear colleagues? [*Name present friends*]
Are you *locos* still here?
Are you . . . my audience tonight?
Do you feel lonely when I speak?
What time is it, by the way?
It's so fuckin' late in the show!
And I am still asking all these existentialist questions:
Is there still time?
Time for . . . making love . . .
For dreaming . . .
For reinventing ourselves . . .
For returning to the homeland, to her arms
Is there enough time?
to wait
to stop the war, another war
to cry collectively
to cry for the world for no apparent reason,
the way Fassbinder used to cry
whenever he took a city bus
and saw other suffering humans?
their perplexed and lonely faces?
"Ish bin ain Mexicanishes monster in Berlin"
Poor German citizens,
if only they had been born in Mexico
they would be less tortured . . . perhaps.
Bad phrase. Delete.
[*To someone in the audience*]
Miss, why were you crying the last time you cried?
You beautiful, you . . .
Were you truly aching or just performing?
Am I really, sincerely aching, or just performing?
Is this a mere exercise in linguistic manipulation?
[*To someone else*]
Sir, are you in touch with your heart?
Can you see mine, hanging out like a wandering viscera?
[*To someone else*]

Carnal, are you in touch with your genitalia?
This guy asked me this question at a party the other night:
What does it mean to be in touch with one's genitalia?
I answered rhetorically with a question:
"to be sensitive to people's eros?
or to engage acritically in sexual harassment
or, in Spanglish, sexual *agárrasment?*"
Is anyone, right this moment, besides me
experiencing incommensurable horniness?
No one?
[*Pause*]
Anyone willing to come onstage and take off your clothes
As a homage to early performance art?
[*To an audience member*]
Hey, do you know your genetic code?
Do you know your civil liberties?
How many have you lost so far?
[*Hindu accent*]
I don't ever recall asking you if you were a foreigner
[*French accent*]
ne me dérange plus ou je vous arrache les yeux
bad French accent, coño . . . *terrible!*
I told you I was a bad actor!
'Cause I was never trained . . .
to perform . . .
your desires
much less to entertain . . .
the possibility of . . .
lying.

[*In a nasal voice*]
***La madre superiora*, remember?**
She returns once again to my room
to offer me confession:
"Confiesa hijo de puta!"
she says, *encabronada*,

as if my death were imminent.
I turn on my inner TV.

News Update

[*Voice of typical American newscaster*]
The war goes on in Baghdad
As the performance continues in [*name of the city where I'm performing*]
Miento:
The war goes on at the US–Mexico border
As the performance continues on HBO
Same war, different performance
Blackout!

[*Blackout/I put on a wrestler mask*]

DAY 7

[*In a nasal voice*]
Carolina comes in with a hidden avocado torta
she smuggled from the corner taco shop.
She breaks the good news:
I'm leaving tomorrow, *orale*!
This epic is almost over.
The older nurse, *la coqueta*, asks me for the tenth time
"Perdone señor, what did you say you were?
Per-for-man-que?"

A contra-dic-tion in terms—*respondo*
A straight transsexual—*elaboro*
a wrestler without a ring
a rocker without a band
a cyber-pirate without "access"
a theorist without methodology

a shaman expelled from his tribe
a poet who writes his metaphors on his body
seven *locos*, locked inside an empty room
my mind, mex-plico?
My mind, not theirs.

She looks at me
with a combination of tenderness and fear and says:
"No entiendo nada . . . del arte . . . mo-moderno."

an artist who sells ideas, not objects, not images, not skills
a per-for-man-ce artist, which means that
when I am pissed
I tend to speak in tongues.
[*Angry tongues*]
Performance is a weird religion, I told you
[*Chant*]
per ipsum ecu nipsum, eti nipsum
et T-Video Patri Omni-impotenti
per omnia saecula saeculeros,
I te watcho
[*Tongues*]
[*I take off wrestler mask*]

This is the way my voice sounds when I'm losing my mind,
Testing, testing . . .
El Phony Shaman.

[*Fake nahuatl*]
[*I sing the traditional Hare Krishna*]
Hare Krishna, Krisnahuatl
Hare grandma, hairy nalga
Ommmmmmm
[*Imitating powwow-like chanting*]
Christian girls, Christian girls,
Christian girls, Christian girls,

Oh how I love, oh how I love, oh how I love those Christian girls,
Oh how I love, oh how I love, oh how I love those Christian girls.
Ahhhhh . . .
New age girls . . . [*repeats chant*]
Skinhead girls . . . [*repeats chant*]
Muslim boys . . . [*repeats chant*]

[*Shamanic tongues intertwined with words*]
[*Tongues*] . . . Tezcatlipunk
[*Tongues*] . . . Funkahuatl
[*Tongues*] . . . Khrishnahuatl
[*Tongues*] . . . Chichicolgatzin
[*Tongues*] . . . Chili con Carne
[*Tongues*] . . . Taco Bell Chihuahua
[*Tongues*] . . . Santa Frida
[*Tongues*] . . . Santa Selena
[*Tongues*] . . . Santa Pocahontas
[*Tongues*] . . . Santa Shakira
[*Tongues*] . . . Virgen Tatuada

NAFTA, Viagra, Melatonin,
NAFTA, Viagra, Melatonin,

[*Screaming*]
Melatonin!!
Now everybody, take your pill.

Ginseng, Gingko, Guacamole,
Ginseng, Gingko, Guacamole,

[*Screaming*]
Guacamole!!
Now everybody, take a dip.

Kava, ecstasy, chili beans,
Kava, ecstasy, chili beans,

[*Screaming*]
Rosarito!!
Now everybody, take a shit.

[*In a nasal voice*]
The day I was released
Doctor Hernandez gave me the bad news:
"Guillermo, you need a total change of lifestyle."
I hate that *pinche* word, "lifestyle" . . . "lifestyle . . . "
I *pinche* hate it.

ONE MONTH LATER

[*In a nasal voice*]
I'm back in San Francisco
learning how to be a laptop intellectual, *coño*!
I miss the road, the troupe,
our dangerous crossborder adventures.
I badly miss Myers rum and Marlboro reds.
I'm filled with millennial doubts, *chingos*!

POST-SCRIPT: MILLENNIAL DOUBTS

Damas y caballeros;
I'm feeling a bit insecure and introspective tonight.
I just turned forty-eight,
and I wonder if I'm still asking the right questions,
or am I merely repeating myself?
Am I going far enough, or should I go further?
North? But the North does not exist,
South? Should I go back to Mexico for good?
Regresar en español a las entrañas de mi madre?
But the Mexican nation-state is collapsing as I speak
so *stricto sensu, Mexico en español* no longer exists

Guillermo Gómez-Peña as El S/M Zorro.
Liverpool Biennial, 2002. Photo: Manual Vason.

'cause everyday Mexico and the US,
like Fox and Bush,
look more and more like one another
and less and less like you *y yo*
which means, "we" are no longer foreigners to one another.
Follow my Kantian logic?
Therefore, as orphans of two nation-states,
we've got no government to defend,
no flag to wave.
We've only got one another
which sounds quite romantic,
I mean, politically speaking,
but it is a philosophical nightmare . . .
I mean, if neither the North nor the South
are viable options anymore,
where should I go? East? *EST*?
Should I go deeper into my global psyche
and become a Chicano Buddhist?
Or should I cross the digital divide west
and join the art-technologist cadre?
How?
Alter my identity through body-enhancement techniques,
laser surgery, prosthetic implants,
and become the *Mexica* Orlan?
A glow-in-the-dark transgenic *mojado*?
Or a postethnic cyborg, perhaps?
A Ricky Martin with brains?
That's a strange thought.
Maybe I should donate my body
to the MIT artificial-intelligence department
so they can implant computer nacho chips in my *&^%^76%78
implant a very, very sentimental robotic bleeding heart
and become the ranchero Stelarc?
What about a chipotle-squirting techno-falo jalapeño
to blind the *migra* when crossing over?
Or an "intelligent" tongue . . . activated by tech-eela?

You know, imaginary technology
for those without access to the real one.
I mean, I'm arguing for an obvious fact:
When you don't have access to power
poetry replaces science
and performance art becomes politics
Mex-plico?
No, I got to get me a "real" job, a nine-to-five job.
But the question is, doing what?
Hey, I could be an intercultural detective?
a forensic expert in X-treme identity analysis . . . *nay*!
Que tal la pedagogía radical?
Translation please?

I can teach "Chiconics" in jail, I mean Yale,
"What's up *esos, chinguen a sus profesores.*
Saquen la mota y el chemo.
Forever, Aztlan nation."
How about posing as a model for a computer ad:
[*I put on my techno glasses and stetson hat*]
"El Mexterminator thinks different, *y que*?"
Or posing as a wholesome eccentric for a Ben & Jerry's poster?
No, I'd have to lose 10 kilos at least
and use lots of coppertone ¿qué no?
Wait,
I could conduct self-realization seminars for Latino dot-commers:
"Come to terms with your inner Chihuahua."
[*I bark*]
Que tal a workshop for neoprimitive Anglos?
"Find your inner Aztec."
[*I speak in pseudo-nahuatl*]
I look the part ¿qué no? . . . kind of . . .
I could write a bestseller for conservative minorities titled . . .
Inverted Minstrel: One hundred ways to camouflage your ethnicity to get a better job
or *Using Make-Up and Wigs to Get a Loan from the Bank*

or to Buy a Home at a Trendy 'Hood
I just don't know anymore.
It's tough to find a useful task for a performance artist nowadays.
In the age of the mainstream bizarre, revolution as style
and globalization gone wrong, weapons of mass distraction,
asses of evil shoved into your face.
In this time and place,
what does it mean to be "transgressive"?
What does "radical behavior" mean after Howard Stern,
Jerry Springer, Bin Laden, Ashcroft, Cheney,
six-year-old serial killers in the heartland of America,
a First World Banana Republic . . . Florida,
tampering with electoral ballots,
an AA theological cowboy running the so-called "free world"
as if he were directing a spaghetti western in the wrong set?
Conan the Barbarian running for governor in California?
Coño, I ask myself rhetorically,
what else is there to "transgress"?
Who can artists shock, challenge, enlighten?
Can we start all over again?
Can we?
May I
Mear . . . los?
Should I burn my bra or my green card?
Damas y caballeros,
I thought maybe I might have one more chance
to make a deal with my personal death
So, I wrote this script
It begins like this . . .

[*Blackout*]

TEMPORARY END

18

Twenty-first-century Chicano newscast

(Performance Radio and Cyber Communiqué, 2002)

Guillermo Gómez-Peña and Elaine Katzenberger

*This performance text was first circulated on the Internet as a "cyber-*placazo*"-tagging. Then it was broadcast on several community radio stations as "real news" and read live on a few occasions. Understandably NPR didn't want to touch it.*

Part I

Newscaster voice: Good evening America; good morning Europe. At the top of the news tonight:

President Bush extends his "War on Terror" to Venus and Mars. Sources in Wachingón confirm that an allied occupation of Pluto has not been entirely ruled out. Operation "Intergalactic Justice" has garnered him a deserved nomination for the Nobel Peace Prize.

Out in California on a last-minute, mega fundraising tour before signing the campaign-finance reform bill, Mr. Bush hosted a series of meetings with Hollywood executives to pitch his latest idea, "a sort of high-tech spaghetti western staged on the wrong set."

Regarding ABC, Fox, and MSNBC-TV's much-awaited merger with the Pentagon, Chairman of the FCC Michael Powell had this to say: "Dad and I couldn't be happier.

Maintaining the optical illusion of a separation between the media and the government was a big waste of time and resources, and now America can get down to business!"

Clear Channel's "We Rule the Airwaves and A Whole Lot More" has announced a date for the live broadcast of *their* new national anthem.

On Easter Sunday, singer-songwriter and devout fundamentalist Christian, Attorney General John Ashcroft will lead a humungous chorus of every single Republican and Democrat in the House and Senate in a singalong of what sources are calling "an anthem a million times better than 'The Star Spangled Banner'!" At his Episcopalian church in Arkansas, Ashcroft comments *en* trance: "Let it be clear! Only twenty-five Enron executives were actually employed by this administration. The pornocommunist press always blows things out of proportion."

We'll be back after the following mock emergency security alert.

Momento. Aquí hay un desfazamiento entre el discurso oficial y la realidad política.

Part II

On the domestic terror front: An Al-Qaeda cell (the fifth one discovered in America so far) was discovered in the saliva of an innocent-looking puppy in Queens, New York. The Director of Homeland Security has declared that "all cloning of pets will be immediately suspended until further notice."

In Los Angeles, what appeared to be an anthrax-laced *pupusa* was found in a subway trashcan. The city's only mass-transit system was shut down for ten solid days, but no one actually noticed. Over 2000 Salvadorean immigrants have been indefinitely detained, says an FBI spokesperson, "just in case."

At the Ronald Reagan Airport in Washington DC, an Arab-looking man passed through security without receiving any extra harassment by airport REP personnel (Random Ethnic Profilers). As a result, Senator Dianne Feinstein is calling for a speedup of the federal takeover of airport security. "This is an outrage!" Feinstein fumed. "Anyone who doesn't look like they're from Norway or Pasadena absolutely must be subjected to a body-cavity search!"

America stands tall in its fight to defend freedom and democracy. An eighty-nine-year-old Mexican national is being held by FBI agents after being observed taking photos of the gardens at the Fresno County Courthouse. The Governor of

La KKK nurse posing for the camera at the laboratory of desire.
Alice Joanou. *El Mexterminator Project*, 1998. Photo: Eugenio Castro.

California called for a statewide maximum-security alert. "We have information that terrorists are planning to deploy horticultural weapons of mass destruction," said Governor Gray Davis in broken Spanish.

America stands tall in its fight to defend freedom and democracy. An ex-icecream-vendor in San José, who is thought to be related to someone whose neighbor might have an Arab friend, has been named as the twenty-first hijacker and perhaps the second serial sniper. FBI director Robert Mueller cited the evidence: "Shit! The INS was about to extend his visa! Case closed!"

The US–Mexico border is now completely sealed. "There are no more illegals coming in," said the Western Regional Commissioner of the INS. "The tourist, food, construction, and entertainment industries are hoping to replace their illegal workers with ethnocyborgs overnight."

Human and civil rights organizations are announcing an epidemic of "compassion fatigue." All political, racial, and ethical implications have been extracted from this newscast for your comfort.

We'll be back after the following commercial . . .

Part III

On the international stage: The mummified body of Osama Bin Laden was found on exhibit at a roadside museum in Montana. DNA tests have confirmed his identity. An FBI actor from the popular TV program *Forensic Files* has challenged the DNA results: "We've encountered these mummies before. This one is not Osama. It's actually . . . Noriega. Don't believe the hype."

For its new "tali-Gap" campaign, mega-store Gap has recruited fifteen ex-Taliban supermodels and a Chicano rap group named Oh Sammy Bien Latin and the Tali-Beaners.

Twenty-five developing countries are fighting over who will be the next to host the exciting military exercises now taking place in the Philippines. Kuwait, Qatar, Colombia, Bulgaria, and Somalia are tied.

Prime Minister Ariel Sharon was caught on camera slamdancing with a group of skinheads in a Jerusalem nightclub. He explained to our reporter "my message is finally getting across to the youth."

News flash: Venezuelan leftist dictator Hugo Chavez was seen eating falafels with Yasser Arafat and a Saddam Hussein look-alike in Ramallah. "Bad timing!" cried the Venezuelan spin department. When Fidel saw the photo he was furious for having been excluded.

In Guantanamo Bay, human-rights organizations are accusing the USA of placing twenty-eight prisoners inside a 4x4 Presbyterian wooden church. "It's small, I know

. . . but they've got Direct-TV, what do these people want?" says US War Chief Tommy Toms.

We'll be back in a few minutes, after a brief word from Texaco Oil, Exxon, and Halliburton.

Generic terrorist.
From a Mexican wrestling magazine.

19

America's most wanted inner demon

(Performance Script, 2003)

I El Archeotypal Greaser

[*I speak in tongues*]
VOICE #1: NORMAL

Hello, my dear audience:
Je suis El Archeotypal Greaser,
born and raised south of the media border
where the continents of fear and ignorance overlap.
Soy yo el mero mero great-great-grandson
of Cortes y La Malinche,
l'enfant de la chingada da-da.
I was . . .
I am . . .
the bastard son of Lone Ranger and Tonto,
el hijo apocrifo de Frida Culo y Freddy Kruger,
the Meskin brother Banderas badly wanted to have,

a true Hollywood refusnik . . .
Soy yo Joaquin, pero el otro
El que se perdió when crossing the border.
Lost and found in the translation,
misinterpreted by both sides.
[*I sing to a cumbia beat*]
"*Un, dos, el* nasty one,
un, dos, the rebel one,
el indomable e intraducible
undocumented/*documentado*" . . .
[*Normal voice*]
shit!, I am a terrible *cumbia* singer
I'll try another persona
[*Tongues*]

II El Mad Mex

VOICE #2: COMPUTERIZED
Soy el Mad Mex, *Chero* psycho-killer;
prototype 187-GQ
conceived at MGM
with body parts assembled in TJ/Taiwan.
'cause all Mexican artists were made in Taiwan;
our body parts assembled by German curators
to perform X-treme art functions
at expos, festivals and TV ads
[*Pause*]
Primary Functions:
100+ identity morphing capabilities
including *el S&M Zapatista*
el galant mariachi rocker
el X-rated *narco brujo*

el transgender dandy *servidor*
que cruza y penetra vuestras
inmensas nalgas transnacionales.
Delete. Open Accessories File:

- chipotle squirting robo-jalapeño phallus to blind the migra when crossing over . . . shift.
- software located in my *&^&% . . . $%&&& . . . shift.
- my intelligent tongue, mastica computer nacho chips imbedded in my *&^&% . . . $%&&& . . . shift.
- my poisonous lips mastican your delicious, delicious white flesh.

"Viva gringuita!"
cries El Chihuahua Chucky
my favorite Mexi-cannibal *colega*
right before devouring your hardware.
[*I bark*]

III El Allatola Whatever

VOICE #3: SATANIC
Estimado publico aterrado:
Due to profound cultural misunderstanding,
America's favorite sport,
Tonight, I am the most suspicious Other around,
the Other on the other side of the mirror, das TV set,
your evil twin, the brown one,
perdido entre las torres gemelas?
[*Rapping*]
I am . . . the bogeyman
of ABC, the INS, the NSA,
and the Homeland Security Gestapo.

Evil Other #27846: El Robowarrior in *The Museum of Fetishized Identities.*
Juan Ybarra. Performance Space, Sydney, 2000. Photo: Hiedrun Lohr.

Motto: Security for you;
inseguridad para el resto del planeta
Neta: I am *que soy* . . . whomever you want me to be
dark, unscrupulous and genetically anti-American,
I am *que fui el capo de capos,*
Brown Vader Escobar
morphing into the Lord of Heavens,
mato luego existo/cruzo luego soy,
and, by strategic association,
or rather perceptual incompetence,
at different times, I can be, I could be . . .
the Mullah One,
Body Snatcher Extraordinaire,
Osama morphing into Saddam
Hussein, Qaddafi, or Arafat,
El Allatola whatever,
I am, I can be, I could be
America's most wanted inner demon
[*Arabic tongues*]
the T-word, Tee, la té de "terror"
embodied by a big, brown, muscular Vato Loco
'cause you know, we know,
Arabs and Latins are
as hard to distinguish from one another
as a Hutu from a Tutsi
or an Irish from a Scot
in the eyes of a Bengali holy man . . .
[*Tongues*]
'Cause at this point in time
outside of Bush's inner circle
we all are "Arabs," or rather
all Arabs are Latin,
Oh Sammy Bien Latin
Sultan de los Tali-Vatos
and please, please, s'il vous plait
do not confuse "them" with the Tali-beaners,

those phonies sponsored by the Gap,
'cause tonight, tonight,
my mind is out of control
and you, my dear audience,
you're caught in the crossfire
[*I speak in tongues*]
Remember?
Remember me?
Remember my original text?
No biggie.
I'm just a nanabush,
a fancy dancer tightrope-walking coyote;
[*Howling*]
and my only privilege here is
to be allowed to cross
the many many forbidden borders that exist
between my mouth and your fears.
And now, with your permission,
I will cross the border between "I" and "we."

20

A declaration of poetic disobedience from the new border

(Performance Text, 2004)

[*Guillermo Gómez-Peña facing the ceiling of the gallery, theater, or auditorium while chanting in tongues*]

To the masterminds of paranoid nationalism
I say, we say:
"We," the Other people
We, the migrants, exiles, nomads, and wetbacks
in permanent process of voluntary deportation
We, the transient orphans of dying nation-states
la otra America; l'autre Europe y anexas
We, the citizens of the outer limits and crevasses
of "Western civilization"
We, who have no government;
no flag or national anthem
We, fingerprinted, imprisoned, under surveillance
We, evicted from your gardens and beaches
We, interracial lovers,

Rito neo-Azteca.
Guillermo Gómez-Peña and Emiko R. Lewis. From a photo-portfolio sponsored by Spanish curator Orlando Britto. 2004. Photo: James McCaffry.

children of interracial lovers, ad infinitum
We, who defy your fraudulent polls and statistics
We, in constant flux,
from Patagonia to Alaska,
from Juarez to Ramallah,
We millions abound,
We continue to talk back . . . continue, continue (in loupe)
[*Shamanic tongues*]

To those up there who make dangerous decisions for mankind
I say, we say:
We, the unemployed, who work so pinche hard
so you don't have to work that much
We, whose taxes send your CEOs and armies
on vacation to the South
We, the homeless, faceless vatos aquellos
in the great American metropolis
little Mexico, little Cambodia, little purgatory
We, the West Bank and Gaza strip of Gringolandia
We, within your system, without your mercy
We, w/out health or car insurance,
w/out bank accounts and credit cards,
We, scared shitless at ground level
We will outlive your project X, Y, Z,
[*Shamanic tongues*]
I speak therefore we continue to be . . .

To the lords of censorship and intolerance
I say, we say:
We, mud people, snake people, tar people
We, Living Museum of Modern Oddities & Sacred Monsters
We, vatos cromados y chucas neo-barrocas
We, the permanently unsatisfied subcultural typos
We, the immoral majority sieging your dreams
of purity and order
We, bohemians walking on millennial thin ice

Our bodies pierced, tattooed, martyred, scarred
Our skin covered with hieroglyphs and flaming questions
We, indomitable drag queens, transcendental putas
waiting for love and better conditions in the shade
We, against the corruption of formalized religion and art
We, the "subject matter" of fringe documentaries
We, the Hollywood refusniks,
the greaser bandits and holy outlaws
of advanced Capitalism
We, without guns, without Bibles
We, who never pray to the police or to the army
We, who barter and exchange favors & talismans
We, who still believe in community, another community,
a much stranger and wider community
We, community of illness, madness & dissent
We, scared and defiant
We shape your desire while you contract our services
to postpone the real discussion
[*Shamanic tongues*]
I speak therefore we continue to be . . .

To those who have conveniently ignored our voice
I say, we say:
We, who talk back in rarefied symbols and metaphors
We, the artists and intellectuals who don't wish to comply
We, bastard children of two humungous nouns:
"heterodoxy" and "iconoclastia"
We, radical theorists in the academic trenches
We, the urban monks who pray in tongues and rap in Esperanto
We, who put on masks, penachos and wigs to shout
We, standing still in our underwear
right in the center of the stage
with the words carved on our chests:
"We, critical brain mass"
We, fuga inminente de cerebros y hormonas
We, spoken word profética, sintética

[*Shamanic tongues*]
I speak therefore we continue to be . . . continue

To those who are as afraid of us as we are of them
I say, we say:
We, generic brown and black males who fit all
taxonomic descriptions
We, who have no name whatsoever in the news
We, edited out, pixilated, censored, postponed
We, beyond the video frame, behind the caution tape
We, tabloid subject matter par excellence
We, involuntary actors of "the Best of Cops"
We, eternally stalking mythical blonds in the parking lot,
We, mistaken identities in your computer memory
We, black and brown nude bodies in the morgue
We, embalmed bodies in the Museum of Mankind
We, one strike and we're out; two strikes and you're in
We, prisoners of war in times of peace;
prisoners of consciousness without a trial
We, prime targets of ethnic profiling (your favorite sport)
We, of the turban, burka, sombrero, bandana, leather pants
We surround your neon architecture
While you call the FBI, and the Homeland Security Office
[*Pause*]
Yes, we are equally scared of one another . . . Your move . . .
[*Howling*]
I speak therefore I continue to be a part of "us"
To the shareholders of monoculture
I say, we say:
We, bilingual, polylingual, cunnilingual,
Nosotros, los otros del mas allá
del otro lado de la línea y el puente
We, rapeando border mistery; a broader history
We, mistranslated señorrita,
eternally mispronounced
We, lost and found in the translation

lost and found between the layers of this text
We speak therefore you cease to be
even if only for a moment
I am, US, you sir, no ser
Nosotros seremos
Nosotros, we stand not united
We, matriots not patriots
We, Americans with foreign accents
We, Americans in the largest sense of the term
(from the many other Americas)
We, in cahoots with the original Americans
who speak hundreds of beautiful languages
incomprehensible to you
We, in cahoots with dozens of millions of displaced
Latinos, Arabs, Blacks and Asians
who live so pinche far away from their land
and their language
[*Shamanic tongues*]
We feel utter contempt for your myopia
and when we talk back, you loose your grounds
[*Shamanic tongues*]
I speak, therefore we continue to be . . . on the same page
on the same strange planet

To the masters and apologists of war and their pitiful "Coalition of the Willing"
I say, we say:
We, caught in the crossfire,
between Christian fear and Muslim rage,
We, rebels, not mercenaries
We, labeled "extremists" for merely disagreeing with you
We, thinking majority against unilateral stupidity
We, against preemptive strikes and premature ejaculation
We reject your arms sales and oil deals
We, distrust your orange alert and your white privilege
We, oppose the Patriot Act patrioticamente

We oppose the largest surveillance system ever,
the biggest prison complex to date
We, oppose your "full spectrum dominance"
We, who are never polled by Fox News
We, who never get to debate Chris Mathews
We, whose opinions are never on the front page
of your morning paper
We did not vote for you, Magister Dixit
do not support your wars, Master Cannibal
do not believe in your Infinite Justice
We demand your total TOTAL withdrawal
from our minds and bodies ipso-facto
We demand the total restructuring
of the world economic system
in the name of democracy and freedom
[*Pause*]
And you, Mad Cowboy, are you taking note?
or are you already on your way to Mars?
[*Shamanic tongues*]
I speak in tongues therefore you evaporate, evaporate, adios

Finale
[*Finally facing the audience*]
We, baaaad poetry,
We, poliglotas en la oscuridad
We, [*Tongues*]
We, the shamans exorcising Enron
the brujos against Microsoft
We, dervishes under the arch of McDonald's
We, the ghosts of the past
in cahoots with the future warriors
in cahoots with all innocent civilians killed
on both sides of the useless War on Terror
We, literally dying for new ideas
performing against all odds
[*Pause*]

We dedicate these burning words
to our homeboys and homegirls;
the rejects of all dysfunctional communities
embarking on a great political campaign
against the enemies of difference
[*Shamanic tongues*]
I speak, we speak, therefore we continue to be . . . together
even if only in the realm of the poetical
even if only for the duration of this unusual mass.

21

Helpful performance tips on how to avoid xenophobia and express solidarity with innocent Arab-Americans after 9/11

(Cyber Communiqué, 2001. Banned by NPR)

Guillermo Gómez-Peña and Elaine Katzenberger

Given the current atmosphere of overwhelming fear and suspicion, with citizen vigilantism on the rise and civil liberties being sacrificed on the altar of "national security," we may encounter the need to protect ourselves and others from the rage of misinformed citizens. We would like to humbly suggest the following performative options:

1. In order to avoid misled racist attacks, all Arab-Americans should wear a mariachi hat and a Mexican *zarape* when going out in public.
2. All Arab-looking Latinos and South Asians should follow suit.
3. Other "looks" which might be useful to try include

    (a) the Native American Dandy—braids, Indian beadwork, and a leather vest;
    (b) the Chicana Matron/Frida Kahlo look—Mexican folk dress with an accompanying "authentic ethnic" hairdo;
    (c) the Tex-Mex *vaquero*—stetson hat, fringed leather jacket, and cowboy boots;

(d) the Andean street musician—panpipes, Bolivian hat, and colorful woven vest.

4. For those Anglo or Anglo-looking people who wish to express solidarity with Arab-Americans and Arab-looking people, we suggest wearing buttons, T-shirts, or baseball caps that state, "We are all Arabs."
5. Arab-Americans should call the FBI hotline to report sightings of suspicious-looking Montana militia or survivalist types, especially in groups of two or more.
6. We would also like to politely propose that those who spout xenophobic rhetoric should be held responsible for their words in the following ways:

(a) Those who believe that racism and ethnic-profiling are "minor issues" in the face of the tragedy must spend an entire day in public wearing a turban and a fake beard or a Muslim woman's headscarf. This will help acquire both humility and perspective.
(b) Those who insist that Arabs in the USA should "go back where they came from" will be asked to name at least five Arab homelands and to find them on a map.
(c) Anyone who states that "those people are fanatics" or "they just don't value life the way we do" will be handed a copy of *The Turner Diaries* and a photograph of Timothy McVeigh.
(d) Those who believe that "security is more important than civil liberties" must name exactly which of the amendments to the US Constitution—known as the Bill of Rights—they are personally willing to sacrifice.
(e) Finally, for all who feel that public dialogue is "inappropriate and divisive" at this time, as in "you're either with us, or you're with them," there will be a simple performative requirement: Wrap a blindfold tightly over your eyes (you may not use a flag), plug up your ears, put a patch over your mouth, and practice marching in a straight, unbroken line with others who have done the same.

22

The post-9/11 "rights and privileges" of a US citizen

(Anonymous Cyber-communiqué, 2003)

1. I may think as I please so long as I don't do anything about it.
2. I may speak or write as I please, so long as I do not interfere with the patriotism and intolerance of others.
3. I have the right to vote. With my vote I get to imagine I actually choose the public officers who are really my servants.
4. I have the right to imagine I choose my work, any job for which my experience and ability have equipped me, even if there are no jobs around.
5. I have the right to a prompt trial by jury, if I should be accused of a crime, so long as I am not an Arab or Arab-looking.
6. I may seek justice in the courts where I have equal rights with others, so long as I am not Black, Latino, Asian, or Native American.
7. I have the right to try to improve my lot through various means, including lying, stealing, and invading other countries.
8. If so, I also have the privilege of sharing in the benefits of all the natural resources of my country and other countries.
9. I have the right to worship a Christian god.
10. I will do my part to make America, once again, "a nation of riflemen."

Please forward this document to other "good citizens."

Before (1978)

After (2000)

track five

CONVERSATIONS WITH THEORISTS

This final section offers another layer of complexity to Guillermo Gómez-Peña's pedagogical project. Always striving to create dialogue outside of the performance field and within a global context, Gómez-Peña tests the limits of his politics and methodologies with Colombian philosopher Eduardo Mendieta. They discuss key issues such as the role of language and the relationship between the body and "global culture." Their connection as philosopher and performance theoretician/practitioner is concretized by their interest in moving theoretically and methodologically beyond "post" analysis, for example poststructuralism and postcolonialism.

In "The Minefields of Utopia," US performance theorist Lisa Wolford and Gómez-Peña discuss the obstacles and possibilities of collaboration, particularly transitions made between theory and practice. In a follow-up dialogue entitled "The Minefields of Dystopia," Gómez-Peña and Wolford discuss how they each adjusted to post-9/11 politics and paranoia.

In a move to disrupt conventional notions of author and editor, Gómez-Peña and I produced the last dialogue. We hope it offers a candid backstage look at the production process of this book. Our relationship as author and editor was saturated in humility and intensity. There were many differences to contend with: Generational, gender, and political differences, to name a few. We redirected the powerful energies backing our differences so that they only enriched our collaborative process. I challenged, he challenged, and so it went.

Elaine Peña

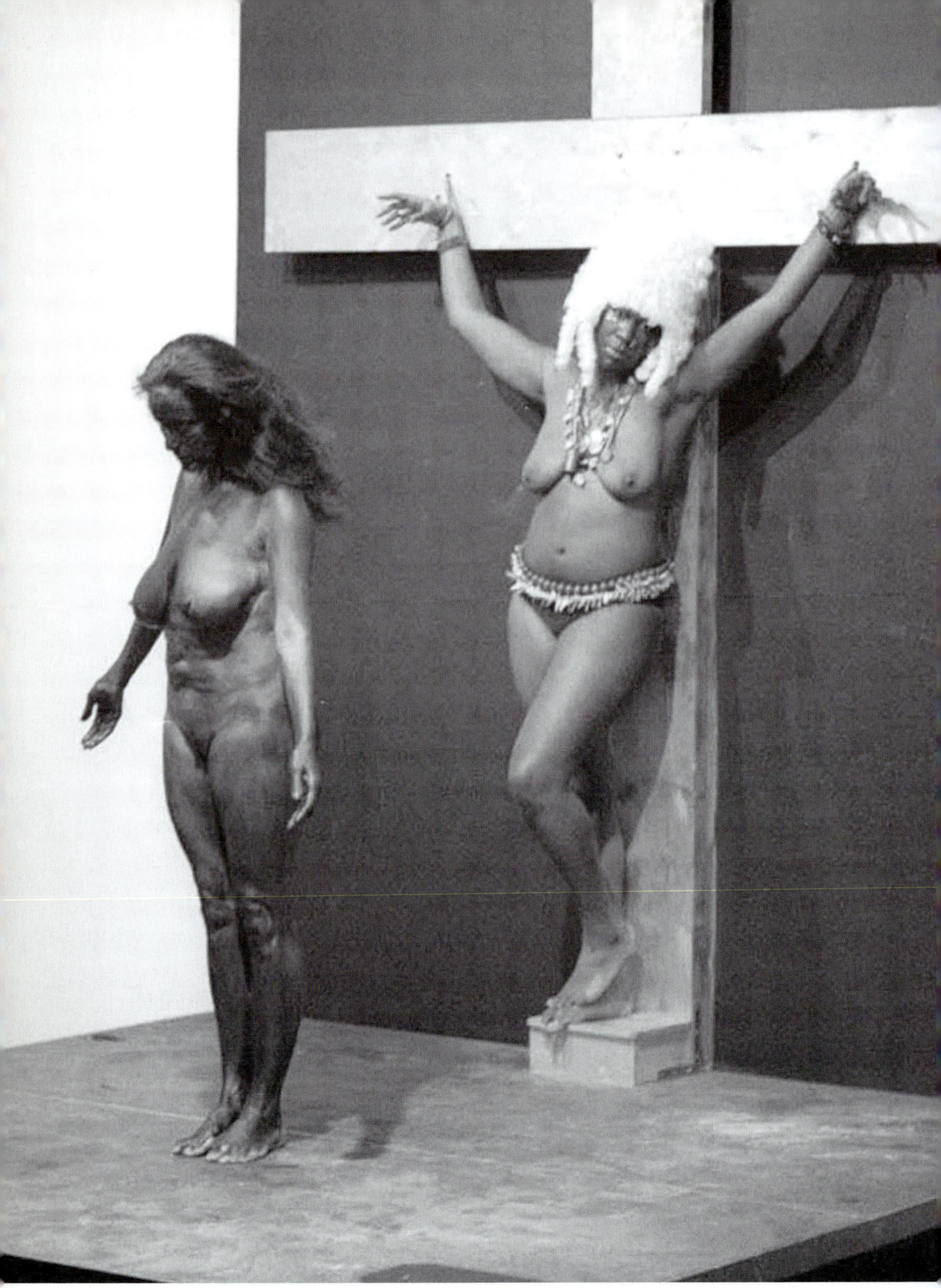

Michelle Ceballos performing a full body minstrel with Barby Asante (crucified) during the final tableau of *Ex-Centris.*
Tate Modern, 2003. Photo: Hugo Glendinning.

23

Theatricalizations of postcolonial theory

A Colombian philosopher interviews a Chicano performance artist

(Interview, 2001)

Eduardo Mendieta and Guillermo Gómez-Peña

Mendieta: Just as Francis Fukuyama was talking about the "end of history," Arthur Danto was proclaiming the "end of art." Neither idea is new: They can be traced to Hegel. Now, one could read some of your recent performances and reflections as announcements of the end of art, as kinds of obituaries for art. Do you think that art has become either impossible at best, or irrelevant at worst?

Gómez-Peña: I believe that in this era of savage globalization and relentless consumerism, politicians, the media, the masterminds of the Internet, and society at large have chosen to ignore the importance of art in our everyday lives. They have chosen to ignore the unique voice of the artist as a social critic, as a reformer, as an ombudsman, as a vernacular philosopher, as a postmodern shaman, as an enlightened fool who always tells the truth in their own particular way. This poses an incredible challenge to us politicized performance artists. What to do if the only roles we have been assigned in the new era are those of programmers, entertainers of a new consumer class, the cyberbourgeoisie, and decorators of the omnipresent horror vacui? These options are equally pitiful, ¿qué no? How can we then reconquer a central role in society, become once again shapers of consciousness and moral advisers? Is this even possible nowadays? I really don't know. My colleagues and I are obsessed with this dilemma. Where are our artists and intellectuals when we need them? It's not enough for us to operate within the art world and academia.

Mendieta: What are some of the strategies you utilize in your work to assume a more central positionality?

Gómez-Peña: One of our strategies is to occupy a fictional central space, fully knowing that it's fictional, and to speak always from this fictional center, to push the dominant culture to the margins, treat it as exotic and unfamiliar. We operate in the realm of contingencies and inversions. The questions for us in this imaginary realm are: What if Latinos were in power and could decide the terms of the debate? What if the United States was Mexico? What if Spanish was the official lingua franca? What if imagination was a form of political praxis? What if Anglo-Americans were mere nomadic minorities? We call this strategy "reverse anthropology." But we are aware that this is a purely conceptual strategy that does not translate into the social sphere. That's why we are also trying to infiltrate more populist spaces such as public radio and TV, to cross over into these realms with dignity, and we don't always succeed in keeping control of our material during the crossover. We are in a trial-and-error stage. As I recently told a journalist colleague of mine, there has to be a third option between Gayatri Spivak and Camille Paglia (with all due respect to Gayatri), between rarefied art for chic museums and *barrio* art, between HBO and pirate media. We are looking for it. My compañera Carolina calls it "la tercera opción" (the third option).

Mendieta: You see, I actually don't think that what you're doing is analogous to what Danto, Fukuyama, or Hegel were saying or doing with respect to art. And you just gave a name to this difference: "reverse anthropology." Furthermore, the question "What if imagination was a form of political praxis?" points in a different direction than that described by the self-appointed prophets of the end of time. On the one hand, I think that there is an infinite amount of hubris in announcing that history and art have come to an end. When a society allows, in fact demands, such kinds of pronouncements, then "imagination" becomes a form of resistance. Yes, indeed, to dream, to dare to produce art, becomes a form of resistance to the relentless and pervasive commodification of everything, even our dysfunctions and most perverse fetishisms. On the other hand, I think that we have to analyze this rare specimen, this imperial creature that abrogates for itself the role of universal timekeeper for all humanity. I mean, we must turn the tables on this culture that must cancel and pronounce anachronistic any and every other culture because it cannot countenance that better futures, more humane futures, might be imagined by other cultures. Sometimes I wonder, after seeing and reading your work, what if the culture of globalization was not coming out of Hollywood,

New York, and Paris, but Bombay, New Delhi, and Cairo? Are you not in fact doing a reverse anthropology in order to liberate our imaginations from the grip of Euro-American culture?

Gómez-Peña: There is another kind of global culture, not imposed from above, but emerging organically from within grassroots communities and the streets. I'm talking about a kind of borderized proletarian *transcultura*, a hybrid culture that often resists, consciously or unconsciously, the "legitimate" forces of globalization. This culture is not theorized. It simply is. I am very interested in the redeeming powers of this "other global project" which no one can control, program, or predict. I am interested in the culture generated by the millions and millions of uprooted peoples, the exiles, nomads, and migrants from so-called Third World countries, the orphans of crumbling nation-states who are moving north and west in search of the source of their despair. In the process, they are redefining both the North and the West. In the process, they are creating a new culture, which by nature is antiauthoritarian, anticolonial, and antiglobal. . . . In our art, my colleagues and I wish to contribute to this other antiglobal/global project. It's a humble contribution in terms of scale but is nonetheless important. We really see our work as part of a much larger project involving artists, activists, and intellectuals from all over the world. Our work only makes sense in dialogue with the works of all these wonderful people.

Mendieta: Sometimes I read your work as announcing not just the end of art—of a very particular type of art, bourgeois art—but also the end of culture. One might say that we are living in a postcultural age, and I think that it is this passing away that is registered in your devastating but right-on criticisms of pervasive commodification, including criticism and contestational reflection. And yet, culture was where society went to reflect about itself. It provided a critical mirror, an atropic and anatropic place, as Foucault put it somewhere, where society could see itself differently. Do you agree with this reading, and, if so, what can take over the critical function that culture fulfilled?

Gómez-Peña: Nothing can replace the critical functions of culture. Advanced capitalist societies like the United States that are spearheading the destruction of critical culture are already in deep shit. The spiritual vacuum and ethical crisis of America are the logical consequences of rejecting critical culture and confining it to extremely rarefied milieux and corners such as academia and the Art World in capitals. The powers that be know it. An example comes immediately to mind: A few years ago during the cyber-gold-rush era, the elite of the dot.com industry, the technologists, were obsessing with the need to recuperate their social dimension and physical bodies and engage in "meaningful" cultural practice and artistic rituals, the very same cultural practice they were helping to obliterate. They suddenly realized that there's life before, and after, cyberspace, and that the acritical cult of the Internet could actually lead them to serious despair. It warmed my heart. The *Homo digitalis* was suddenly interested in live arts, in spirituality, and in sex. They were interested in critical culture, in what they called "content." Whatever could bring them back to their bodies and senses and challenge their minds and greedy hearts was suddenly welcome. They were tired of their own social Darwinism. And they didn't even know how to begin the great project of recapturing their sociocultural dimensions, their humanity, and their physical bodies. They tried everything, cybershamans, extreme sports, and escort services, and the fact that they tried real hard was symptomatic of the desperate need for critical culture, for transcendental artistic experiences . . . Now, the problem is that when the corporate elite or the political class decide to look at their own image in the mirror of critical culture, they don't really like what they see. Those who choose to look at themselves in the mirror of critical culture and critical art may find no reflection, or a very ugly one. That's why it's much easier for the rulers and masterminds of Global Culture to sponsor a culture of escapism, in which we all pretend to experience vicariously "real" emotions, "real" danger, "real" depth, "real" Otherness.

There is also the more basic question of the destruction of the infrastructure of critical culture, the de-funding of the arts, of public radio, and public access TV, the closing of alternative spaces and small presses. It's happening all over the world. If we don't stop this madness, the masterminds of globalization are in for a big surprise. If they manage to successfully destroy the infrastructure that supports critical thought and bohemia, its utopian spaces of contestation, deviation, and invention, they will find themselves existing alone in an obnoxiously unlivable world, one sponsored by Microsoft, Sony, Dreamworks, McDonald's, and Starbucks, and that is a real and quite scary possibility. Let's look at this city [San Francisco]. If the gentrification of culture generated by the cyber-gold rush does not derail, San Francisco may very well become a bohemian entertainment park . . . without bohemians, a museum of literature . . . without living writers, a heritage park of difference . . . but without real difference. Then the dot.commers and the technocrats will wake up one day in a world of unbearable sameness. They will look at one another and say: "Shit! This is unbearable . . . It's only us left! What have we done?" Luckily, there are hopeful signs. The "land-grab" era of virtual capitalism seems to have reached an end, and the dot.commers are beginning to drop like flies.

Mendieta: Your performances are about marking the body, the marked body, the branding of bodies. Your dioramas remind me of auction blocks and the parading of bodies for consumption, whether voyeuristic or literal, the way one might check out the bodies of prostitutes. Your bodies are hypereroticized, but this eroticization seems to have overflowed its channels of containment and ruptured out into superorgans and prosthetics. But your marked bodies are also about maiming, wounding, and torturing. Some of your creations include women in wheelchairs, El Mexterminator on crutches, El Veteran Survivor with his tattooed chest and limbs, and so on. Can you talk about this type of branding and marking, which one might say is different from the type of branding and marking that goes on when we are gendering and racializing someone through marking their bodies?

Gómez-Peña: We are attempting to both parody and subvert the strategies of corporate multiculturalism and of what I term the culture of the mainstream bizarre; this superficial fascination that the media has with everything "extreme," with high-definition images of hardcore violence and explicit sexuality; this fascination with revolution-as-style, with stylized hybridity and superficial transculture. This new relationship that the self-proclaimed center has with its margins is one of total voyeurism, of cannibalism and erotic fascination. In this new epistemological relationship between subject and object, between mainstream and subculture, there are no more ethical implications whatsoever—no more guilt, no more sensitivity to cultural difference, no more passionate debates about power and privilege. The backlashers won, *punto*. Ethical dilemmas are perceived as passé, as a black-and-white film on the History Channel, and as politicized artists "of color" we are trying to understand why this has happened. As performance artists we try to offer to the audience the sacrifice and the spectacle of our brown bodies distorted and exaggerated by the media, wounded by pop culture, eroticized by cultural tourism and, at the same time, distanced, mediated by technology, in the hope of triggering a serious process of reflexivity . . . No, when we perform, we are not actors, not even human beings with a fictionalized individuality. We are more like Mexican Frankensteins, artificial freaks, or what I term "ethnocyborgs." In other words, we are one-quarter human, one-quarter technology, one-quarter pop-culture stereotype, and one-quarter audience projection. In fact, the audience completes or alters our identities in situ with make-up and costumes. We even offer the audience the opportunity to directly intervene in our bodies and alter our identities on site. We give them permission to cross that dangerous border. They can touch us, (symbolically) inflict pain on us, point weapons at us, or tag our nude bodies with spray paint. They can even replace us for a short period of time and experience the pleasure of "calling the shots," of determining the fate of the performance. In our recent performance practice, the audience gets to co-direct the piece. And of course they love it. It's more "real" and "real" is good for them. It's a dangerous performance game for us, I know, but we are willing to put ourselves on the line, so to speak, to make an important point: Our physical bodies and social selves are being controlled, manipulated, wounded, surgically intervened, politically mutilated, and we don't seem to mind. It's so sad . . . We actually like it. We love to laugh at the spectacle of the mutilation of our identity and our bodies. That's what media is all about. Whether it is comedy, a talk show, a fiction movie, Reality TV, or a Playstation game, the most popular forms of entertainment nowadays almost always involve some kind of "extreme" humiliation of people of color, women, gays and lesbians, the working class, foreigners, the physically challenged, the unemployed. And people don't seem to mind. Now, how does this affect our performances? Our own audiences are constantly asking us to turn the gaze 180 degrees and inflict violence on them, or humiliate them. No matter where we perform, whether it is in a museum or in a community center, here or abroad, there are always a few audience members who beg us to hurt them. When this happens we have to remind them that "it's only art," that "it's just a symbolic game." Times have really changed in the past four or five years. This has engendered a tremendous ethical dilemma for us.

Mendieta: Technology plays a duplicitous role in your artistic productions. You use it, play with it, reflect on it. Some of your most recent work is precisely about claiming technology. El Webback is about a politics of technological access. But you are also quick to point out how technology is also our curse. Our creations are always turning on us. The Frankenstein curse, if you will. On the other hand, your work seems to suggest that we are borgs who are always being betrayed by the cybernetic in us. Or is it the other way around—that is, is it the biological in us that betrays the synthetic and technological in us?

Gómez-Peña: When Stelarc, the Australian performance artist, created his famous robotic third arm in his attempt to prove that the human body was becoming obsolete, I came up with my own Mexican version. My *robo-garra*. They looked kind of similar, but the main difference was that mine was made out of plastic and it would have a poetic life of its own and rebel against me. It would attack my features, betray my will, deform my identity. Why? In our work, we are interested in what I term "imaginary or poetical technology." The premise is simple: Since Latinos don't have real access to new technologies, we imagine the access. All we have is our political imagination and our humor to interject into the conversation. It's an imaginary act of expropriation, and it is imaginary because reality is simply overwhelming. Less than 3 percent of the population of Latin America is wired, and less than 10 percent of the Chicano/Mexican population in the United States is wired. So what are we really talking about when we use terms like *global* or *access*? Whose global project are we talking about? Access to what? Cyberspace reproduces almost identically the geopolitical cartography of nonvirtual reality. There are borders and there are people south of the digital divide . . . Latinos. That's why I often describe myself as a "Webback," illegally crossing the digital borderline and facing the "cybermigra." Once in cyberspace, my only weapons are my humor, my *linguas polutas* and my political imagination.

Mendieta: Your recent creation, the "Spanglish opera" *Califas 2000*, is subtitled *Jurassic Aztlan*. Here, however, we have a dystopia—the hell of synthetic authenticity, if we can use this oxymoron. One of the projections in this multimedia opera reads, "We manufacture difference." Are you afraid, are you warning us, that the different and heterogeneous, the really different, will be extinguished and replaced by domesticated and manipulated difference—difference à la carte? Are you suggesting that the discourses of difference have been already coopted and have therefore become passé—even de rigueur and establishment—and thus perhaps suspect?

Gómez-Peña: Perhaps the only places where a politicized discussion on difference is taking place are the elite universities and the rarefied theoretical journals. But only a few hundred people are participating in this discussion. In other realms such as the "international" art world, pop culture, and the media, the new fetish is mild difference, tamed difference, stylized difference, low-cal Otherness, stripped of all political implications.

The subjects of identity politics are passé. The new dominant discourse states: We are already installed in a postracist/postsexist society. The new cultural impresarios want sexy images of race and hybridity, but without the political text. Unlike their multicultural or postcolonial predecessors, the new impresarios and self-proclaimed experts of Otherness are no longer interested in the articulation of the tensions and clashes of cultures. They no longer wish to discuss issues of power and privilege. They know better. They don't want their neocolonial positionality questioned by angry primitives and strident women. They suffer from the Vietnam syndrome of the cultural wars. Besides, what they really want is to market Otherness, not to understand it. What the impresarios of global culture want is mild salsa, vegetarian burritos and tofu tamales. They want Zapatista supermodels, not "real" Zapatistas. They want Salma Hayek to play Frida Kahlo. They want "Livin' la Vida Loca" sung by Ricky Martin, not enacted by gang members. If they could, they would have Jennifer Lopez performing the role of Rigoberta Menchú and Jimmy Smith or Banderas performing Subcomandante Marcos. It's ludicrous, but they're getting away with it. They've outsmarted us. As Latinos, our only option, if we want to participate in this new kind of corporate multiculturalism, is to provide them with glossy images of mild difference; if we complain, we are immediately perceived as self-righteous ideologues. In this respect, the pertinent question for performance artists is: How do we continue raising crucial issues without scaring our audiences or without facing deportation back to the margins? My answer, for the moment, is that we must mimic mainstream culture, and when the mirror is standing between them and us, reflecting their fantasies and desires, we break it in the audience's face. If parts of the mirror get in their eyes, that's their problem.

European anthropologist posing with a group of Amazonian women.
(Note the placement of his left hand.)

Mendieta: Wait, don't you run a danger here that people will confuse your mimicry for the real thing, and thus miss the critical potential of your exploding the "caricatures" of Otherness that you parody?

Gómez-Peña: There's always that danger, of course, but we try to provide non-specialized audience members with various clues and coded messages to help them slowly discover the other rooms in the house, so to speak, the hidden meanings and critical edges. But they have to work hard. I don't like to spoon-feed messages to my audience. I want them to engage in an exercise of critical thinking, to participate in a truly democratic exercise. That's why some of our most ambitious performance works last three to four hours, over a three-day period, and people have the option of walking in and out of the space, of designing their own journey, of returning later on, or the next day. It's a multilevel journey, a hypertextual adventure. During this time, people go through various changes of positionality vis-à-vis our work, and the performance triggers various processes of reflexivity. These processes don't get resolved right away. At different times audience members become voyeurs and objects of desire. They may be cultural or sexual tourists at one point and then, when they return later on, they themselves are suddenly placed in the uncomfortable position of exotic creatures or objects of analysis. We are constantly refracting back to them their own projections. In this sense, it's hard for them to escape our work. When an audience member tells me immediately after a performance, "*Ese*, I love your work," "I really understood it," or "I totally agree with you," I always tell them, "Wait, wait for the piece to sink in, to create a sediment in your consciousness. You might not agree with me in a week."

Mendieta: Languages, like biodiversity, are under serious threat. We are witnessing the death of languages at an unprecedented rate, which should make us take serious steps to safeguard linguistic diversity. I think that you are one of the very few performance artists who reflects on the role of language in culture, personal identity, in the politics of exclusion and oppression. Still, from the outside, people are stymied by your apparent noncommittal stance. You are neither a monolingualist nor a bilingualist. If anything, one could say that you are for a kind of multilingualism that seeks to dispense with all grammar and pronunciation cops.

Gómez-Peña: My generation uses Spanglish in a very different way than, say, the previous generation of Chicano poets and performance artists did. With a few exceptions, in the 1970s and 1980s, the combination of Spanish and English in a text was very formulaic: Spanish was reserved for the private realms of home, intimacy, love, family, and memory, and English was meant for the public realm, for politics, for the streets. What my generation did in the late 1980s, early 1990s, was to create a new formula: Spanish and Spanglish would be languages of occultation and complicity, partially forbidden zones, so to speak, and only those fully bilingual would have access, temporary access, to these zones. We, the artists and writers, would determine the nature and content of these zones and broker between audience and content. The objective was to make the audience members or the readers experience how it feels to be partially excluded, to be minorities in their own city, foreigners in their own country, even if only for the duration of the performance. We wanted everyone, at one point or another, to feel partially excluded, because we felt that partial exclusion was a quintessential contemporary experience, a quintessential American experience. Besides, the idea was to create various levels of complicity with different sectors of the audience. So at any given moment some people would be laughing and others wouldn't; some people could access certain political or symbolic meanings that were unavailable to others, and so on and so forth. And we could control this "semiotic alchemy" at will. This is a very different proposition from that of the first generation of Chicano and Nuyorrican writers, who were using bilingualism and Spanglish to map a binary cartography, in which Spanish and Spanglish meant "us" and English meant "you."

Mendieta: What would you say to the accusation that your Spanglish, your patois, your linguistic transgressing and mixing is aiding in the extinction of language diversity? Basically, I am asking what you think is the role of language in a global society.

Gómez-Peña: It is true that my strategic use of Spanglish has engendered some criticism, but curiously this criticism is coming mainly from self-proclaimed purists of Spanglish who believe that there's "real Spanglish" and fake Spanglish, which is totally ludicrous. I mean, how can you be a purist of impurities, *carnal*? To me the real power of Spanglish, all forms of Spanglish, vernacular and self-consciously experimental, is that it destabilizes monoculture, and I am all for it. My job as a Spanglish performance artist is to help all *linguas polutas* circulate and infect the *logos digitalis*. There is also the fear that certain fragile communities express, in the face of rampant globalization, that hybrid culture and Spanglish will destroy their traditions. But let's loosen up: Spanish is not exactly a frail language spoken by ten thousand people in the mountains of southern Mexico. It is one of the main neocolonial lingua francas. So to contaminate it a bit won't hurt it. Besides, Latino culture is cannibalistic in essence. One of the powers of Latino culture is its capability to expropriate colonial culture, to infect and devour imposed cultural forms and turn them inside-out and upside-down. Since the arrival of the Europeans to the not-so-New World, Latin American culture and the Spanish language have always been "impure," syncretic, and hybrid. Latino culture has always fed on the flesh and form of the Other, and this cannibalism might be the very source of our strength. Chicano culture is a prime example. I mean, there is nothing more "impure" and at the same time more powerful than the blending of German polka with Mexican norteño, corrido, and rock and roll to create the sounds of Tex-Mex. Despite the fact that Tex-Mex has created a noble tradition—again, old impurities become new purities—nonetheless its forms are constantly incorporating new ingredients and influences. We now even have Tex-Mex hip-hop and "nortech" (a combination of electrónica and norteño). The same is true of performance art. We are the illegitimate *mestizo* children of art, theater, and literature, of "high" and "low" culture, and our job is to remain open to new influences, not to set fixed theoretical parameters. In fact, the strength of performance lies in its indefinable nature, in its hybrid and ever-changing nature. The day you can define it, it stops being performance.

Mendieta: Guillermo, sometimes you identify yourself as a Chicano artist. What do you mean by this term if we keep in mind your creations, like the ethnocyborgs and El Webback, and other such personifications of metonymy that militate against ethnic and racial essentialism?

Gómez-Peña: Performance art has taught me that I can reinvent my identity at will, that we are not necessarily straitjacketed by identity. Performance has taught me that props, make-up, tattoos, costumes, fashion, hairdos, constructed social behavior, and language also determine how we are perceived by others, and that we can be creative about this. In fact, a big part of my body of work is an exercise in the reinvention of identity. To me ethnic identification can be both strategic and contextual. When it is pertinent and politically necessary, given a certain context, I choose to define myself as a Chicano, meaning a politicized Mexican-American, and this implies that I am occupying a certain conceptual space when I speak. Other times I strategically choose to define myself as a Latino (any person of Latin American descent living in the USA), or as an American in the widest sense of the term, as a continental "American." It really depends on my audience, the site, and the nature of the debate.

Mendieta: Give me a few concrete examples.

Gómez-Peña: When I go back to Mexico to perform, in order to challenge Mexican ethnocentrism, I choose to present myself as a Chicano. However, if I'm performing for an all-Anglo audience in the United States, I choose to present myself as an American to fuck with their narrowminded notions of Americanness. When I am engaging in a dialogue with non-Chicano US Latinos, it is better for me to define myself as a Latino, a wider conceptual territory, in order to establish alliances and connections. When I go to Europe, in order to avoid exoticization, I present myself as a "diasporic artist." This way I am able to establish connections with British Pakistanis, French Algerians, German Turks, and Spanish Moroccans. Am I being clear? Deep inside I really believe that all terms to articulate complex identities are imperfect and dated. Our new realities and multiple repertoires of identities demand a new nomenclature.

Mendieta: I would like to close with this question. Everything is dragged along and pushed forward by the iron logic of relentless innovation; everything must be made new, newer, everything has to be the newest thing. But in the euphoria of this temporal fix—for we are junkies of futurity—everything has become old; the new turns out to be no more than the newest old thing recycled. Our new newest is the new or newest of the old and oldest. Everything is already old precisely because everything wanted to be the newest of some already bygone time. Such premature decrepitude and aging characteristic of our times is reflected in the fact that we can't think past the "post." Everything is post this or post that. How do we escape this logic? How do we begin to dream and think beyond the "posts" that weigh on our dreams like nightmares of the dead?

Gómez-Peña: *Ay loco*, that's the ultimate question: How do we escape this post-posty labyrinth we've gotten ourselves into? Our relentless desire for innovation seems to be like a Moebius strip. As a performance artist, this dilemma becomes even graver since, unlike any other art field, the performance field defines itself in direct opposition to both the immediate tradition and the prior generation. We are supposed to be the vanguard of the vanguard, and our job is supposed to be to explore the outer limits of culture. So, in order for performance artists to remain at the table of debates, we are forced to constantly reinvent ourselves and come up with an entirely "new" and "original" project. Every year we need to come up with a brand-new conceptual proposal that emerges out of the most current debates and theoretical trends. *Que joda* (What a burden), *¿qué no*? Because of this acritical cult of innovation and originality, performance artists are often trapped in a vertiginous dynamics of perpetual reinvention, but since there's nothing really new or "original" anymore, all we do is reinvent a "new" language to rename what we are already doing, to come up with yet another framing device, another subtitle so to speak. And if we don't do the new, new thing ourselves, the art critics will do it for us. And when others begin to label you and you lose control of the naming process, that's your kiss of death. The question gets even more complicated when we realize that theoretical trends in the art world only last a few years, which is ridiculous. To give you an example, in the early 1980s when I got started as a young artist in California, I was considered just a "Mexican artist." Then in the mid-1980s I was a "multicultural artist." In the late 1980s I suddenly became "el border artist" extraordinaire. Later on, in the early 1990s, I was rebaptized a "community artist," which at the time was a euphemism for a non-Anglo artist, remember? And then, when hybridity became chic, I became a "hybrid artist." When the backlash era began in 1993–4, and the debates on identity politics were declared passé by conservative esthetes like Arthur Danto and Robert Hughes, many of us experimentalists were forced to redefine ourselves as "techno-artists," which was a more politically neutral term that avoided all the highly charged terminology of identity politics. Now even "techno-art" is passé, and we all are looking for new adjectives to name what we do. Nowadays everything is retro-, meta-, neo-, ultra-, and posmo-. The serpent is not just biting its own tail, but devouring itself and replaying the video tape obsessively.

Our philosophical and political dilemmas are always reflected in the symbolic territory of language, and for the moment we seem to lack a language that can help us articulate complexity and depth with clarity. This semiotic crisis is complicated by the fact that corporations, media conglomerates, and computer firms have hijacked all progressive language. And so has the Right. Today words like "revolutionary," "radical," and "progressive" are being overused on MTV and the Internet. So, we "progressive artists" are constantly asking ourselves, how do we rename the world if corporate America has hijacked all progressive languages? How do we heal the word? How do we escape elliptical theoretical discussions and solipsistic terminology in order to find a new clarity? Marcos once told José Saramago that the Zapatista revolution was first and foremost a language revolution. The genius of the Zapatistas was to create a fresh new language, a poetic language that could cut across ideological bullshit and still articulate theoretical complexity, but in a way that could appeal to a wide spectrum of people, from *campesinos* to intellectuals. *Zapatismo* was essentially a framing device, a new way of naming the world that suddenly made sense to a lot of people. We need to learn that lesson from them. Where are the *pinche* poets when we need them, *carnal*?

Zapatista supermodel crucified by the IMF.
Michelle Ceballos. Gran Canaria, 2000. Photo: Nacho Gonzalez.

24

The minefields of Utopia

A dialogue on the dangers of artistic collaboration

(Excerpts, 2000)

Lisa Wolford and Guillermo Gómez-Peña

Introduction

Lisa Wolford

The material for this interview was distilled from conversations that took place over a two-week period in late May and early June 1999, while La Pocha Nostra was in residence at the Centre for Performance Research in Aberystwyth, Wales. In contrast to more formalized interview situations, Guillermo and I spoke in the midst of quotidian activities, as people smoked, drank coffee, exercised, and otherwise prepared for rehearsal and daily life. While I have tried, in the editing process, to smooth over fragmentation in the text, both the occasional discontinuities in the interview and the relatively charged nature of certain topics discussed can perhaps be attributed to the dynamic of informal conversation among artistic colleagues who know one another well. In the months since this conversation was recorded, various changes of personnel have occurred within La Pocha Nostra, with certain collaborators becoming progressively more present in the work and others moving in directions that allow them to explore independent creative projects. By the time this text gets published, most likely La Pocha Nostra will have new membership.

Wolford: For much of the course of your work, you've tended to collaborate for long periods of time with various ensemble companies—first Poyesis Genetica, then Border Arts Workshop, and more recently La Pocha Nostra. What draws you to collaborative work, and what are some of the challenges, especially when artists work together in ways that push them to negotiate various axes of difference—of gender, ethnicity, culture, or professional background, for example?

Gómez-Peña: I was very influenced by the *grupos* in Mexico City in the 1970s, the interdisciplinary collectives of the generation prior to mine. Felipe Ehrenberg was one of my godfathers. Very much in the spirit of the times, his generation created interdisciplinary collectives and utilized the streets of Mexico City as laboratories of experimentation, as *galerias sin paredes* (galleries without walls). At the same time, in the late 1970s, when I moved to California, I was surprised to find that there were also many Chicano collectives, such as ASCO and the Royal Chicano Airforce. It was the spirit of the times. I think that the spirit behind it was a kind of utopian impulse, believing that to share visions, resources, and efforts could only multiply the impact of art in society. Also, the belief that collaboration is a form of citizen diplomacy, which later on became the original impetus behind the creation of the legendary Border Arts Workshop (BAW/TAF). If a binational, multiracial, crossgenerational collective can in fact function in the real world, then maybe it's possible on a larger scale to sort out our differences and cultural conflicts . . . I think that it's this kind of utopian impulse that has led me to work in a collaborative manner.

Wolford: What have you found to be some of the challenges of collaborative work?

Gómez-Peña: You are asking me to walk on a minefield . . . But hey, it's important stuff to deal with, and I'll do it. I think that this very utopian impulse I'm talking about carries its own seed of destruction, the fact that no matter how hip and progressive we think we are, we inevitably end up reproducing autocratic, separatist behavior . . . It's basic human nature. If you work within a collective devoted to crosscultural or crossgender dialogue in an effort to create a more enlightened model of racial and gender relations, trying to deal with these issues directly, in this very quest it's possible to end up hyperintensifying the problem, and being devoured by one's own utopian dreams. Sadly, BAW/TAF was not able to erase the borders amongst ourselves, the very same borders we were attempting to erase in the larger society, so we succumbed to our own sexism, our own racism, our own cultural prejudice, our own fears and stupidity. Chicanos and Mexicans within the group were unable to overcome our mutual resentments so as to understand one another and develop a new mode of relationship. The men's attempt to be more egalitarian with our women colleagues failed. And as you know, this has happened to so many collectives . . . There is also the thorny issue of mixing artistic collaboration and intimate relationships.

Wolford: Isn't it true that in BAW/TAF, at a certain point, most of the people in the group were involved with other collaborators? How did this contribute to the tensions within that group?

Gómez-Peña: Some were involved, not everybody . . . but that was inevitable, especially when people are young, full of hormones and rage, and committed to a political cause. I call it the Rock and Roll Syndrome. See, you share so much of your time touring and working late hours that your life revolves around the collective. It's almost inevitable that people end up being sexually involved with members of the group. And this creates friction, favoritism, jealousy. If a relationship breaks within the collective, that ends up affecting the group dynamics and poisoning the entire collaborative process. It's a recurrent problem in most collectives. It's part of the untold history of collaboration, how sexual desire ends up getting in the way of utopian ideas . . . Shit, I'm sounding like a Chicano Foucault!

Wolford: Better that than a Chilango Freud. But seriously, no one in La Pocha Nostra is involved with any other member of the group—not just within the core ensemble, but throughout the company. Everyone has committed relationships outside of the group, and that has to make a huge difference in terms of interpersonal dynamics.

Gómez-Peña: We're militant about that. It's probably the only thing that we're militant about, and I'm convinced that's why we have survived for so many years. We are extremely close, but the first commandment of La Pocha Nostra is to not get sexually intimate with one another for the wellbeing of the work. We respect each other's personal lives and decisions. We protect each other's backs.

Wolford: And each other's privacy.

Gómez-Peña: Precisely. We respect each other's spiritual eccentricities and the eccentricities of each person's sexual relationships outside of the group, but we keep them outside the rehearsal space. It's quite healthy. We no longer operate on the model of the family, the clan, or the leftist or swinger collective, which is very healthy. In prior collectives, it always seemed like the group really became the center of everyone's lives, and this isn't at all the case in La Pocha Nostra. Each member of the company has a full life, keeps other jobs, and takes separate vacations. Our public and social lives overlap, but we also have different milieux of friends . . . Also, we work with an outer circle of collaborators who live in different parts of the USA, Mexico, and Canada. See, Juan [Ybarra] is living in Canada, Leticia [Nieto] in Seattle, Michelle [Ceballos] in Phoenix, you're in Ohio, Violeta [Luna] is in Mexico City, and the rest of the *flota* is in San Francisco. We usually work intensely with these wonderful people for short durations on specific projects, then each person goes back to their own home and their own life. As a general notion of artistic community, this seems much healthier. We're like a global collective, in the best sense of the term "global". It took us many years and lots of mistakes to discover this fluid and highly functional model.[1]

Wolford: I want to switch topics somewhat and also time periods. In La Pocha Nostra, all of the people you're working with define their professional identities in terms of some aspect of performance—performance artists, dancer-choreographers, etc. You make a clear distinction between core collaborators and more peripheral or occasional contributors to the process, and also between members of the group and what you call "involuntary performance artists"—people that you bring in for a specific project. It seems to me that all the people you work with now have strong, independent professional identities outside of the work you do together. How does this affect the collaborative process? I mean this in terms of both the advantages and disadvantages of working in a situation where everyone defines themselves largely in relation to outside projects, as well as the fact that everyone is bringing to the table what they do well and not running the risk of becoming a dilettante by crossing outside of their own milieux.

Gómez-Peña: The structure we have found that really works is very simple. You have three core collaborators, Roberto Sifuentes, Juan Ybarra, and me, who are involved in most of the performance projects. And Nola Mariano, of course, our beloved agent/manager and holy protector of our backs in the mean streets of the art world. It's like the first circle, the *flota pesada*, so to speak. I still do some solo work, but it's really a small portion of the work we do, maybe 30 percent. Most performance projects involve at least three core collaborators.

Then we have this outer circle of people like Sara Shelton Man, Michelle Ceballos, Rona Michelle, and Gustavo Vasquez, who are involved in about half of our projects, and who still have their own work outside. And then there is a third circle of people involved in specific projects, like actress Norma Medina and performance artist Carmel Kooros, who worked on *The Temple of Confessions*, and Violeta Luna and Yoshi Maeshiro, who worked on *The Mexterminator Project*, and so on and so forth. Then there's yet another, very ephemeral outer circle that involves local artists and eccentrics who join the process a week or two before opening night. They join a workshop. There are usually ten to fifteen of them. It's only for the major projects that the whole community comes together, for the really large-scale versions of *The Mexterminator Project*, *Borderscape 2000*, or the opera . . .

1 See "Crosscontaminations," pp. 77–93.

Wolford: Earlier, when we were talking about the utopian impulse of collaboration across métier, across culture, across gender, you said that you believe this impulse carries the seeds of its own demise. Do you think that the seasonal, periodic nature of La Pocha Nostra, the rhythm of the work with the core collaborators and the intermediate and outer circles, makes it easier to sustain this impulse over a longer period? People can work together for a month or two, but then they go away for six months, and then they come back. Is that part of what makes it easier to have these collaborative relationships, or are they still difficult? I'm looking at this from a more distant place, as someone who participates in maybe three or four projects a year, so I don't necessarily always see where the tensions are within the group.

Gómez-Peña: There are some difficulties. Mainly because I carry on my shoulders the sole financial responsibility for La Pocha Nostra, and that is a problem we haven't been able to solve, a sort of paternalistic structure which can become a drag. I sometimes feel like Buffalo Bill's Wild West Show, dragging the caravan on my shoulders. And of course people don't mind it. When the shit hits the fan in terms of money, understandably, no one is there to help. I have to face the IRS. I have to go to the lawyers. I have to get out of debt. I have to go on the road as a solo performer for a couple of months to bring back money and pay our debts. It's a pain in the *culo*. But I assume full responsibility for not preventing this problem. La Pocha Nostra is currently embarked on a process of reinvention in an attempt to decentralize this model after all these years. We are making all performers more accountable and proactive . . .

Wolford: Are there other sorts of issues beyond the financial that you sometimes find difficult to negotiate?

Gómez-Peña: Another problem I think has to do with cultural and methodological differences, which are potentially dangerous at times, but which we don't shy away from. We have managed to survive these differences. For example, Roberto and I come from more activist backgrounds. I see myself as a public intellectual first, then a performance artist. Roberto is the same. Our work in the public sphere is completely connected to our work onstage. To do a benefit for La Galeria de la Raza or for a farmworker organization is as important for us as to perform for the Corcoran Gallery of Art, if not more so. To do a workshop with Latino youth at La Peña or at MICA [a Native American community arts center in Montana] for Native Americans is as important as to go to an international performance festival. Our other colleagues don't necessarily share this attitude toward art . . . Another occasional problem is the fact that our extremely irreverent working methodologies don't necessarily jive very well with people who come from highly trained backgrounds, especially actors and dancers. So a lot of wonderful collaborators go crazy when they are in the rehearsal room with us. They want more discipline, more direction, they want more rehearsal time, and less blah-blah . . . You know, when conceptual artists who use performance as a strategy get together with trained performers, major negotiations have to take place. It's inevitable. We now allow for the coexistence of a multiplicity of methodologies and preparation methods in our performance.

Wolford: For example?

Gómez-Peña: Before we go on stage, Roberto and I might be toasting with the crew in the dressing room and talking with friends, while Sara and Juan are talking to the Great Spirit, doing tai chi, or stretching somewhere in the theater. We are learning to make room for each other's ways of preparing. Also, after years of working with them, Roberto and I are becoming increasingly more conscious of the importance of training our bodies and developing a performance pedagogy, while our colleagues are engaging more seriously with the philosophical, esthetic, and political dilemmas inherent in the work.

Wolford: Believe me, I understand what you're talking about in terms of feeling a little . . . off-balance, I guess, relating to La Pocha Nostra's creative methods. It was very difficult at first for me to get used to the ethos of your rehearsals, and I've often joked that the biggest crosscultural negotiation I've had to make in working with you has nothing to do with ethnic or national differences but rather with the expectations and conditioning that come from working in very different sorts of performance cultures. I would imagine that it's often a difficult adjustment for actors and dancers not to have a director in the conventional sense who tells them what to do.

Gómez-Peña: It can drive actors crazy. But at the same time, what attracts a lot of physical actors and dancers, even opera singers, to work with us is precisely the lack of hierarchy and authoritarian structures in the work, and that is exactly what they end up missing in the moment of truth. So many people have told us that. So many people have said that they came to us in the first place because it was such a relaxed and democratic process, a decentered process, a fun process, and then in the middle of the process they started getting nervous because they were not receiving clear commands and direction. I think it's a scary proposition to assume more political and esthetic responsibility for your actions onstage, to become more autonomous as an artist, to become a better collaborator. I see it as part of a democratic process . . .

Wolford: Moving back and forth among different professional realms as you do—working as a performer, an *animateur*, a cultural critic, a radio commentator, a journalist, an activist, not to mention occasionally as a sound designer—definitely requires a particular and unusual combination of skills. How do you negotiate your different roles, and specifically how do you balance the aspects of performer and public intellectual?

Extreme fashion show at *The Museum of Fetishized Identities.*
María Eugenia Chellet. Museo del Chopo, Mexico City, 2003. Photo: Enrique Gonzalez.

Gómez-Peña: After twenty years of crossing interdisciplinary borders, I have managed to get good at it, to somehow solve this crisis of professional identity. No matter what I do outside the realm of performance, whether it is recording a radio commentary for *All Things Considered*, teaching a theoretical class, conducting a hands-on workshop, or organizing a town meeting, I try to do it from the positionality of a performance artist. Conceptually, I always occupy a performative space, and my voice in that particular realm is an extension of my performance voices. As corny as it may sound, for me, everything I do is performance, of course with the exception of love—my love for Carolina, for my son, for my mother, for my friends, that's not performance. It may be performative—extremely performative—but it's not performance per se. . . .

Wolford: No, of course not, not if you're thinking of performance in the sense of something fake.

Gómez-Peña: No, I didn't mean it in that sense. For me performance is never fake. It's just a different way to tell the truth.

Wolford: But even in your most intimate relationships, you bring people into a theatricalized realm. I'm thinking of photos of your mother and son in costume in different performance personae . . .

Gómez-Peña: Sure, my family is very eccentric. But I understand that this is my *onda*, my trip, and not necessarily other people's, especially people who tend to operate in a more monodisciplinary mode and whose notions of the borders between performance and other realms are more fixed. In other words, I know that if I need to invite someone to speak to a specific political issue, I won't choose a preverbal dancer or vice versa. I would never invite Carlos Fuentes or Henry Giroux to be part of a performance piece strictly as performers and ask them to wear punk mariachi suits so as to be more effective as intellectuals, the same way I would never invite a *zapotec* shaman or a Chicano activist to participate strictly as performers in one of our pieces. Though there are always exceptions to the rule, I understand the clear differences and the contextual problems involved. I'm tempted to cross these borders, but I won't do it. For me respect is essential.

Wolford: Of course, Giroux is a good example of an intellectual who has a clear sense of how to present his ideas in a dynamic, performative way, a way that's compelling and captivating and doesn't leave people in the audience thinking "nice ideas, but I'd rather be reading this." I can also think of a couple of occasions where you've included Baldemar Velasquez, who's a very important Chicano activist, in some of your pieces, in one instance as a musician as part of a spoken-word performance in Toledo, and also in your performative town meetings, though there (if I understand correctly) it was basically the framing of the event that was performative rather than the way that the activists participated.

Gómez-Peña: Exactly. Within the larger realm of the performance, we opened a space for political debate in which activists and scholars could perform their ideas, or, better said, where they could be a bit more performative as speakers. After all, they needed to compete with skilled spoken-word poets and performance artists, so they became acutely aware of presentational matters, of efficiency and timing, even of costuming. They all showed up dressed to kill. However, there is a difference between intellectuals and activists trying to present their ideas in a performative way, which is extremely desirable and which I think is the case with people like Giroux and Baldemar, versus esthetic theoreticians who want to become performance artists overnight, which is not in itself a bad thing, but it rarely produces any interesting art, *¿qué no*? Am I being clear, sister?

Wolford: Very clear. It can be very risky for people to work in a performative way if they don't have some degree of training or background, or at the very least a kind of innate aptitude that gives them a sense of whether or not what they're doing creates the effect they want.

Gómez-Peña: I think it's inevitable that intellectuals in the performance-art field want to perform their ideas, since one of the many paradoxes in the field is that traditionally people have been dealing with radical ideas in very conservative formats. So the question here is how can you reconcile the fact that radical theoreticians are presenting two-hour long papers dealing with radical ideas in the most traditional and authoritative way, standing behind a lectern under neon light in horrible rooms at nine in the morning? I think the field is hyperaware of this problem, and they want to jazz it up a little bit, to make it sexier, and to find more radical formats to present innovative ideas. That is an extremely legitimate goal and I wholeheartedly encourage it, even if not all of their experiments are entirely successful. Most radical theorists have to figure out more performative ways to be compelling and innovative in how they present these radical ideas, otherwise there is an inherent contradiction. I don't want to sound so frivolous as to think that if an intellectual is not charismatic and performative and doesn't know how to deliver their ideas that we shouldn't pay attention to them. I understand that intelligence, in the era of spectacle, is also spectacle. To see intelligence at work can be extremely seductive and compelling. I just happen to believe that often radical intellectuals don't acknowledge the importance of context, of staging, when presenting their ideas.

Wolford: But even though intelligence is a spectacle, if someone has great ideas and a beautiful text but no vocal or performance skills, their points aren't going to get across.

Gómez-Peña: Nowadays, particularly since we are living in an information-based society, a highly visual, mediatized society, intellectuals should understand that we all have to learn how to package our ideas, how to make them sexy and more accessible to larger audiences, how to present them in interesting ways. Otherwise we will be condemned to speak only to our immediate colleagues, to remain trapped in academia, a self-referential concentration camp of the mind. Of course this is dangerous, because if we take this task too seriously we might lose the complexity of our thoughts and end up creating inventories of sound-bites, which seems to be the only possible way one can be an intellectual in the US media . . .

Wolford: What I sense running through this conversation as an almost unspoken but foundational subtext is an understanding that different types of communicative strategies function in different venues. In a spoken-word performance, one kind of writing is going to be successful, in a critical text something else, in a radio piece for *Latino USA* something else yet again . . . Even though you recycle material and create different montages by creating various juxtapositions out of a certain set of building blocks, there is always a sense of strategy in your work. You know what is going to get across to an audience on radio, and you know very well how far you can push the envelope on *All Things Considered* as opposed to what you can get away with saying on *Latino USA*. This kind of strategic understanding of different media and formats seems to me extraordinarily crucial, and yet in many ways not sufficiently acknowledged by a number of intellectuals. If you're going to operate in different venues, you have to know each of those venues very well and understand who your listener is, who your reader is, what the boundaries are in that specific forum, what kind of knowledge base and level of engagement you can presume.

Gómez-Peña: Sure, I think this is one of the spooky byproducts of globalization: The more globalized the world becomes, the more unable we are to communicate across borders. But at the same time performance artists have become extremely savvy linguistic alchemists and semioticians. We understand the importance of cultural context and translation in the shaping of a message, and we know that art does not necessarily translate to different contexts and audiences in the way the art world wishes us to believe. Art is not universal. We know that the meaning of our actions and symbols changes when crossing a geopolitical border, sometimes dramatically so . . . But then again, we operate as border semioticians. So our performance strategies are different, for example, when we perform in Mexico as opposed to working in the USA. The proportion of English and Spanish shifts. The amount and nature of humor shifts, the notions of transgression and radicalism shift as well. The positionality we assume within the work shifts. I mean, when a performance crosses a border, it becomes a different piece.

Wolford: I can see these kinds of shifts even when you move from, say, a university campus to a prominent art gallery or a Chicano community center.

Gómez-Peña: In certain Chicano contexts, our politics become more present, more overt. In other contexts, say in the art world, we can be more formally experimental or more sexually explicit. In certain circumstances, we have to do pieces that aren't language-based. One of the reasons why *The Mexterminator Project* doesn't have spoken text has to do with the fact that we wanted to take this performance to other parts of the world, so the performance needed to be more visual and experiential.

Wolford: How do you contextualize the culturally specific imagery of *Mexterminator* when you move away from the Mexican border region? Here in Aberystwyth (Wales), for example, people can't be assumed to share the same points of reference as an audience in the southwest of the USA.

Gómez-Peña: The images of our diorama performances are strangely familiar in other countries because these multihybrid stereotypes have been successfully broadcast by US media to the rest of the world. Am I clear? The context for *The Mexterminator Project* has become strangely internationalized thanks to global pop culture . . . but still, we have to make some changes, strip the hyper-regional specificities from the performance, and add some pertinent program notes. Our local collaborators also help us to anchor the piece in the new site. They provide site-specific imagery and local issues to the work. Now, when we deal with a language piece in Spanglish, the alchemy we have to engage in is even more complicated and the borders we must cross are much more extreme. If we perform a language-based piece in Hamburg or Helsinki, we definitely have to make major changes and strip the text of all its regional references, translate certain sections into their language, and create conceptual connections with local diasporic communities. It's a major translation challenge. That's why my language-based work takes place mostly in English-speaking countries.

Wolford: To what extent do you have to worry about context and the kinds of references people will bring to your work when you're dealing with radio pieces?

Gómez-Peña: I have developed an interesting consensual agreement with my editors at *All Things Considered* (National Public Radio). They understand the uniqueness of my voice: I am first and foremost a performance artist who also happens to be a cultural critic, as opposed to a performance artist trying to impersonate a journalist. They like that uniqueness, the fact that I speak as a performance chronicler. At the same time, I understand that I have to mimic the format of public radio to a certain extent. If I'm too experimental and too crazy in one of my radio pieces, I know that my editors will call me back and say, "Gómez-Peña, it doesn't fly. It's too weird." There is a constant negotiation, and I don't always win. The same goes for our work in TV. In order to operate in multiple realms and cross over with dignity into more populist domains, performance artists have to be pop-cultural semioticians before anything else, even before we are performance artists, otherwise we are out of the game . . . It's a double challenge: Mainstream culture has to open up to include critical intellectual voices and experimental artists, and we ourselves have to develop populist strategies that don't compromise the complexity of our ideas. We badly need a third option.

Wolford: Going back to what you said before about your editors at NPR understanding your voice, that you're a performance artist who happens to be a cultural critic . . . You understand that distinction very well because you've also worked as a journalist.

Gómez-Peña: As a performance artist I am allowed to have a frantic voice, to be as strident as I can, and to be as contradictory as I am. As a journalist, I'm not allowed any of these privileges, and it's very difficult for me. In America, there's still the myth of "objectivity," the naïve belief that we can document or chronicle "reality" in some way that's beyond ideology, and also a sense that your ideas have to be narrative and monodimensional when it comes to journalism. With a few exceptions, journalism in America is very poor. I am perplexed by how naïve people are in terms of accepting this optical illusion of distance and objectivity. Journalists treat citizens as infants, and we let them treat us as such . . .

Wolford: There's often a tendency to freeze artists at a particular moment in time.

Gómez-Peña: Art history basically wants to list artists by tricks. You become known for a trick, for a style, for one piece you did, for a bombastic incident with which you were involved, and then your wings get pinned against the wall, you are given a taxonomy, and you become part of art history. Perhaps this was inevitable during modernism, but nowadays, an artist has to be constantly redefining themself and their strategies, metaphors, and languages. Our capability to reinvent ourselves must be as rapid as the changing cultural realities we wish to address. Still the art world wishes to freeze us in one particular instance, put us inside an ice cube, and we're constantly fighting to get out of the ice cube. It's a neverending ritual.

25

The minefields of Dystopia

The pervasive effects of 9/11

(Excerpts, 2001–2)

Lisa Wolford and Guillermo Gómez-Peña

Introduction

Guillermo Gómez-Peña

This series of conversations took place in cyberspace in the months following 9/11. The ideas presented, as well as the tone of the conversations, reflect the challenges and uncertainties that US artists and intellectuals faced during this period. Though times have since changed in certain respects, we felt it was important to publish this text as it represents a crucial paradigm shift in the way artists and intellectuals think about our work.

Early November, 2001

Gómez-Peña: Following the events of September 11, the fetishization of Otherness by the global media and the sanctioned culture of extreme behavior as depicted

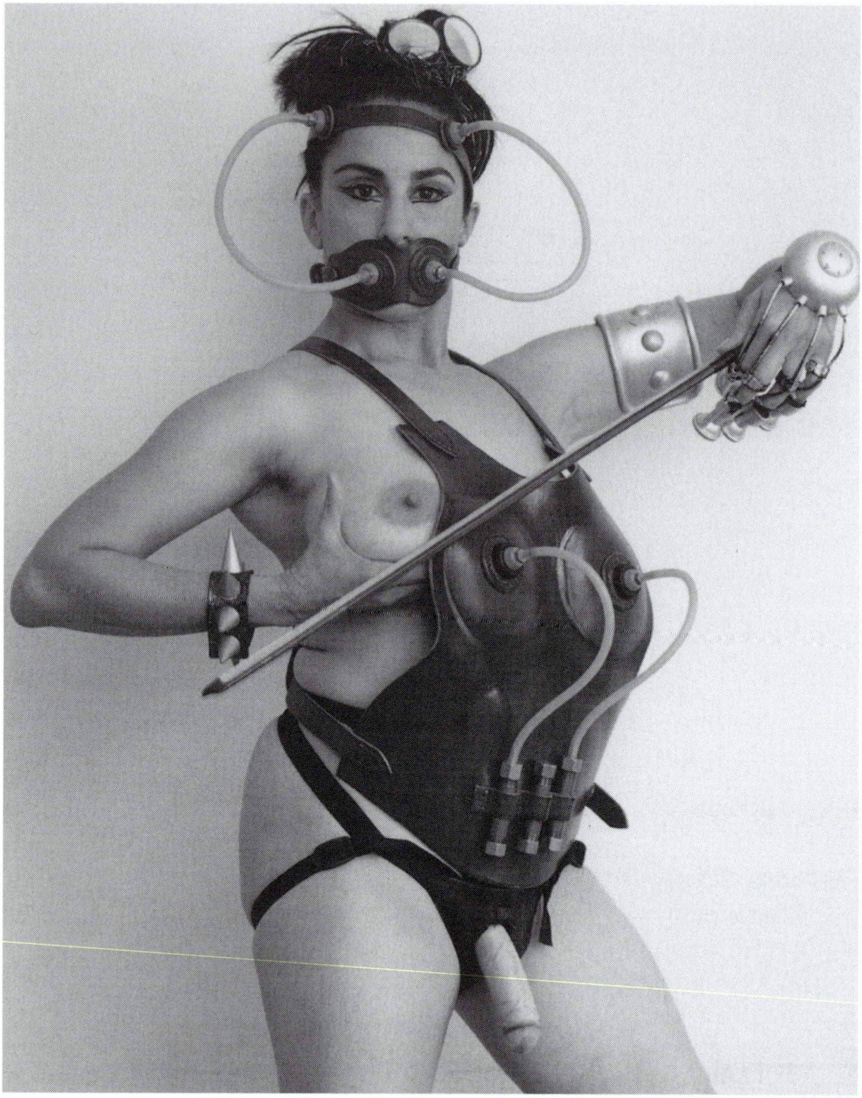

Cyborg violinist made in Taiwan.
Michelle Ceballos. Liverpool Biennial, 2002. Photo: Manual Vason.

on TV, movies, and the Internet have suddenly become unfashionable again. The Other is once again perceived as seriously threatening, as "un-American." There's been a total overnight shift of parameters and attitudes toward, say, brown people. We are no longer hip, sexy, and exotic creatures on the global menu. In the world according to Bush and his evangelical cowboys, we are all "suspicious."

The "mainstream bizarre" has been temporarily deported back to the old silent margins, and dominant culture has become once again extremely centralized, authoritarian, euphemistic, and artificially wholesome . . . like in the 1950s. It's back to the pre-civil rights era. It is no coincidence that the two most popular movies of the season are *Harry Potter* and *The Lord of the Rings*. Americans want to escape. The world seems too incomprehensibly frightening.

Wolford: What I find truly startling about the extreme popularity of those movies is the extent to which political discourse in this country echoes the rhetoric of those films. Americans are being encouraged to consume *The Fellowship of the Ring* as a kind of political allegory; there are actually advertisements for the film that make a pointed citation of the events of September 11. Hearing Bush speak about "the evil one," it's as if he imagines himself as a hero out of Tolkien's stories, sending his minions off to do battle with the Dark Lord. I enjoy science-fiction and fantasy literature, but I worry when CNN starts sounding like something from a sword-and-sorcery epic.

Gómez-Peña: Contemporary US electronic media seems like a huge Hollywood war production sponsored by the Pentagon in cahoots with big entertainment corporations. It's also a huge propaganda machine, the biggest ever, the most efficient ever. It has nothing to do with real investigative reporting. Those guys at Fox News and MSNBC are practically receiving orders from the generals and the puppeteers of the Bush administration, orders about what to say and what not to say. Their ideological biases and ethnocentrism are so obvious that the whole world is laughing at us.

Wolford: Government control of broadcast media has been quite overt in the past few months.

Gómez-Peña: This is outrageous if we consider that one of the main ethical functions of the media in a self-perceived "democracy" ought to be to monitor the behavior of the government, not to sanction it uncritically . . .

Times are really strange. Artists are being asked by Washington to suspend all critical thought and to not voice our disagreements. We are also being asked to revise our artistic vocabulary and tone it down. Words that were part of our performance lingo like "radical," "revolutionary," "transgressive," and "extreme" have now been overlaid with the demonizing meanings of the Bush doctrine and the Patriot Act, which means we are no longer in control of their meaning. Suddenly everybody is tiptoeing around delicate issues, and artists are being forced to revise our repertoire of images and metaphors to either make sure we don't "offend" American patriots, or that we don't get a sudden visit from the FBI. It's wild.

Wolford: What kind of impact has all this had in terms of your work as an itinerant performance artist?

Gómez-Peña: The USA reminds me nowadays of the way Mexico used to be twenty years ago, when we were all scared of the PRI. A few American presenters have politely asked me to please retitle my piece, or to not bring up certain issues during the post-performance discussion with the audience. One presenter openly told me, "Guillermo, let's wait one more year to bring you to our city. Things right now are . . . delicate." "What do you mean exactly?" I asked him. He answered after an eternal pause: "You know . . . I don't want to lose the little funding we have left." "Poor coward," I thought to myself.

Wolford: So does it seem to you that there's a general movement back toward a more Disneyfied, feelgood multiculturalism, even among educational and arts institutions?

Gómez-Peña: In some cases, yes. Those presenters who are scared of losing their funding or getting their boards and sponsors angry are, in fact, taking the safe route and canceling any potentially controversial programs and replacing them overnight with apolitical art, with escapist or euphemistic art. Exhibits and film festivals dealing with politically sensitive issues, or simply with "Arab" culture, have been indefinitely suspended . . . But to be fair, many other presenters, I must say, are quite valiant. I've heard some presenters say: "Today, more than ever, we need to present this kind of work." So, both things are happening. It's a time of major readjustments. We are all facing major ethical dilemmas.

Early January, 2002

Wolford: I know that you've sometimes been subjected to ridiculous harassment when you've entered the USA from Mexico, like the time when you were traveling with your son and the border guards decided you must be a child-pornographer and went through all the raw video footage you were in the middle of editing for a performance project. I'm sure you hoped that once you officially became a binational citizen, that sort of thing would stop. Evidently in the new world order of surveillance, that hasn't been the case.

Gómez-Peña: No, it's actually gotten worse, much worse. Ethnic profiling is now accepted behavior, official policy, and "Arab-looking" people, including most Latinos and brown people, have become an ongoing source of anxiety and mistrust for true "patriotic" Americans. One of my recent performance personae is the "Tali-Vato" a Chicano hipster who morphs back and forth into a generic Arab terrorist. Because of this new racism, brown people are being forced to overstate their patriotism as a mere survival strategy. It's sad to see so many Chicanos, Salvadoreans, Arabs, and Pakistanis putting humungous flags outside their businesses and homes just to avoid getting harassed by "patriotic" neighbors. . . .

Touring has actually become scary. We lost one of our Mexican collaborators for a while. When flying from Montreal to Mexico City to take a break between projects, our colleague made a stop in Atlanta, and a border guard, empowered by the state of "maximum alert," saw our colleague's intensely ethnic features and decided to invalidate his multiple-entry visa. Just like that. Despite pressures from the Mexican consulate and from top cultural officials in Mexico, our colleague wasn't allowed to return to the USA and join us in our next project. It wasn't until late December, two months later, that he was able to obtain a new visa. It's crazy, and the US politicians want us to go back to "our normal lives." They must be kidding.

Last week in my NPR commentary I whimsically mentioned that in order to survive the ongoing harassment of TWAL (traveling while Arab-looking), my colleagues and I have developed a repertoire of hyperethnic "amigo" looks such as the gallant mariachi, the Tex-Mex rocker and the Native American dandy.[1] Carolina [Ponce de Leon] and Michelle [Ceballos] now travel as hyper-Latinas, wearing lots of make-up and bright colors to not be mistaken for generic Arab women . . . But still, our props keep getting confiscated. A few weeks ago, Michelle and I were to perform in Boston. When we arrived at Logan airport, our trunks, filled with ethno-techno gear and weird fetish artifacts, were immediately confiscated by airport security. They kept them for three days. Give me a million breaks! I can imagine those forensic experts examining each and every prop with their chemical kit: our wrestling masks, our donkey jawbones handpainted with withcraft-looking symbols, our jalapeño dildo. I can see them thinking "What the fuck?" . . . If it wasn't for a nice security officer who Michelle befriended, we probably would have never been able to get them back in time to perform. The props arrived two hours before our opening, which means that the actual performance had to be postponed for several hours. Luckily, the audience understood our predicament and waited patiently. Those *politicos* in Washington have taken all the romantic pleasure out of traveling. It's a drag. What about you? How has the political climate changed at the university where you teach?

Wolford: Well, if Lynne Cheney and the conservative watchdog groups she's connected with are concerned about a liberal bias in the academy, they obviously haven't been spending time in northwest Ohio. There were a couple of teach-ins and public discussions at BGSU[2] in late September, with a handful of politicized faculty trying to provide students with a historical context to better understand the root causes behind the attacks. There have also been a few events sponsored

1 See "Touring in Times of War," pp. 157–8.
2 Bowling Green State University, Ohio.

by the Islamic student group on campus. I suppose the American Council of Trustees and Alumni would consider the teach-ins and student gatherings to be examples of "unpatriotic speech."

Gómez-Peña: What about your colleagues?

Wolford: I've been grateful that a number of my colleagues, especially in cultural studies and media studies, have voiced a more critical perspective on the events of the past few months, but I've become hyperaware of the extent to which students and even some other faculty view me as a fringe radical. I've always thought of myself as a rather innocuous left-leaning socialist, but when I mentioned to some of my doctoral students that my email correspondence and phone messages had been surveyed—you remember when Echelon or Carnivore was so fascinated by our conversations for *TDR*—they seemed to think I was the kind of person who needed watching. And I suspect the US government continues to think so as well, if for no other reason than because I've assigned writings by Edward Said and Noam Chomsky in my classes, which I understand is enough in itself to get red-flagged in Bush's America. I'm really astonished by what happened to your collaborator. This country gets attacked by a group of mostly Saudi nationals and so they decide that a performance artist from Mexico City poses a threat to national security? That's insane. What has it been like in the Bay area? Has the mass impulse toward xenophobia and conservatism managed to gain a foothold there as well?

Gómez-Peña: San Francisco is no longer the haven for progressives, visionaries, and bohemians it used to be. The new economy (1997–2000) had already transformed the spirit of the city, from a culture of political compassion, of artistic and sexual experimentation, to one with a Darwinian spirit of survival of the digital fittest. What remained of the old bohemian San Francisco was just the set design, the storefront, the mirage. September 11 only made things worse. We now hold two very sad records: The largest number of guns purchased since 9/11—yes, San Francisco—and the largest number of Latinos profiled and detained at any airport in the USA. A paradigmatic case study in paranoia took place not long ago in the Pacific Heights district. An upper-class white lady called the FBI hotline telling them that "an Arabic man was outside [her] window with a rocket launcher." Patrol cars were immediately dispatched. They cordoned off her entire block and, after a few hours of high drama, they finally found the source of her anxiety: A Chicano journalist on assignment with a telephoto zoom lens (the alleged rocket launcher) taking photos of mansions for the *SF Chronicle*. Situations like this are happening all over the country. I think that the great challenge America has right now is to deal with its inner demons. That's the other war on terror. I still have faith that when the arts community finally breaks this incommensurable silence, San Francisco will recapture its spunk and put up a good fight.

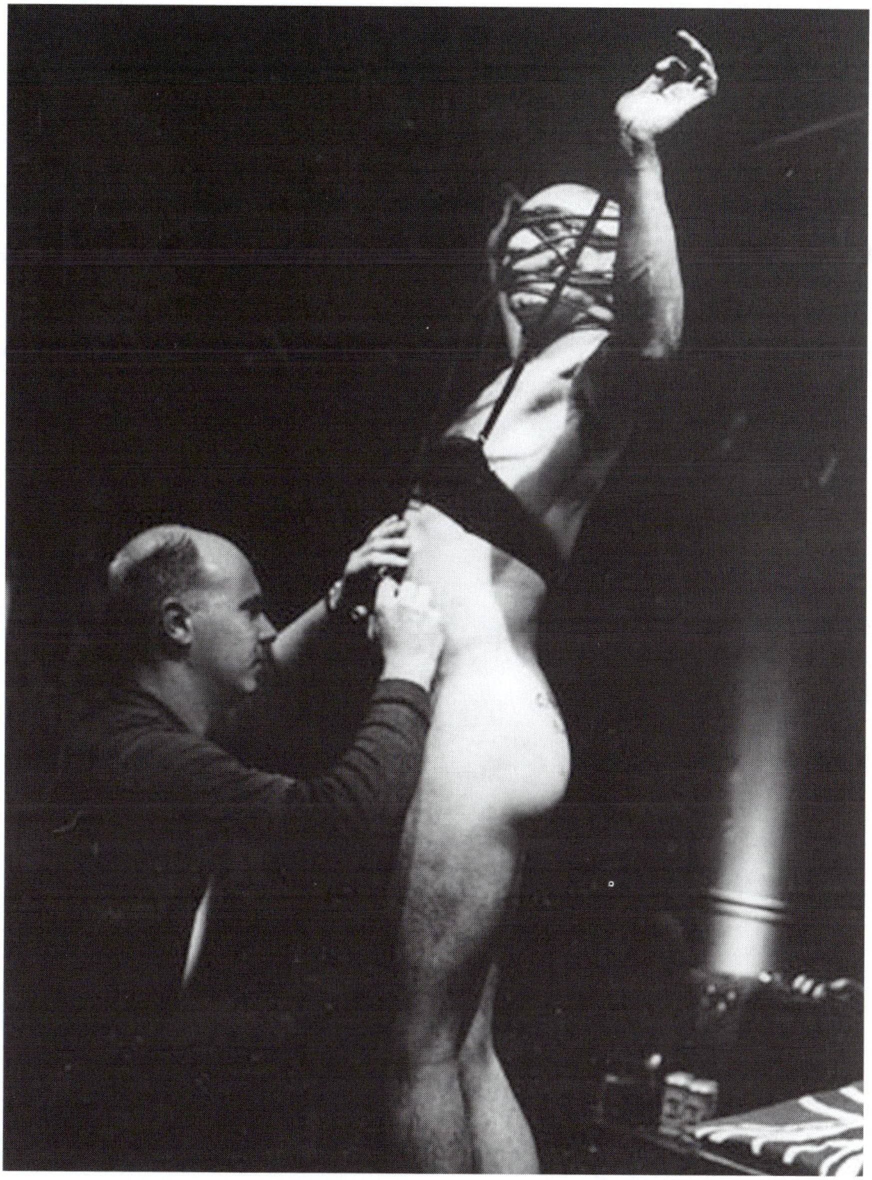

Audience interaction during *The Museum of Fetishized Identities.*
Juan Ybarra and audience member. Performance Space, Sydney, 2000. Photo: Heidrun Lohr.

Wolford: One of the things that I've found most distressing in the past few months is the complete evacuation and silencing of dissenting viewpoints, even those that I would consider the most moderate and benign. I'm infuriated by the implication that any critique of the US government's actions is necessarily an expression of support for terrorism. I shouldn't even call it an implication, since in the days following the attacks, Ari Fleischer stated outright that there was no appropriate time for criticism of the national agenda.

Gómez-Peña: But luckily there are a lot of dissenting voices on the Internet . . .

Wolford: And in the international press, thank goodness. But that's the sort of thing that people have to go out of their way to find, so it's not exactly interfering with the indoctrination process that's being so effectively facilitated by broadcast media. While it's true that there are some voices that haven't been silenced altogether—critical intellectuals like Said and Žižek—they're given no access to mainstream media, so precisely the perspectives that we need to be listening to as a counterpoint to rabid nativism are marginalized. Instead, we get Pat Buchanan on cable news talking about immigration, and people are treating him as if he were a rational human being with a valid point to make.

Gómez-Peña: We are clearly caught in "the crossfire," to use a cheesy Pat Buchanan metaphor, but between two forms of dangerous fundamentalisms—the Islamic and the Christian, "the two bellicose desert religions" as Richard Rodriguez says—and for the moment, we simply don't know what will happen next. We don't know if and when those fundamentalists on both sides will make yet another dangerous move that will threaten the whole world even more. We just don't know who is potentially more dangerous, Osama or George W.? The script of the latest Hollywood thriller is pretty scary.

Wolford: How is all this affecting your sense of the future?

Gómez-Peña: My sense of the future has diminished considerably. Like a Colombian journalist once told me, history nowadays starts when you wake up and ends when you go to sleep. That's how it feels. There seem to be no metahorizons left, at least for the moment. Of course the real challenge is to not succumb to fear and despair, to live as if the Patriot Act didn't exist, as if we actually lived in a true democracy.

Wolford: It's difficult to do that, especially since the Patriot Act has done so much to erode civil liberties. I don't want to sound completely paranoid, but it seems to me that the Bush regime would be happy with a sort of old-style Soviet society, with controlled media and ubiquitous surveillance by the state. I have a hard time understanding why so many Americans feel comfortable with the kind of "security" that Ashcroft, Cheney, and their henchmen are trying to impose. How has the ideological climate affected your own work in the context of the art world since we last spoke?

Gómez-Peña: The chilling effect of this epic drama has made many US art presenters a bit apprehensive about the content of art.

Wolford: Give me some concrete examples.

Gómez-Peña: Some want to make sure that during my lectures and performances I don't overtly present my opinions about the "War on Terror," or that my message and tone is not "negative" or "divisive." I think I understand them. The unspoken dominant narrative seems to state: Why do we need art right now when we are fighting formidable enemies abroad and inside? That's the stupid logic of the administration. But what this really means is that art will soon be thoroughly de-funded. In fact, a lot of our projects are being canceled or "downsized" due to impending funding cuts. We have lost several major commissions which we were counting on to keep the doors of our organization open. But I am not complaining bitterly. Luckily, other projects, mostly in other countries, in Europe and Latin America, have appeared. If this de-funding trend continues, I just fear that La Pocha Nostra will become an expatriate troupe. The idea of Chicano expatriates in Europe is a weird one, *¿qué no*? If Bush gets reelected, kaput! There will be an unprecendented brain drain. Artists, intellectuals, and scientists will flee to Canada or Mexico, or . . .

Wolford: I don't know; for me as well, emigration is starting to look like a very attractive option. My colleagues in Wishhounds Theatre are also being affected by this funding crisis, even though their performance work isn't intended to intervene in the social sphere in such a direct way as La Pocha Nostra's. Raymond Bobgan and the company have been working on a devised piece based on the writings of the Founding Fathers, called *The Hidden Twin*. In this cultural moment, drawing attention to the rhetoric and vision on which this nation was allegedly founded is necessarily a political act, since it highlights the incommensurable distance between that idealism and the reality of what America has become and what it represents in the larger framework of a community of nations. But things just keep getting worse in terms of funding prospects. Money that used to be available for educational programs, like Cleveland Public Theatre's summer workshops and classes for urban youth, even that type of funding is much more difficult to secure. I used to think that the alternative arts sector in this country was such that only artists with a certain degree of cultural capital and celebrity status could survive financially, but given what you're saying, I gather that the situation is even more difficult than I'd realized.

Gómez-Peña: What is scary is the uncertainty and the ambiguity. I mean, the borders between compassion and fear, and between sensitivity and censorship—those borders are very subtle, almost indistinguishable nowadays. This has profound psychological and spiritual effects on our frail communities. We all have to constantly fight the existential despair, the unbearable silence, the self-censorship, and face with tremendous valor the disbanding of entire artistic communities. I have never seen so many unemployed artists and so many talented artists working in shitty nonartistic jobs. We all have to work twice as much just to pay the basic bills. It's worse than in Mexico, my other country. It's clearly a defining moment for the US avant-garde . . . But paradoxically, in my experience, audiences in the USA, are more than ready to discuss important issues, to engage in a critical conversation with the artist.

Wolford: How can you tell?

Gómez-Peña: We are getting huge audiences, wherever we go, and, after our shows, they want to ask flaming questions, they want to know where we stand vis-à-vis the crucial issues of our times.

Wolford: Why?

Gómez-Peña: I can only speculate. It is as if the performance stage has become, by default, a demilitarized zone, a sanctuary for critical culture and progressive behavior, a space where people can really talk about important issues, the issues that aren't being raised in the media, in the workplace, or at home.

One would think that what might come out of this medieval nightmare is that people's priorities would get straightened out again, that more artists will become politically active again, and that we will soon be forced to deal with issues that really matter, not just which is this month's art fad or who is fucking whom in the bla-bla Biennial. In times of acute crisis, society often recaptures the compass, so to speak. It sounds a bit trite, but I really feel that the USA just woke up from a dream of undeserved privilege and is now clumsily learning how to live in a world of uncertainty and danger, the world in which 95 percent of humankind lives. The fog of uncertainty won't dissipate anytime soon. It will be the dominant weather for years to come.

Mid-March, 2002

Wolford: I'm afraid that I don't see much hope for an alternative to the prospect you mention of arts-funding being eliminated entirely. Even in the best of times, the USA is light years behind other nations in terms of the value that it places on art as an integral part of the social fabric. There's been such a strong push toward corporatization and private-sector funding for the arts, which has tended to privilege ideologically conservative and Eurocentric types of work. In this economy, I don't see corporate funding as a viable alternative even for more traditional artists and arts organizations. If we continue to move in the direction of a consumer-driven art market without any concomitant effort to ensure the continuance of an alternative sector, the future looks very bleak. On the other hand, there are so many examples, historically, of extraordinary artwork emerging during moments of social and political crisis. I'm still optimistic enough to believe that important, politicized artwork will continue to be created, though I'm more dubious about the financial survival of the artists.

Gómez-Peña: Critical culture has never been part of the global project. The role assigned to art in the global project is actually to numb us, to help us escape from the everyday social hardships, to make sure we remain apolitical, and confused. Art in the era of globalization is either meant to entertain, decorate the horror vacui of the upper class, or perform the role of conservative diplomacy. Politicians don't see any use for us other than dancing ballet, or singing opera for yuppies, or performing the roles of glossy bohemians on the Bravo channel. They certainly don't find our unique voices and progressive perspectives necessary. Not only that, they actually find us annoying. That's why when funding-cut time arrives, critical artists, experimental artists, politicized artists are the first ones to go *à la chingada*. The rationale they utilize to de-fund us is that we are "decadent," "elitist," and "un-American," but the reality is that they know they can't domesticate our voices and make us sing along with the official mantra. Performance artists are like wild animals. We simply can't survive captivity . . . I truly believe that in times of crisis, the performance artist can perform many necessary roles. Since we are not accountable to the art market, we have the freedom to raise the questions that no one else is willing to raise, and to create spaces for tolerance, difference, pluralism, and dissent. But of course there are no grants or commissions for this endeavor. It's something we just have to do *a contracorriente*—against the stream, with or without funding, with or without the blessings of the art world. We have to do it because it needs to be done. That's our job! Period.

Wolford: What strategies have you and your collaborators adopted to fight against forms of tacit silencing?

Gómez-Peña: We are in a permanent process of reinvention, constantly trying out new ideas and models. We are trying to operate within a new conceptual triangle created by the vertices of community, experimental art, and radical pedagogy. In this sense we are placing more emphasis than ever before on process, context, and education. We are starting a number of educational projects for rebel artists to help them sharpen their performative and analytical skills. La Pocha Nostra is good at it. We are also trying to cross over with dignity into more populist terrain and fight the isolation of the art world and academia. Besides our occasional incursions into the realms of public radio and satellite TV, we are now in the process of designing an interactive performance DVD series to be used as a teaching tool in universities, colleges, and museums. Our goal is to demystify the performance-art field and hopefully make it understandable, sexy, and "hip"—for students, young artists, and general audiences. Each DVD in the series will contain forty to fifty short performance videos created by performance artists in collaboration with independent filmmakers. And the user will be able to retrieve them by author, chronology, subject matter, or language.

Another important project we are involved in is a multigenerational performance lab in San Francisco called Regroup.

Wolford: How did it come about?

Gómez-Peña: The San Francisco performance-art milieux felt that we badly needed to rebuild our community which was in disarray due to the profound impact of 9/11. La Pocha Nostra put out a convocatory and people responded right away. We formalized our call in November of 2001. Something was extremely unusual about this new "laboratory." Without prescribing it, and without the pressures of grant deadlines, it so happened that "El Lab" was truly multiethnic, multigender, multigenerational, and multidisciplinary. The ages of the fluctuating members ranged from the early twenties to the late fifties. There were Mexicans, Chicanos, Iranians, Colombians, Filipinos, Koreans, Anglos, and hybrids in between. Participants were coming from the visual arts, theater, dance, and music—and at least half were gay or self-defined "poly-sexual." A second circle of "guests" from out of town included performance artists from LA, Arizona, Portland, and Mexico City. A third circle included occasional visitors and friends who were too busy to be permanent members but couldn't resist an occasional visit to our mad jamming sessions in search of inspiration and energy. As of now we have approximately seventeen artists from different ethnic and professional communities jamming, brainstorming, developing new material. We meet twice a month. It really warms my heart. Though I'm fully aware that Regroup is a temporary experiment,[3] it is precisely projects like this one which give me the strength to continue walking in the dark forest of the twenty-first century.

3 Regroup disbanded in late 2003.

26

Loose ends

The fluid borders between author and editor

(Phone conversations and email exchange, 2004)

Elaine Peña and Guillermo Gómez-Peña

"The point is not to shy away from the borders."

Phone conversation, June 2004

Gómez-Peña: People keep asking me if you are my "real sister" *por lo de* Peña. And I tell them that in a sense you are. We both are artist theorists, relentless experimentalists with a social conscience, cabrones obsessed with crossing all kinds of borders. *Pero* sister, I'm curious, why did you accept my invitation to edit this book?

Peña: I needed a space to strategize. Teaching privileged students, I desperately tried to connect critical pedagogy, performance practice, and political analysis, but was met with apathy and lackadaisical attitudes. Many of my students could not connect or they feigned naïveté. I thought that writing and reading about critical performance pedagogy framed by your innovative style would help me work it out . . . Why did you offer?

Gómez-Peña: I wanted to work with an editor who understood in a guttural manner the predicaments and complexities of being a transcultural artist; someone who

Transvestite mohawk.
Juan Ybarra. Performance Space, Sydney, 2000. Photo: Heidrun Lohr.

could understand from the inside my bicultural esthetics and biconceptual concerns . . . Besides you were young, very smart, and tough. I also thought that our generational differences could add another layer of complexity to our working relationship. I wanted this book to speak to at least three generations of students, artists, and intellectuals. So far, you've kept me on track.

Peña: But I don't think our differences were entirely generational.

Gómez-Peña: True. There were other healthy necessary differences. You operate in the context of academia; I don't. You place more emphasis on the textual aspects of race, class, and gender. These paradigms are implied in everything I do, but I had to make them more textual. At times you made me aware of my shortcomings in those territories . . .

Peña: At times I was aware of the similarities and differences of our gender politics. For example, sometimes it was a challenge to negotiate my feminist perspective. Particularly when I thought your work was not attuned to the way gender is always at work in performance. There were times when I asked you to refocus or broaden your frame of reference and other times I refocused mine.

Gómez-Peña: True. As a male Latino interested in dismantling his own machismo, my job is to collaborate with powerful women both onstage and in writing. That's the only sincere way I think I can effectively rework my own gender politics. The rest is pure rhetoric . . .

Peña: I agree. Yet, I think it is important to be aware of our rhetoric and its effect outside the context of this project. Performance scripts, chronicles, cyber-*placazos* are consumed and reproduced. Each reincarnation is a product as well as a constant look back.

Gómez-Peña: What I'm trying to say is that just to theorize about gender or racial equality without practicing is pointless, a mere rhetorical exercise ¿qué no? Only through a dialogical relationship, a true collaboration between men and women, Anglos and Latinos, and artists from different generations can we get to a new place. A place which is empowering but not self-righteous or accusatory.

Peña: OK. Are you sorry you invited me to edit the book? I know I was a bit much at times, challenging many points. I have to ask because we debate a lot. Of course we are always civil, no fistfights, black eyes, or bloody noses . . .

Gómez-Peña: Are you kiddin'? I am thrilled that we are constantly debating. It's been intense but polite, bien Chicano, and I love polite intensity. Besides, you are meticulous and very demanding of clarity. And I badly needed to test my crazy ideas against your academic rigor . . . though I must say that at times the intellectual rigor celebrated in academia can border on *tapadismo*—narrowmindedness. It happened a few times, and I had to politely remind you: *Esa*, think as an artist for a while, change hats, or rather headdresses.

Peña: That's interesting. I do agree that academics can be somewhat closeminded, but I do not think I ever disregarded my artistic senses. In fact, sometimes I thought I was paying you the same favor.

Gómez-Peña: Interesting [*pause*]. Collaboration at times can be a distorting mirror, *¿qué no*? In collaboration there are rivers of subjectivity which crisscross the common ground we wish to map consciously. I don't mind them as long as we realize they are part of any intellectual dialogue. Subjectivity is a big part of collaboration . . .

Peña: But let's get back to the challenges we faced.

Gómez-Peña: Another big challenge for me was to insist on the importance of humor in this manuscript. Your insistence on pushing out of the book texts which I considered playful or, say, more "indirect," made me get a bit defensive and restake my territory.

Peña: I noticed.

Gómez-Peña: *Serio*. I was afraid that my quintessential irreverence was going to be confined to the "Performance Literature" section. I must confess that at times I felt you had little patience with some of the texts which weren't overtly political. Am I wrong?

Peña: Not entirely . . . *pero* . . . I never thought that all the texts had to be Gramscian political manifestos, or that your humor was not effective or engaging. I think your rhetorical strategies are brilliant, but there is a time and a space for them. The truth is that some of the texts that I "censored" were not directly connected with the issues at hand. I cut for clarity. Also, some of the texts I rejected veered so far off that they negated your earlier claims. But you are a contradictory *vato*, *¿quéno*?

Gómez-Peña: And so are you, because as a person you are hilarious, and your own performance ideas are quite outrageous. I remember when we first met in Chicago and I invited you to join the La Pocha Nostra troupe at the last minute. You showed up on opening night as a bare-chested Guadalupana covered in mud—not exactly a conventional image. The thing is that we are sometimes different people in writing than in performance mode, *¿qué no*?

Peña: There are certainly differences. It is hard to pin down the distinction between these performance modes because they are so site-specific.

Gómez-Peña: True. As a performance artist I am much more *locote*. Whereas I tend to be more reflexive when I write, much more self-critical and solipsistic. I tend to have many doubts. *Por ejemplo*, during the process, I kept asking myself, are there any texts which Elaine felt she had to accept simply because I was too passionate about them, and she felt she had to respect my artistic integrity or my heart? Now I am asking you, was that the case?

Peña: There were a couple of texts, rather parts of texts, that I accepted because you were so . . . so . . . romantic about them: Some parts of "In Defense," *Brownout*

2, and the conversations. They are powerful, emotionally charged pieces of yourself that you offer the audience. Realizing this, I decided that I would be doing your readers a disservice if I cut them.

Gómez-Peña: Thanks for telling me four months later, *cabrona*.

Peña: I did tell you! But I was in polite Chicana mode, not in super-*cabrona* Chicana mode. Maybe I was trying to package my comments too delicately. Anyway, I loved the texts secretly.

Gómez-Peña: Alright. In your opinion, now that the book is almost finished, which were the toughest aspects of our collaboration?

Peña: The toughest was definitely the geographical distance. I was in Chicago and you were either in San Francisco or on the road. We had to deal primarily through phone calls and email. What a fucking nightmare. It's like, okay, so Mac and PC are not related, not compatible, just like Mexico and the USA, one can say. Yet, I'm sure that all the global-mafiosos are on the same system. Unfortunately, we were not. They have clear lines of communication.

Gómez-Peña: Besides the technical worries . . .

Peña: I think the second toughest challenge was dealing truly and effectively with the multiple themes running through the book. I mean performance, pedagogy, *and* activism is not an easy task. Another concern was that I definitely didn't want our engagement to be superficial. We needed to get down and dirty. Was this hard for you?

Gómez-Peña: Definitely not. I believe in the power of true collaboration. I mean, two or more minds working together can have a larger scope of perception and imagination. Let's take the structure as an example. If it had been entirely up to me, I would have created a more hypertextual, experimental structure. But you insisted—rightfully so—that if pedagogy was at the core of this book, we needed to be more systematic, comprehensive, and therefore, "pedagogic," in the way we structured the book. I ended up complying because you were . . . right. Talia's structural suggestions also helped tremendously in this respect. We needed her "bird's eye view" of the performance field, especially since we all wanted this book to touch the infected wounds of the field.

Peña: And also hopefully work outside our field, to appeal to other fields like anthropology, cultural studies, Chicano studies, media studies, etc.

Gómez-Peña: That is always the trickiest situation.

Peña: It was very convenient that we finally agreed over the choice and order of the texts. We made many structural changes which could have led to very different books, but I believe our final conception was the best. That is one thing I really liked about our collaborative process. It was great to make a decision after rowdy point–counterpoint discussions, but it was really wonderful when we both agreed on instinct. What do you think was the toughest section to work through?

Gómez-Peña: Certainly the one on pedagogy. It's all new material written within a span of three months in collaboration with Rachel Rogers. The manuscript went back and forth in cyberspace at least ten times. And then you cut the text with your own scissors, adding other layers of complexity. I mean, it was definitely written on the fast lane, almost as a journalistic piece, with a clear deadline and a clear purpose: To make our performance methodologies available to other artists and teachers. I knew that our methodology worked very well in the rehearsal space, but it's a different thing to have it written on paper.

Peña: You're completely right. In retrospect I think it is the most generous text. Yet, dealing with the fast-paced writing style and multiple collaborators was challenging. There were so many ways to organize and present the exercises. It was exciting but tough. I had to constantly remind myself that pedagogical texts are always working drafts. They cannot be prettily packaged.

Gómez-Peña: I remember when I first showed it to you I thought you were going to reject it. I was a bit insecure, since neither Rachel nor I have formal training as pedagogues. When you, Talia, and later on the readers had a positive reaction it really made me happy. I felt the same kind of happiness and relief I feel when I premiere a new performance and the audience gets it.

Peña: What reaction did you have when you finally read the whole manuscript in order?

Gómez-Peña: I liked it a lot. It was tight and *picante*, but I became aware of the fact that certain ideas that appear, say, in the main introductory essays, later on reappeared in a performance text or during a conversation with Eduardo or Lisa. Similar ideas, different genre, angle, or writing style. First I thought, *coño*, I am repeating myself, and flipped out. I even tossed out a few texts which I found repetitive. But then I realized: Hey, I'm sampling, and my performance work samples and recycles constantly. It's a border strategy.

Peña: Repetition was a pressing issue. It is difficult to get a handle on the scope and details of the manuscript, especially when one is so passionate about the ideas. At one point we were so obsessed that the manuscript was massive. Remember?

Gómez-Peña: Four hundred *pinche* pages at least.

Peña: It was overwhelming, but I did not think we were doomed. We faced the cuts bravely. That is always the hardest part of writing: Giving it up. It paid off because we now have a much sleeker version.

Gómez-Peña: But there is still the issue of repetition.

Peña: Repetition without cause is usually annoying, but I believe it is a key component of any pedagogical project. The abundance of recurring ideas in different sections and in different formats enriches and tests them. For me, this is the core of pedagogy. Each reincarnation makes the idea more accessible.

Gómez-Peña: Besides, I don't expect readers to navigate the book in order. They know my past books. They know that my performance country does not have straight freeways. Some readers are going to go to the index and say, I want to check out the infamous La Pocha Nostra methodology and try it out in my class. Others will be more interested in the performance theory or in my experimental writings. There's many ways and directions to enter the book . . . just like performance.

Peña: Accepting this idea was our strongest connection. Both of us understand that creating and shaping performances, on paper or otherwise, is maddening. Its form is dependent upon the borders that manifest themselves at a specific time and place . . .

Gómez-Peña: . . . and in the maddening attempt to articulate the fluid borders between pedagogy and madness, between performance and accessibility. It's a formidable challenge. The implied question for us throughout the editing process was how to be accessible and yet remain complex and experimental; how to be clear without sacrificing the venom and the *chile*, without destroying the metaphorical and performative aspects of the work.

Peña: Especially given the context of emergency we are living in . . .

Gómez-Peña: It's *cabrón*; I mean to write a book about art in a time when there are so many irrational wars going on and when the government is exercising censorship and violating our civil rights every day. It's quite a backdrop. The world is a political mess, a cultural hurricane, and everyday life has become dangerous. We are losing friends to suicide, joblessness, spiritual despair, illness, deportation. This is not a poetical statement. We are definitely operating in a context of emergency and I really want my readers to experience this sense of urgency, which means . . .

Peña: . . . which means we can't afford to be unnecessarily obscure. It seems as if we are at a point when things could escalate to irreparable levels. I don't want to get on a soapbox about it. Everyone knows what's going on. I think the worst part is that justifying mounting violence will be easy for those in power. It is for this very reason that we have to give of ourselves, selflessly, in our every endeavor. We need to be able to explain our ideas and methodologies in a thousand languages, to teach and be taught.

Gómez-Peña: *Oye*, what lessons did you learn in this editing process that you will carry into your live performance work?

Peña: Where do I begin? It would take me pages to articulate them all. I won't because I'm sure that it would turn into a self-indulgent mess. The most basic and important lesson: The importance of process, of working relentlessly for precision and complexity. But those things are definitely good advice in most situations. And you?

Gómez-Peña: Thanks to this book, it is becoming very clear to me that teaching performance, sharing strategies and methodologies, is as important as performing . . . it is now clear to me that building community through performance pedagogy is, can be, an extremely political act, and this is a true epiphany. I knew it way deep inside, but it wasn't conscious, or wasn't as clear to me as it is right now. This book is definitely my clumsy attempt to articulate an epiphany.

Peña: *Ay* Guillermo . . . it's just the first step.

The apocalyptic geisha.
Emiko R. Lewis. From a photo-portfolio sponsored by Spanish curator Orlando Britto. 2004. Photo: James McCaffry.

index

Page numbers in **bold** denote references to illustrations.